Cultivating Dissent

SUNY series in National Identities

Thomas M. Wilson, editor

CULTIVATING DISSENT

Work, Identity, and Praxis in Rural Languedoc

Winnie Lem

State University of New York Press

Published by
State University of New York Press

For information, address the State University of New York Press,
State University Plaza, Albany, NY 12246

Marketing by Patrick Durocher
Production by Bernadine Dawes

Library of Congress Cataloging-in-Publication Data

Lem, Winnie.
Cultivating dissent : work, identity, and praxis in rural
Languedoc / Winnie Lem.
p.   cm. — (SUNY series in national identities)
Includes bibliographical references and index.
ISBN 0-7914-4187-3. — ISBN 0-7914-4188-1 (pbk.)
1. Languedoc (France)—Social conditions.   2. Country life—
France—Languedoc.   3. Capitalism—France—Languedoc—Influence.
I. Title.   II. Series.
DC611.L32L46   1999
306′.09448—dc21   98-54770
                                                       CIP

1   2   3   4   5   6   7   8   9   10

for Timothy

Contents

Preface

This book begins and ends by considering the question of rural resistance, class consciousness, and the politics of culture. It is a study that attempts to illuminate the multiplicity of ways in which rural people—in this case the small family farmers in the Languedoc region of Mediterranean France—struggle against the processes of disintegration brought on by the development of capitalism and the modernizing imperatives of the state. *Cultivating Dissent: Work, Identity, and Praxis in Rural Languedoc* examines the problem of how small-scale family farmers sustain themselves, their livelihoods, and their way of life by engaging in a wide repertoire of forms collective action. It also explores these actions as self-conscious acts informed and inflected by distinctive subjectivities and understandings of the forces of change in the political and economic landscape.

While the book is concerned with the political and social practices of a rural population as well as problems of consciousness in the 1980s and the early 1990s, the questions addressed, in fact, draw their inspiration from the early work of Eric Wolf, Eric Hobsbawm, and Barrington Moore on the nature of agrarian struggle and revolutions in the twentieth century. Since I first encountered their work as an undergraduate in the mid-1970s, and began to reflect on how rural women and men become involved in social change and revolutionary movements, my research has moved in many directions, each of which has given some shape to this study. My investigations of these issues began with an attempt to explore class struggles and the development of class consciousness among rural women and men in prerevolutionary China. My preoccupation with China was stimulated, quite simply, by a desire to explore the historical conditions that created a Chinese diaspora in the first half of the twentieth century, of which my immediate family was a part.

After completing a period of work focused on the transformations wrought on China by the forces of capitalist change, my attention then shifted to Europe, the heartland of capitalism itself. By studying European history, culture, and politics, I was keen to apprehend the essence of societies that engendered a particularly predatory form of colonialism expansion—one that was informed by the development of capitalism. From the work of such writers as E. P. Thompson, Louise Tilly, and E. E. Le Roy Ladurie, I absorbed an elementary lesson that was all too obvious to many more established students of European society and history. That lesson was that the dynamics of capitalist transformation and expansion did not only produce distinctive histories of conflict and accommodation between differing classes of people *across* borders and *across* continents. But *within* the boundaries of European countries they also engendered confrontations between classes, between women and men, the powerful and the powerless both at the centers as well as the peripheries of nations and nations being formed. As a student of anthropology with an interest in agrarian societies and cultures then, my studies of Europe became inclined toward its rural population and they lay particularly in trying to fathom above all how forces of history shape and were shaped by ordinary people in their everyday lives, and further how the forces of historical change were assimilated and understood by people in the quotidian world. My work then and now, is driven quite simply by a desire to extend current appreciations of the complexities of rural struggle and the complex understandings that drive rural women and men to contest, accommodate, or collude with the forces of capitalist transformation—concerns pursued in such seminal studies as *Peasant Wars of the Twentieth Century* and *Primitive Rebels*.

In the 1960s and 1970s, when such works were first published, the political and cultural climate was conducive to predispositions toward investigating the nature of revolutionary change and studying questions of human agency. Moreover, that time was also more hospitable to the whole the enterprises pursued by the *intellectuel engagé*—a scholar with political purpose—and many academics, for example, dedicated their efforts to examining how transformative social movements could be forged among people who occupy rather disparate subject positions. However, in the 1990s, the integrity of such a political project has become somewhat dissipated in the fragmented world of postmodern abstractions. As the new millennium approaches, many intellectuals seem eager to distance and to disengage themselves from the questions and the political commitments that emanated from a bygone "modern" era. Overarching questions of how structural changes have occurred or how they may be brought about have become eclipsed by a narcissistic preoccupation with identity politics in many quarters in the academy and also in society at large. If indeed such interests rule the day, then it is clear that what lies at the heart of the book—the concern with the struggles of the powerless and marginalized classes to change the status quo—seems manifestly out of step with the times. However, in reflecting on recent trends on the global landscape, I would argue that studies of the struggles of powerless classes, old and newly emerging and considerations of forces that contest the status quo are more in step with the times than they may first appear. In the light of the triumph of capitalism in the new world order and especially with the demise of any political and economic system that poses a challenge to the hegemony of neoliberal ideologies and practices, I would suggest that there is indeed an imperative that *intellectuels engagés* remain faithful to their projects, defying criticisms that dismiss such work as being the outmoded relics of history. It is worth remembering particularly in the light of the such developments as the economic restructuring of China, the rise of nationalisms in Europe and the reemergence of peasant insurgency in Mexico—that history does repeat itself, though in rather novel guises. Therefore, it was with the firm conviction that the study of popular struggle, consciousness, class resistance and the politics of culture has a heightened immediacy in these old new times that I pursued my fieldwork then and now present this extended essay.

On Fieldwork

With these scholarly commitments and political concerns, I was drawn particularly to the region of Languedoc after reading in various presses and academic articles of the 1980s about the protests of family farmers, who refer to themselves as Occitan wine growers. Wine growers, in various localities throughout what was often called the "*Midi Rouge*" (Red South),[1] were protesting vigorously against the entry of Spain into the European Economic Community (EEC), as it was then called. Spanish and

other foreign wines, so they feared, posed a threat to the
Languedoc economy, which was based on family-run viticultural
enterprises in a highly competitive wine market. In the years
immediately preceding Spain's membership in the EEC (now the
European Union [EU]), which actually became formalized in
January of 1986, the protests of the Occitan growers escalated
and they staged mass demonstrations, as well as small-scale
assaults. The drama of their acts of defiance rendered them
especially newsworthy and images of angry wine growers on the
rampage regularly graced the pages of *Le Monde, Le Figaro,* the
Guardian, and the *International Herald Tribune.* My curiosity
about Occitan growers was piqued by the spectacle of their sometimes very colorful and always intense forms of popular protest.
I became keen to know more about what lay behind those rarefied
moments of heightened political engagement in which growers
mustered all their energies to defend their livelihoods. I became
eager to explore the more mundane aspects of making a living
in rural Languedoc and to understand the nature of the everyday life and local culture that growers thought particularly
worthwhile defending. With a determination to get behind the
spectacular and a concern to penetrate a world that lay beyond
the realm of public performance, I descended on the region of
Lower Languedoc to set my sights on observing through fieldwork
the more ordinary preoccupations that govern the everyday life
and struggles of the small, family wine grower in a wine-growing
village.

The Observer Observed and "Other" Puzzles

Conducting fieldwork in the village of Broussan, a pseudonym,
posed several challenges to an Asian woman from North America.
Like many "first contacts" between anthropologists and their
subjects, my initial interactions with villagers were laden with
misunderstandings about codes of conduct and local mores.
Mutual confusions multiplied on several fronts—on the question
of gender, cultural identity, and language. After explaining to
villagers that I was a researcher from Canada interested in rural
life in France, many people were perplexed by the fact that I did
not speak with a "Canadian accent." Their expectations were
that I would speak French with a Quebec accent and not with
the Anglo twang acquired in a Canadian-classroom setting that
marks my accent. Villagers' familiarity with "Canadian" culture

reflected the stronger cultural ties that exist between Franco-phone Canada and France. Villagers' images of Canada then were largely shaped through media representations and trans-missions of music, theatre, films, and television programs issu-ing from Quebec; and inasmuch as many Anglophone North Americans are not cognizant of the cultural and historical distinc-tions that exist between Occitania and the north of France, many villagers considered Quebec to be coterminous with Canada.[2] It became necessary to explain that I was from Anglophone Canada—the other side (*l'autre coté*) of the country, with which villagers were less familiar, hence my unusual accent.

Inasmuch as villagers were rather puzzled by my first efforts to communicate, I was also initially confused about French as it was spoken in Broussan. The limitations to my fluency in French, notwithstanding, after becoming familiar with the lilt of the *accent du Midi* (the Midi accent) in Languedoc, I was nonetheless often stymied by various items of vocabulary that punctuated the conversations. After noting some of the terms used and failing to locate them in my dictionary, it became clear that many villag-ers, especially the elderly, often spoke a linguistic pastiche of French and Occitan—Francitan. When pressed to explain cer-tain items of vocabulary, some interlocutors would then admit that they often unreflectively slipped back and forth between French and Occitan or what they called "patois."

Another source of confusion, which in many respects encap-sulates one of the issues tackled in this text—the complexities of locating self and others in a cultural pantheon—presented itself in the early weeks of my research. One day, shortly after I ini-tiated my contact with the villagers through a door-to-door ap-proach, I descended into the main street of the village to be greeted by wide smiles and friendly nods from passing people. Feeling that I had "broken through" one of the barriers that keeps outsiders outside and that I was, at last, receiving a friendly welcome after word of my arrival had circulated in the village, I approached some of the people who smiled at me. I introduced myself and asked if they would like to meet me some time to talk about village work routines, how people make a living, and the village itself. They looked rather taken aback by my request, hastily gave me their phone numbers and walked off. This scene repeated itself several times, as I approached other individuals who were casting smiles in my direction. The source of their bewilderment was again due to a misapprehension about my identity. Their friendly gestures were not meant for me, an

inquisitive social scientist from North America, but rather for
members of several families, refugees from Vietnam who had
come to settle in the village. My arrival in the village coincided
with that of the refugees and I was initially perceived as part of
the Vietnamese diaspora. This situation called for further efforts
to position myself in the global social and cultural order. After
locating myself in space as a person from Canada and, in time,
as a person whose presence in Canada was determined by the
events in twentieth-century Chinese history, I eventually, became to be known as the Canadian, *la Canadienne*. It was established that Canada is my country—*mon pays* and *mon pays* is
where I live and work. My efforts to position myself through self-
definitional statements that made allusions to place and work
held an immediate resonance for the small farmers of Lower
Languedoc, precisely, as I was to discover, because of the primacy of work experiences in their own of sense of identity.

Such initial confusions about each "Other," then vividly encapsulated some of the issues surrounding the notions of identity that I wished to explore—particularly, how collective identities
are negotiated and constructed through concrete work experiences and also, how they are defined and redefined in the light
of changes in national and global political economy. Moreover,
beyond parameters of the specific issues addressed in this study,
these interactions, in fact provoked some reflections on other
issues that relate to the enterprise of anthropology itself, particularly who its practitioners tend to be and who usually constitute the anthropological subject. In the context of European
ethnography, they reminded me of how uncommon it is for a
"non-European" and, a woman at that, to undertake an anthropological investigation in a European culture. Indeed with very
few exceptions, anthropologists of Europe, by and large, have
been white Europeans and perceived by European subjects to
belong, in a wide sense, to the category of "Us."[3] In the light of
the history of European imperialist expansion, and more particularly of France's domination over certain countries and peoples
in Asia or *Indochine* as French colonial territories in the East
were collectively called, it is somewhat an inversion that a person who might be perceived as a "(post-?) colonial subject" has
ventured into the territory of the "colonizers" to engage in an
anthropological study. In a way, it overturns the historical order
of things in the sense that anthropological investigations of non-
European people were once undertaken by principally European
ethnographers working for colonial governments. Furthermore,

despite being culturally assimilated to mainstream Anglo-Canadian culture (and somewhat "Occidentalized"), as a "transnational," "cosmopolitan" subject, I became ever cognizant of the implications of visibility and difference in a context where racism has been reaching a crescendo fomented by the National Front under Le Pen. Although this study neither explicitly addresses these larger epistemological problems, nor indeed, the issue of racism and constructions of difference itself, I anticipate that the concern with identity, regionalist and minority nationalist sentiments, and political practices will serve in a general way, to shed some light on the question of racism and chauvinism in their various forms.

Acknowledgments

Many people contributed to the completion of this book in a number of direct and indirect ways, both in North America and in Europe. In North America, I would first like to express my gratitude to advisors, colleagues, and friends. Shuichi Nagata, Stuart Philpott, Harriet Friedmann, and Pierre Beaucage read a draft of this book in its earliest incarnation as a Ph.D. thesis. While what I have produced in these pages is rather far removed from what they originally read, I hope that it somehow reflects their criticisms, suggestions, and objections. I would also like to thank Michael Keating, Sean Loughlin, Harriet Rosenberg, William Roseberry, and Gerald Sider who helped me work through some of the ideas and problems presented here. Thanks are due also to the participants in the Anthropology and History seminar at York University, especially Marilyn Silverman, Philip Gulliver, and Malcolm Blincow, whose enthusiasm for informal gatherings and cross-disciplinary work spawned many enjoyable evenings. I am grateful to Tom Wilson and to the anonymous reviewers of the manuscript whose acute comments provoked me to refashion some of the arguments in the book in interesting ways. Also, I wish to thank Zina Lawrence at SUNY press for her encouragement and enthusiasm for this project.

Many people in France facilitated my research by offering guidance, stimulation, incisive criticism, and hospitality. They include Jacques Andrieu, Louis Assier-Andrieu, Maurice Aymard, Christian Fages, Christina Horko, Geneviève Ossard, Hervé Ossard, Martine Segalen, Geneviève Santoro, and the late Olga Fages. I would like to acknowledge the many people in Broussan who welcomed me into their community and their homes. Above all, I thank Henri Durandeu, Célestine Cot, the late Henri Cot, Berthe Pigassou, the late Jean Pigassou, Pierre Escande, Claude

Escande, Françoise Pistre, and Bernard Pistre. Words cannot express the depth of my gratitude for their kindness and generosity and I hope they will not mind that I have used fictional names for their friends and neighbors.

I also wish to thank Rebecca Comay, Wenona Giles, Peter Murphy, Leslie Martin, Victoria Lee, Joachim Voss, and Villia Jefremovas whose friendship sustained me through the various phases of completing this work. I am truly indebted to my mother, Fay Hing Lem, and my late father, Fred who encouraged me to press on in my studies so that I would find a secure place in a country where they lived but never called "home."

Research for this book was generously funded by grants from the Social Sciences and Humanities Research Council of Canada; the Ministère des Affaires Etrangers (France), the Wenner-Gren Foundation for Anthropological Research and Trent University. For assisting in the final stages of preparing the manuscript, I am grateful to Laura Sworn, Nora Lem, and Glynis George.

Finally, my greatest debt of gratitude, as always, is owed to Gavin Smith.

A Note on the T ranslations

The Occitan and French versions of the anthem in the epigraph to chapter 1 appear in Napo (1971) *"Les Chansons de la Révolte"* [Songs of the Revolt]. The epigraph to chapter 2 is a passage from the Manifesto of the *Comité d'Action Viticole* (Cazes and Castéra 1976, 26). These translations as well as translations of interview material and technical vocabulary relating to viticulture are my own.

INTRODUCTION

A Disappearing World?

On a warm spring evening in the village of Broussan I arrived for dinner at the home of some friends, Annie and Roger. I offered to help with the preparation of the meal, since Annie was frantically rushing around stirring pots and sampling sauces. She was anxious to finish the busy part of the cooking before Roger returned from work and drinks were to be offered. Feeling flattered that a fine supper of *coquilles St. Jacques*, followed by roast pork was being prepared on account of my visit, I became a bit humbled by noticing that I was not the only guest. The table was set for six.

I knew that Annie and Roger's children were visiting friends for the evening, so I became curious to see who the other diners would be. As I was sipping an aperitif of pastis and shelling peas, Roger arrived at the door accompanied by three men who were wearing heavily soiled work clothes. I recognized one of the men, Jacques, a part-time farmer and who also worked for Roger as a laborer. The other two villagers were Raymond and Jean, also farmers.

Each of the men greeted me in turn by extending either the back of their wrists or elbows for me to shake, since their hands and lower arms were covered with grime. They had just come back from the fields. Roger said teasingly to his friends that I was really a good sort (*une brave*) because I did not mind shaking

1

hands with "grubby peasants like us." Raymond and Jean had spent the day helping to spread fertilizer on Roger's vineyards. He invited them to join us, partly because they were curious to meet me and partly because their wives were not home to prepare the evening meal. They both worked as cleaners at the hospital in Béziers and had been scheduled to do the night shift. Jacques was single and often had supper with Annie and Roger. Raymond joked that it was a good thing they liked each other because today they had spent more than 12 hours in each other's company and what's more they were going to be together every day for the next little while. Roger explained their plans to work together on Raymond's farm on the following day. Then they would be spreading fertilizer on Jacques's fields keeping up the rotation between holdings until the task on each of their vineyards was completed. The men took their turns washing up then sat down to have their drinks while I helped Annie put the meal on the table.

Dinnertime chat took on a rather serious note when Annie mentioned that she had seen some tourists buying Spanish wine from the supermarket in Béziers. Roger exploded on hearing this, virtually roaring with indignation about how abominable French supermarkets were to stock foreign wines when there were ample supplies from local producers. Jean, also flew into a rage. He pounded the table, adding that they never seem to be able to let things rest and that they will have no choice but to mount their campaign again.

My curiosity was aroused. I asked what they meant by their "campaign."

"Wait. I will explain," said Roger, who had composed himself a bit as he disappeared into another room. After a few seconds, he emerged clutching a photo album. Roger placed the album on the dinner table in front of me and immediately flipped to a page with a newspaper photograph of a small group of men whose faces were blacked out. They were running through the doors of a supermarket, pushing past store customers who were wheeling grocery carts and wearing startled expressions on their faces. The caption read "Mad Wine-Growers! Again!" Roger pointed to one man in the photograph and indicated that it was Raymond. He then, rather proudly, showed me that he was the figure who was racing toward the photographer. Each of them, competing for my attention, began to talk, all at once, about why they were in flight. I gathered from the chorus of explanations that they were photographed in the midst of a bottle-smashing escapade that involved dashing into a supermarket and gathering up as many bottles of Spanish or Italian wine as they could carry in their arms in order to shatter them on the floor. What had provoked this attack, was the news that shipments of foreign wine had arrived in local supermarkets.

I heard Jean's voice above the others as he said: "The market has no loyalty or morality! Business is business!"

"There, so you see!" Jean continued stabbing at the news photo with his finger, "That's one of the things we do in our campaign!"

I could see Roger's fury mounting again as he punctuated the discussion with: "We peasants are going to have to cause some trouble again if we want to defend our future!"

Considerably sobered by thoughts of organizing their next assault, all nodded in silent agreement.

Paradoxes of French Modernity

Roger and his guests felt themselves to be living in a world where the future of their way of life as small wine growers was threatened and their identity as Occitan family farmers was at odds with the imperatives of a French society insistent on a "modern" future. Modernity in France would involve a cost-efficient agriculture, on the one hand, and the creation of a homogeneous citizenry, that assimilated itself to the economic and cultural imperatives of neoliberal states, on the other. As we enter the closing years of the twentieth century, however, and turn to France, we find a country in which problems of social integration are at the forefront of the national agenda. Whether or not we envisage the civic citizen as positively as did the policy makers of postwar France, the fact is that the country remains riven by marginalized groups, from women to immigrants to regional nationalists. While as a result of France's modernizing imperative, the small family farm has indeed been consigned to history in certain places, in other areas it remains the focus of vigorous discussion and energetic efforts to sustain it—as on the occasion of my encounter with Roger, his companions, and their representation of one of their past campaigns.

Discourses of "the way forward"—of what would make a better society—change. As the 1960s turned into the 1970s, the discourse of the day held that the small-scale family farm (often branded with the mark of the past [and incidentally the Third World] by being referred to vaguely as "the peasantry"[1]) should be condemned to extinction. This was as prevalent in the corridors of power as it was in those of the academy and hence pervasively through much of French society. Over those decades, studies such as *The European Peasantry: The Final Phase* (Franklin 1969); *The Vanishing Peasant* (Mendras 1970) and *Peasants into Frenchmen: The Modernization of Rural France, 1870–1914* (Weber 1976) all confidently foretold of the demise of these small-scale, family-based farms faced with a rapidly industrializing nation. As the initial hesitant strides of the Marshall plan turned into the confident march of the new, Cold War capitalism, a contented industrial workforce was to be produced, supported by a welfare state so as to protect Europe from "the East" by eliminating urban communism and rural radicalism. Policies promoting structural changes in the rural milieu were to encourage an exodus from the countryside by fostering the transformation of the "peasantry" into a proletariat.[2] The swelled ranks of the proletariat would then power development in a France that was embarking on the path of rapid industrialisation.

The way, then, was paved for the emergence of a prosperous capitalist farmer, economically integrated into the market and culturally assimilated to a modern French national identity as "peasants" were also to be transformed into Frenchmen (Weber 1976). Those small-scale farmers, who remained in the countryside of the provinces and the regions, so it was envisioned, would retain a residual function as virtual caretakers of the artifacts of France's rural past. They were to become what Franklin (1969) called "park-keeper peasants"—geriatric custodians of a cultural heritage, rapidly disappearing under the assimilationist forces of French cultural integration. The diversity of regional cultures would then be eroded while collective identities would come to be consolidated through the strengthening of national culture and galvanizing citizenship.

While this was the thrust of many postwar dialogues on the development of modernity in France and Europe, more recently by contrast, in the discourse of the 1990s, we hear much talk of development in terms of "a Europe of the regions" in the context of the creation of the EU. Indeed, an academic industry has arisen to address the question of forms of "regional development" that build on extant institutions in social and economic peripheries. Much of the discussion is premised on ideas of what might be done to push a country's more "disadvantaged regions" along on the road of progress. A political discourse can be detected that is somewhat more delicately phrased than in the

1960s and 1970s, that focuses on the role that regional identity might play in the making of the French citizen or, more recently, an European citizen, rather than outrightly dismissing it as irrelevant to modernity's agenda. The discourses of the two periods are interrelated of course: "regional development" is in part the state's response to the clamber of the regional discontent that has grown apace over the past years. And conversely regional discontent is itself a function of peripheral people's perceptions of threats to their way of life that have emanated from the center over the postwar years.

But as academics and policy makers seek new ground on which to build their models for the future, together they share the modernist and planner's impatience with history. It is frequently forgotten, for example, by today's advocates of regional development in France and elsewhere in Europe who seek to experiment with new economic forms (Piore and Sabel 1987) and build on existing institutions of family enterprise and interpersonal networks to encourage capitalist growth and development, that those enterprises and networks only exist (insofar as they exist at all) because of the resilience and political energy of people like Roger and his cohort of friends. Individuals who maintained such networks often did so as part of a constant struggle to resist a model of capitalist growth that is as vigorously pursued in policies of the 1990s as in those plans of years gone by. If those earlier policies "failed" to achieve the goals of eliminating cultural "backwardness" and economic inefficiency, that may partly be because of their inherent poor formulation. However, it would only be to plan further failures for the future, were we not to recognize that much of that "failure" was the result of the agency of the regional and rural recipients of those policies.

By presenting an ethnography that focuses on a village in one region of contemporary rural France, where "peasants" have not entirely become transformed into "Frenchmen" to borrow from Weber, I seek to recover that history and the agency of a group of people as they confront modernity. In doing so, it is worth remembering, what is all too easily forgotten in the intellectual fashions of the day. It is one thing to condemn our modernist past *in toto*. It is quite another matter to try to draw some lessons from it. So here I prefer to retrieve the details of its specificities as they were felt in the Languedoc region of Mediterranean France, by small farmers who engage with their political worlds by struggling to preserve the agrarian economy

and the particular way of life associated with family-based production against the development of capitalism in agriculture.

The Problems

It is particularly striking that within a country that is at once
modern and capitalist, agricultural enterprises owned and operated by the family remain salient. Despite intensive industrialization since the Second World War and despite France's present
position among the most modernized countries in Europe, the
country remains largely an agrarian nation, representing one of
the most important agricultural producers in the European Union
and the western world (Muth 1970; Zeldin 1983; Hoggart et al.
1995). Moreover, it occupies this position with an agricultural
sector that continues to be dominated precisely by those small
family-run farms slated for disappearance.[3] This is especially
the case in the country's southernmost regions.[4] Despite both the
competitive pressures of a highly developed market economy *and*
the presence of a sector of larger-scale capitalist farms that are
run using a permanent force of wage laborers, small-scale family
run farms persist.

   The ability of family-based agriculture to persist, especially
under modernizing forces and state policies that are manifestly
dedicated to its eradication begs the question of how small-scale
farmers manage to sustain themselves, their holdings and their
families in the face of forces fostering their demise. Moreover, it
is equally striking that while small-scale family-based farming
remains, at least in the present, a consistent feature of rural
France, it is distributed throughout a country that is composed
of regions marked by significant differences in social institutions, languages, and cultural practices. Moreover, such regional
distinctions do not persist as mere artifacts, but are themselves
animate, animated by the commitments and practices of rural
people. Noting such regional distinctions, many writers have
recognized in their studies that the homogenizing forces of cultural assimilation that accompany the processes of modernization, building a nation-state and consolidating a national identity
have failed to erode the diversity of life in social and cultural
spaces removed from the centers of power. Rogers (1991) and
McDonald (1990), for example, each wrote of the complexity of
local social and cultural institutions and of the distinctiveness of

local practices in different regions in France. For France, as for many other European contexts, this diversity reflects the fact that far from implying homogeneity, the very processes of modernization have produced segments of society that are distinctive and people who maintain their distinctiveness and indeed alienation from national culture and society (Heiberg 1989; Keating and Loughlin 1996).

In these pages, then I present a case in which that sense of alienation and distinctiveness is often translated into action taken to contest structures of power and forms of domination that contour and constrain local life. The study focuses on a village of Occitan wine growers who, since the beginnings of the development of commercial monoculture, have been engaged in a concerted struggle to resist the various forms of domination that have accompanied capitalist transformation, while trying to negotiate a way of surviving within a market driven economy. My purpose is to attempt to apprehend the social practices and conventions which have moved people to engage in dramatic displays in the theater of public protest. To accomplish this, I focus on the internal social world of family farmers in Broussan to interrogate what I propose is a dialectic between work, political practice, and collective identity. The discussion illustrates the ways in which local social and cultural practices involved in struggling to put together a livelihood are implicated in political practices. It also shows how the vigor of their political campaigns in league with social practices of making a livelihood in everyday life invigourates local culture and sustains a sense of distinctiveness. This cultural sensibility, in its turn, fuels and galvanizes political efforts and also strengthens a commitment toward maintaining distinctive social practices and relations in everyday life. A virtuous circle is established between work, identity, and praxis in which each realm of social action and interaction constitutes and is constituted by the other.

This book then engages with the problems of a small-scale family farmers who will not go away, on the one hand, and the persistence of rural people who consciously maintain their sense of distinctiveness, often as a defiant political act, on the other hand. It is an investigation into what appears as somewhat of a paradox of modernity in France. The more there has been a drive toward economic modernization and cultural homogenization, the greater the efforts made by some of those consigned to the past to resist capitalism and defend their distinctiveness, as a group of people who share a way of life and ways of making a living. While these issues are treated, here, through a study of one group of small-scale family farmers in the context of Languedoc, such forms of agency and these particular problems and paradoxes, of course, are not unique to France. Indeed, in recent years, there has been a proliferation studies problematizing the relationships between cultural diversity, modernity, the emergence of nationalism and regionalist sentiments in France, Europe, and elsewhere. This has emerged in many respects as a effort to understand the forces that have led to the formation of nation-states in the past and the dissolution or the threat of dissolutions of many contemporary nation-states in the present. The rise of nationalism and minority nationalism and regionalist sentiments that assert cultural differences in the context of changes in the nation-state have led scholars to rethink the relationships that might prevail between nation, state, region, and culture.[5]

In this voluminous literature, significant attempts have been made to define nationalism, develop theories explaining the emergence of nationalism and the resurgence of nationalist sentiments both in history and in contemporary contexts.[6] Nationalism is both linked to the formation of the modern state as well as its destruction. In one of the most influential recent exegeses on the nature of nationalism and its relation to the formation of the modern nation-state, Hobsbawn have spoken of nationalism as an "invented tradition" established through such forces as education, public ceremonies, commemorations of national figures and events, as well as standardization of the administration and public law. In the case of France, for example, the secularization of education under the centralizing forces of government under the Third Republic, Bastille Day, and the proliferation of republican monuments in the city and the country worked together to transform subjects into the citizens of a country (Hobsbawm and Ranger 1983). Yet nationalism and nations are not necessarily coterminous with the state. In an early and one of the most elegant statements on the nature of nationalism, for example, Renan proposed the nation is simply a moral community, whose solidarity is built on historical consciousness both of common triumphs and common sufferings (Renan 1996). National ties unite from within the cultural and territorial boundaries of the moral community, they divide from without. Geertz (1994) sheds further light on what this solidarity and, indeed, this dissonance rests on by proposing that nationalism is based on ethnic ties or "primordial loyalties" that confer to members of this moral community a distinctive identity based on particularistic ties. National disunity can be attributed to the "longing not to belong to any other group" especially those, such as citizen, class, party, and union that override those primordial loyalties. Hence, sentiments based on those primordial loyalties can be aroused to oppose those larger forces of nation-state formation and centralization, which threaten to erode those distinctions. In the case of France, and other territories, regionalism, ethno-regionalism or minority nationalism have emerged to challenge the establishment of cultural universalism or the overriding of primordial loyalties, which is a project that had been fundamental to the formation of the modern nation-state. However, the question of the emergence of regionalism or regional nationalism does not rest simply on the issue of traditions being defended or cultural loyalties, being asserted in the face of threats. Hechter (1985), for example, through his thesis of internal colonialism has proposed that such movements emerge to contest the centralizing tendencies of the state in a context in which the state is seen to appropriate the resources of disadvantaged regions within its territorial boundaries. Regions and regional cultures are likened to African or Latin American colonial territories who have experienced a history of conquest, political subjugation, and economic exploitation. Similar to movements that have emerged in colonies that have contested colonialism and imperialism, regional and regional minority movements have emerged to reclaim cultural resources and to extend more local control over regional economies. To Hechter, these movements spring from a bedrock of what he calls "traditional culture" rooted in ceremonies and rituals, diverse language societies. While these and many authors have produced a rich dialogue on the nature of nationalism, there is a tendency to view regional culture and tradition as rarefied field, almost *sui generis*, persisting, for example, in the case of France, beyond the efforts made by the state to act on its official intolerance of diversity. Many lessons can be drawn from the current attempts to grapple with the complexity of nationalism, but also many more questions seem to be raised. For example, many current interventions incite investigators to determine how regional cultures manage to persist, also how traditions are "invented," and further how nationalist sentiments and consciousness emerge among ordinary people. This study is an attempt to shed light precisely on these questions.

My own approach therefore in trying to negotiate a way through the intricate and often troubling questions on identity, cultural diversity, regional distinctiveness, and nationalism is to employ a materialist approach. I argue in this study that local culture, regionalist, and nationalist sentiments are produced and reproduced through the actions and activities of people in their everyday livelihood pursuits. I focus on the social relations of production and study the nature of the politics and consciousness that emerge around the production of things. In using this approach to understand the nature of work, politics, culture, and praxis among wine growers in Broussan, I am in fact exploring two broad themes. The first is concerned with the complexities of the relationship between political action and collective consciousness and this is explored in Part 1: Place, Politics, and Identity. In Part 2: Work, Social Relations, and Everyday Life, the chapters are focused on the theme of the social relations involved in the organization of rural livelihoods. The two themes are intertwined revolve around the larger concern to apprehend the relationships that prevail between the quiescent arena of everyday life and the much more clamorous arena of public political performance.

Part 1 begins with an introduction to the village of Broussan. In chapter 1, the social structure and economy of the village is presented along with a brief historical discussion of the development of commercial monoculture in the region of Languedoc. In this chapter and, indeed, throughout the study I make no claim to be able to represent Broussan as a whole. Any ethnographic text can really offer only an incomplete image of the social and cultural fabric of any ethnographic context. So here attention is directed only toward the women and men of the community whose lives revolve around vine cultivation. The focus in *Cultivating Dissent* is on the population of farmers, which is a group united by their livelihood activities, but differentiated in terms of class into petty commodity producers, capitalist farmers, agricultural laborers, tenant farmers, as well as landlords. It is also a group that is differentiated in terms of gender, consciousness, and political practice. The implications of these forms of differentiation are addressed throughout the book, beginning in chapter 2 with an examination of the nature of the political practices that prevail among the vine-cultivating smallholder of Lower Languedoc.

By focusing on the ways in which small farmers have been consistently aroused to engage in forms of militant protest and collective action, I present a case that poses itself against representations of agrarian populations that stress their individualism, hidebound character and innate conservatism. In studies of rural society, the image of the impassive rural subject has appeared in many analyses from that written by Foster (1964) on the Mexican peasantry to Banfield (1958) on the Italian peasantry. Indeed, the limits of rural conservatism and its potential for radicalism has been the subject of much controversy among academics, political organizers, and thinkers alike—from Marx to Mao to Amilcar Cabral. In contemporary, scholarly circles, the arguments continue among social scientists and historians of developing countries and also of developed countries in Europe.[7] I emphasize here that the subjects of this study are in fact heirs to a vigorous tradition of what can only be called class struggle, fused with persistent acts of confrontation with the state, to resist the terms of its modernity project. These acts of confrontation involve activities that cover a wide spectrum of forms of action, from making demands formally through due political process to launching protests that regularly fall outside the domain of due political process. In chapter 2, then I discuss the diverse forms of collective confrontation that have been pursued by family farmers both within and outside due political process. I suggest that confrontations outside due political process became the quintessential means for expressing and defending the livelihood and way of life of smallholders, since the essence of the state's programs for the modernization of Languedoc viticulture meant a Malthusian process of the elimination small family farmers. Since the interests of the state represented through the modernization programs of successive French governments tended to stand in diametric opposition to the interests of small-scale family farmers, the formal political forums and the discourses of political parties were seen by family farmers to fail to articulate the life experiences and interests of the small-scale farmers. Smallholder then were compelled to engage in political activities and conducting campaigns outside the formal and legitimized channels. The nature of the activities and militant actions that form part of what has been referred to as the "hidden transcript" of resistance and struggle in the village of Broussan is examined (see Scott 1994).

In chapter 3, I explore the question of subjectivity, collective identity, and the forms consciousness that inflect political practice. The chapter is largely concerned with the ambiguities of collective identity and I discuss the multiple ways in which subjects locate themselves in a cultural and political universe. Among the small growers of Lower Languedoc, this ambiguity and multiplicity is manifested in the intertwining of apparently mutually exclusive forms of solidarity premissed on class consciousness, on the one hand, and cultural consciousness, on the other. Among the family farmers of Lower Languedoc, a collective identity as members of the "working class" prevailed. Self-definitional statements not only revealed a working-class consciousness, but in many cases this consciousness mirrored concrete experience. Narratives that recounted work histories also often reflected direct experiences of work and making living as a member of the laboring classes in Languedoc society. However, claims to class identity were also metaphorical and the positioning of people as members of the "working class" often existed beyond any individual's direct or immediate experience of work as a laborer within agriculture or industry. In the context of Lower Languedoc, where a tradition of left politics and working-class struggle prevailed, the discursive practices of class politics in a number of ways resonated with the life experiences many rural people, with and without a laboring past, who felt exploited by or excluded from the process of modernization.

While distinctive class identity prevailed and influenced the forms of political practice among family farmers, a specific cultural consciousness also contoured the acts of protest and confrontation undertaken by the family wine growers of Lower Languedoc. Small farmers of the region located themselves in France's cultural universe as members of Occitan culture. Though seldom absolutely rejecting French national identity, an inclination existed among the small farmers of Lower Languedoc to position themselves against national culture and to challenge the hegemony of the modernity project of the French nation-state. Occitan family farmers initiated and sustained forms of action in the political and mundane realms of social life to contest the extension of absolute state control over the economic and cultural affairs of the region as well as the imposition of a homogenous, dominant national culture.

The small growers of Lower Languedoc therefore asserted their place in the social and political world by synthesizing working-class consciousness with a cultural consciousness as Occitan people. A universalistic identity is interlaced with particularistic loyalties or to use Geertz terms the "primordial" solidarities of regional sentiments. In this chapter then, I explore several issues. First, I examine the ways in which the diverse yet interlocked collective identities focused on class, culture, nation, and region are constructed both discursively and also politically through practice. In focusing on discursive practices, I examine the significance of the key words, metaphors, and rhetorical claims in self-definitional statements by situating them within the concrete experience of work and political practice both in the past and in the present. A final issue that is broached here is concerned with the processes and historical conditions that engender the salience of specific forms of collective identity and foster the occlusion of others. So an attempt is made to situate the construction of collective identities in terms of changes in the local, regional, and national political economy.

Part 2: Work, Social Relations, and Everyday Life turns attention from the sphere of political practice and consciousness to the sphere of everyday life and it focuses on the organization of rural livelihoods. It explores the nature of social practices and relationships that are maintained by small-scale farmers to enable the continuity of their farms both on a daily basis and inter-generationally. The issues addressed are informed by two general and related concerns. The first is to understand the effects of the commodification or the penetration of the market on social and cultural life. The second is to expose some of the implications of populist visions and practices in development by exploring the power dynamics of small-scale operations, that are run by the family.

It is often suggested that the effects of the market are to isolate and individualize both individuals and units of production, liberating people from the bonds of kinship, community, and particularistic attachments.[8] Social relationships become governed by an instrumental rationality and capitalist calculation motivate exchanges of goods, labor, and services between individuals. My argument throughout the chapters of this section, drawing on the example of the ways in which labor is mobilized both within and between households in Broussan, is that even in those contexts where the market is highly developed, relationships are not entirely divested of social bonds. An instrumental rationality or a market ethic, may be present but it tends to be offset and counterbalanced by values and ethic of belonging to family, community, and neighborhood. In Broussan, social interactions and exchanges within the household and between households are governed by an intricate blending of the ethic of the market with the ethic of belonging to kin groups and community. Moreover, as I will seek to demonstrate, through the case material from Broussan, even in those contexts where the market is highly developed, few social spheres tend to be governed exclusively either by market calculation or by "primordial" attachments.

The general issues of the effects of market penetration and the nature of the social relations involved in the production of livelihoods investigated here are relevant to an important debate that has emerged in the study of agrarian societies on the question of the persistence of family farming or more accurately petty commodity production. Many analysts of petty commodity production have sought to explain the viability of family-based enterprises by focusing the nature of the social relations of production. It has been argued that the mobilization and use of family labor that is unpaid accounts for the sustainability of family farms in the competitive atmosphere of a market economy (see, e.g., Friedmann 1980 and 1987; Bernstein 1979 and 1987). It is posited therefore that there is a structural absence of a need to produce profits to pay wages on production units that rely on the unpaid members of domestic arrangements and this allows for its resilience. In this way, the household is seen as a sphere that remains free of the process of commodification and also a rather stark distinction is drawn between the spheres that have been penetrated by the market and those social spheres that lie beyond the reach of the market. This preoccupation with structure in this literature has led critics to comment that while much attention is focused on the implications of using unpaid family labor, scant attention has been paid to question of how precisely labor is mobilized on the family farm. In other words, the microdynamics of domestic life that influence the ways in which labor is secured, is neglected fostering a rather mechanistic view of the ways in which the family farm operates. To move beyond this image in which people are presented as mere labor units in a production process, requires the problematization of the ideological dimensions family-based production (see Scott 1986; G. Smith and J. Barker 1986; Lem 1998).

My own point of departure, therefore, in seeking to explain how family farmers sustain their livelihood is to emphasize, on the one hand that not only do people enter in relations with one another to transform materials into useful things, but they do so as humans beings who live in a social and cultural universe. Labor is embedded in social relationships and those relationships are saturated with values, ethics, and codes that prescribe modes of commitment, duties, rights, and obligations. I suggest therefore that to understand the dynamics of the reproduction of family farm in Lower Languedoc, it is critical to grasp the ways in which particular values govern the mobilization of labor. But this focus on value and meaning is not to insist on its unilateral determination. Because small growers in Lower Languedoc participate in a highly developed market economy, the ideological and social universes of family farming have not remained impermeable to the effects of market or the rule of instrumental rationality. I also stress, therefore, the considerable ambiguous and dimorphic quality of social relations generated by the tension between the "unfree" character of labor, especially in those contexts where family relations imply work relations and the forces that foster its liberation from ties of family, neighborhood and community. In Part 2, overall, I focus on the ways in which both cultural practice and capitalist calculation contours work relations.

In chapter 4, these issues are considered by analyzing the dynamics of the social relations of production that prevail within the context of the household. I emphasize that the interaction between members of the household tended to be governed by a "familistic" ethic. Cooperation, reciprocity, mutuality, and generosity are the norms that regulate exchanges of labor, goods, and services between members of the household as an organic unit. However, I also stress that the domestic sphere is an area that was not entirely free of the rule of instrumental rationality. Capitalist calculation tended also to influence the ways in which family labor was secured and deployed both in the everyday context and over the longer term. The effect of the market was to promote the differentiation of interests between member of the household. It reinforced differences in status of household members and fostered the tendency for members to pursue their individual interests, which often came into conflict with the interests of the collective unit. In this chapter then, attention is directed to the tensions that result from the moral prescription of kin ties and the rationality of the market which often produced dissension between parents and children over attempts to run the family farm on a day-to-day basis and particularly over succession, in the long term. In this chapter, I also expose the hierarchical character of the household which is often masked by the use of such emotive terms such as "family" and "kinship." Values that prescribe the normative behaviors attached to membership in families and kin groups often concealed the dynamics of domination and exploitation of juniors by elders and women by men. I argue that this inheres in a milieu, such as agrarian Languedoc, where the relationship between property and men, as heads of households is *de facto* privileged. The family, then, can exist as a structure which reinforces the power and authority of men. The importance of grasping these dynamics, which I suggest are intrinsic to family-based enterprises in rural Languedoc have broader implications. It contributes to an ongoing critique of populism in development theory and practice. The discussion here casts further doubts on the virtues of establishing small-scale family-run operations in developed and developing contexts advocated by neopopulists. The hierarchical and, indeed, patriarchal tendencies of the household exposed and emphasized in this study challenge the cherished view that such institutions are democratic and empowering.[12]

In chapter 5, the dynamics of patriarchy are examined further in relations to gender relations and the gendered division of labor. I also explore the political consequences of changes in the gendered division of labor to explain what has become the political quiescence of women in a context characterized by political clamor. In present-day Broussan and indeed, in Lower Languedoc, women seem to have relinquished the once prominent place they occupied on the political stage. In the early part of the century, women consistently participated in public and open confrontation with landowners, merchants, and agents of the state. Now, women seem to have withdrawn into a more private world of political expression. In this chapter, then, I suggest that the attenuation of women's political practice can be linked to changes in the gendered division of labor, on the one hand, and on the other, to the absence of a political discourse that articulates with the forms of domination and exploitation that women suffer in their roles as wives and workers who labor in what has become a multiplicity of workplaces, that encompass the domestic sphere and a arenas of work in many and varied spaces outside it.

I argue that the control exercised by men over the means of production and therefore the power employed by men to direct the ways in which households are reproduced become particularly pronounced with the changes in the division of labor that have accompanied the penetration of capitalism in Languedoc agriculture. Women became increasingly alienated from the process of vine production, the economic mainstay of the region. They also gradually came to be excluded from participation in farmwork as not only as agricultural laborers on local estates, but also from work in the fields on family smallholdings. A division of labor emerged in which women became increasingly consigned to perform the tasks associated with the running of domestic life. Women became increasingly constituted as "housewives," while men assumed the identity of "farmer." Women, in these respects, were subjected to a process of "domestication" their work experiences became altogether more individualized and isolated. Yet, simultaneously, their experiences of work became more dispersed and fragmented, in terms of both time and place as they were compelled to undertake many different forms work in a variety of forums, in different and changing workplaces as they pursued other activities for putting together a livelihood in an economy of pluriactivity. The alienation of women from wine growing through these processes is reflected in their retreat from the public political stage. This alienation is furthered by the fact that there is an established hegemony of political practice, which in a viticultural milieu revolves around viticulture, a livelihood activity in which women tended to participate only indirectly.

In chapter 6, I continue to examine the implications of labor's embeddedness social relations by examining the ways in which interactions and exchanges between households are located in a nexus of communal sanction. It has been argued by theorists of the market and its effects that competition and individualization tend to mark relations between enterprises in a capitalist economy (see Carrier 1997, e.g.). This assumption is reflected in the more specific studies of petty commodity production and family farming (see Friedmann 1987). In this chapter, these assumptions are challenged. From analyzing the organization of Languedoc livelihoods, a rather complex and almost paradoxical picture emerges in which one of the responses to the individualizing and competitive forces of the market is to pursue collective and cooperative strategies. In other words, in Broussan social ties between units of production tended to be maintained and relations between units were not wholly governed by competition. The complexity of the relations between units of production are exposed through a conceptual separation of two spheres in which household interact and engage in the exchange of goods, labor, and services—the market and the community. In the sphere of the market, households producing commodities for sale must compete with other enterprises producing the same commodity. In the context of commodity production, therefore, competition characterizes the relations between enterprises. However, the sphere of the market defines only one mode of interaction. The social context of the community defines another. Petty commodity producers must also coexist and cohabit in a small-scale, face-to-face community. Household in the context of the village are bound together as members of a distinctive community and particular culture, which along with the material conditions of living also must be reproduced. In this chapter, then, I examine the ways in which relations of community were sustained through the participation of people in a series of social networks involving a series of cooperative exchanges in their efforts to make a living. These exchanges served both to ensure the continuity of each farm in the competitive atmosphere of the market, and they also served to reproduce a sense of community, an ethic to defend the community and also to resist the penetration of the culture and logic of capitalism. In Broussan, the networks that were forged together through such exchanges often cohered into political coalitions that initiated the political campaigns. The activities undertaken by people within these networks and coalitions, on the one hand, served to get the job done in the everyday world of producing a livelihood. On the other hand, they also served to galvanize cultural ties by reinforcing the values and ethic of cooperation and solidarity in the face of the hardships created by the market. In turn, exchanges and the understanding of the importance of these exchanges conferred a sense of political purpose and meaning to the actions and activities pursued in lives of small wine farmers.

In chapter 7, a different facet of that ethic of cooperation is examined. I explore the formalization of that ethic of cooperation and its consequences for smallholders. Cooperatives in Languedoc are commonly acknowledged by villagers as having their origins in the ethic and practices of cooperation that prevailed among small-scale producers. They were founded under different waves of socialism in the early half of the twentieth century when, a spirit of finding common solutions to the difficulties of small-scale wine production spawned a number of local, endogenous and ad hoc forms of collective organization in viticultural villages. Emerging from this climate, vinification cooperatives were meant as a means for defending small growers interests against merchants and dealers in the market. While serving this purpose, cooperatives sponsored and set up with subsidies by the state, simultaneously became the instrument par excellence for extending state control over the viticultural economy. The establishment of the cooperative also resulted in fundamentally altering the nature of wine production. Wine growers became both alienated from the product they produced, while being subjected to increasing forms of state regulation and control. Moreover, cooperatives as the instrument of the state, also became the vehicle for realizing the state's agenda of agrarian modernization. They participated in promoting the demise of small-scale family-based farming by implementing policies, programs and subsidies that fostered the disappearance and transformation of petty producers into capitalist farmers. In chapter 7 then, I examine the ways in which the mechanisms for monitoring wine production came to be multiplied and how through the cooperative, the state was able to realize its agenda of fostering a modern, capitalist viticulture. This has resulted in a shift in perception of the cooperative. Growers once saw the cooperative as an instrument that served their efforts to resist exploitation and maintain control of their means of making a living in the face of market competition. Now it is seen simply as an appendage of the bureaucratic structure of the state and many growers decry the condition of dependency on the state that has emerged.

In chapter 8, the book concludes with some reflections on the questions identity, praxis in political economy, situating *Cultivating Dissent* in discussions of agrarian resistance, the relationship between culture and class, as well as regionalism and nationalism.

PART 1
PLACE, POLITICS, AND IDENTITY

praxis Refers in general to action, activity, and in Marx's sense to the free, universal, creative and self-creative activity through which man [*sic*] creates (makes, produces) and changes (shapes) his historical, human world and himself.

Tom Bottomore, *A Dictionary of Marxist Thought*

The Languedoc has a distinct character all of its own, quite unlike anywhere else in France. It has its own language, the *langue d'oc*, and the way of life of its fiercely independent people has strong undercurrents of violence and savagery which would never be found in Normandy or the Loire.

James Bentley, *Languedoc*

CHAPTER 1

The Place, the People, and the Land

The village of Broussan is located in the department[1] of the Hérault on the coastal plain of Mediterranean Languedoc.[2] It is situated northwest of the town of Béziers in a nearby canton.[3] The village is enclosed on all sides by fields of vines and farmers make a daily trek from their homes in the village to their minute parcels of land that are often widely scattered over the calcareous hills, valleys, and the exposed briny plains that are characteristic of the landscape of Languedoc. Indeed, throughout this region, seemingly endless expanses of vineyards yield the notoriously low-grade wines—the *"vins ordinaires,"* of France that have periodically glutted the national market and contributed toward the creation of the notorious "wine lakes" of the European Union. Reaching crisis proportions from time to time throughout the twentieth century, this periodic saturation of the wine market was a consequence of the development of the commercial monoculture of vine growing, initiated around the midnineteenth century.

Before the mid-1800s, an essentially subsistence-oriented peasantry generally prevailed throughout Lower Languedoc and farmers in villages like Broussan practised a mixed agriculture of wheat production, animal husbandry, and grape cultivation. Wine produced both on peasant holdings, as well as the large estates of the region was meant primarily for domestic consumption. Only

23

surpluses of wine that remained after the satisfying the needs of the families of the smallholders and estates owners, as well as those of the workers on the estates were sold on the market. As the mid-1800s approached, however, smallholders and estate owners alike began to convert increasingly from a mixed agriculture to the cultivation of grapes alone. For example, in Broussan, from about the beginning of the 1800s to the beginning of the last quarter of the nineteenth century, the land devoted to viticulture more than doubled, rising from about 280 to 600 hectares out of a total of 2,500 hectares of arable and nonarable land (Durandeu 1983). The economy of Broussan, like that in many other villages on the Languedoc plain was becoming progressively transformed from a subsistence-oriented polyculture to a market-oriented monoculture.

Several developments stimulated owners of both large estates and small farms in Languedoc villages to expand vine holdings and transform plots that produced wine largely for domestic consumption into vineyards that produced a commodity primarily destined for sale on markets. Crop conversion was originally initiated by the growth of an international sea trade in the mid-1800s as well as the decline of local wheat production. Competition from cheaper Russian imports reduced the demand or higher priced local grain and the market collapsed for Languedoc wheat, giving impetus to producers to switch to the cultivation of a more saleable crop.

Later in the century, the increased conversion to commercial monoculture was hastened by the opening up of the national market, through the construction of a railway system that linked producers in the south to centers of consumption in the north. Growing demand for Languedoc wines in urban centers of France prompted growers to switch over to vine cultivation en masse especially in the face of unsaleable wheat. While the decline of wheat production and the opening up of the international and then national market accelerated the development of Languedoc vineyards, the thorough transformation of agriculture to monoculture in the region was in fact induced by the phylloxera[4] blight of the last quarter of the nineteenth century. The blight that destroyed France's vineyards resulted in an acute shortage of wine on the national market and prices soared in the last half of the 1800s for available stores.

In the aftermath of the epidemic, the restoration of France's devastated vineyards became an imperative both for growers and the state. The state offered various subsidies and forms of aid to producers to help defray the costs of reconstituting vine-yards. Languedoc farmers, who were already on the road to conversion were poised to take advantage of government schemes and subsidies, and they undertook replantation on an unprec-edented scale. Not only did they replant with more and more vines, but because they had incurred heavy debts over the years of crisis and also because subsidies only partially offset the costs of vineyard reconstitution, growers replanted with varieties of grapes that would ensure maximum yields per hectare in order to take advantage of the high prices wine was commanding. In viticulture, the cultivation of high-yielding varieties of grapes necessarily produces low-grade wines. In Languedoc, then the production of great volumes of low grade wines has contributed to a series of crises in the economy of wine growing, in which periodic booms were often followed with busts and crises of over-production.[5]

Languedoc farming then became transformed from a largely subsistence-oriented polyculture to a market-oriented monocul-ture and a peasantry became transformed into petty commodity producers. Languedoc, itself, not only came to be a region that specialized in a monoculture of grape cultivation but it also became a region that specialized in the production of large quan-tities of *vin ordinaire*. Now on the littoral that spans almost the entire shore of the Golfe du Lion, in villages like Broussan, volumes of plonk are produced by a highly differentiated rural population with the labor of smallholders, agricultural laborers and tenants on the small-scale family-run farms and large es-tates that characteristic of the region. Viticulture and wine grow-ing then has become central to the social, cultural, and economic fabric of Broussan and the lives of a good majority of people in the village orbit around the cultivation of grapes and the manu-facture of wine.[6]

Work and Belonging in Broussan

The collective experiences of working in the vines and living within a community whose daily and yearly routine was orga-nized around the viticultural cycle made farming fundamental to a sense of the shared identity as people of Broussan—*"les Broussanais* and *Broussanaises."* While, in fact, most of the in-habitants of Broussan, farmers and nonfarmers alike, actually made a living through a variety of means, the social, political, and cultural life of the village revolved around grape growing and the manufacturing of wines. Everyday talk was replete with concerns about viticultural policies, the prices of wines, the conditions of the soils, how to execute specific tasks, recruiting labor, the price of land, equipment, inputs—in short—every aspect of viticulture.

One particular topic that loomed large as a conversation piece among villagers was the lingering fear about the decline of Languedoc villages and viticulture, which was a byproduct of the changes experienced by villagers in the immediate post–World War II period.

In the 1950s and the 1960s, the aging of the farm population combined with the flight of young families, as well as the failure of many farmers fueled concerns that Broussan would stagnate. The introduction of the tractor, which reduced the need for laborers and displaced women on wine-growing estates, combined with the revival of the industrial economy under the Marshall Plan as well as efforts made to restructure agriculture through various state programs (see chapter 2) prompted an exodus from the countryside in many parts of France and its reverberations were felt in Broussan. During those years, the population of the village fell significantly, while the proportion of elderly people increased over the years rather dramatically.[7]

In the 1980s this worry continued to find expression among the people of Broussan in discussions and conversations about the future of the village and farming. In interviews with women and men of the village whose experience of work in agriculture spanned the postwar period, gloom-and-doom scenarios were frequently offered on the future of the village and Languedoc farming. One elderly grower, Henri Boher commented about his son, André, who had taken over the family holding:

> André belongs to the last generation of people who will have work in the vines. After, his generation very few, maybe only the rich, will be able to stay in farming. Anyway, the young don't want to stay. I have watched them leaving for a long time, since farmers started buying tractors. There is no future here.

Despite the tenacity of this particular view of future of farming and village life in Broussan among a certain generation of farmers, the threat of stagnation was declared by many to have been stemmed. Indeed in the Municipal Bulletins of the 1980s, village officials were at pains to emphasize the importance of the small but significant rises in the population of Broussan after several decades of decline. In-migration clearly acted as one of the factors that allayed fears that the village would suffer the fate of many rural settlements that had become almost deserted villages of dilapidated houses, boarded-up shops inhabited only by the elderly found in the more mountainous areas of Upper Languedoc and the Massif Central.

New migrants to the village accounted for some of this "recovery," however, a second related development also served to diminish that haunting specter of ghost villages. Village sons and daughters were returning to settle in Broussan. The economic recession that gripped France in the 1980s and 1990s, as well as the restructuring of the national economy, which initiated the deindustrialization in urban areas gave impetus to these developments. Factory closures and the down-scaling of industries have resulted in high levels of unemployment in industrial centers, propelling many out of the cities to search for work elsewhere. Moreover, the relocation of industries to the regions as well as the promotion of regional poles of development in the 1980s has fostered a detectible urban exodus of sorts in which members of the urban working classes are relocating to the regions in a search for work (Jenson 1988, Lem 1997). In contrast to the postwar decades, in which village youth were forced to search in the north for employment in industry, many of the young now either arrive, return or remain in or nearby Broussan. Such developments in the national political economy brought of Anthony Giraud a native of Paris to Broussan. Anthony was 25 years old, unmarried, and worked as a day-laborer in the village. He briefly sketched his work history:

> After finishing two years of military service in 1977, I began to train as a shepherd in the Aveyron. It was part of a course of study for an agricultural diploma. I decided not to return to Paris after serving in the army because the possibilities of employment in the city were not very good. Also, I found the overcrowding and the general pace of life too hectic in the city.
>
> I left the Aveyron finding husbandry very difficult as I was not used to the lifestyle it demanded, not having been born on a livestock farm. I gradually made my way to Broussan after finishing the agricultural degree to look for work in viticulture. I found a job in the vines and began to

train as a vine worker. I want to be able to save enough money to buy a small parcel of vines.

I want to stay here in wine country, since the life of a wine-grower suits me. It has many advantages over the kinds of work that were available to me. In viticulture one can work unsupervised and in the open air and there exists the possibility of one day owning a vineyard. I can set myself up as an independent grower someday with some careful planning. This is much preferable to the life of a factory worker, since you would never become your own boss. One would be crazy to choose that over wine growing, if one had the choice.

In many respects, Anthony occupied an ambiguous status, in the village. While he was from Paris and the north (see chapter 3), he was an outsider to be viewed with some suspicion. Nevertheless, he also participated in the viticultural economy working as a laborer. Like many agricultural laborers who arrived in the village and region before him, Anthony aspired to landownership. Like many of the labor migrants from the mountains of Upper Languedoc and Spain, Anthony was on the road to becoming assimilated to the way of life of those who have committed themselves and their labor to vine cultivation. Unlike other migrants unconnected to the economy of wine growing, he perforce partook in the concerns and priorities that govern the world of Languedoc wine growers by virtue of his work.

The limited possibilities for securing work in cities in the 1980s have also prompted men and women who had originally left the village of Broussan in the 1960s and 1970s to return. Philippe Dolques is one example of a native son who had returned to Broussan from other parts.

Philippe left the village in 1975, at the age of 20, since there was little work for him to do on the very small holding run by his parents and work as an agricultural laborer was scarce. After his father retired in 1980, Philippe inherited the small family vineyard and a house. He retained this property despite his absence from the village, intending to make enough money by working in the city to eventually take over the family holding and to begin to expand it into a more substantial enterprise. However, his efforts at securing lucrative forms of work were only partially successful as he was tossed about by an unstable labor market:

When I first left Broussan, I worked as waiter in a restaurant in Paris. I didn't like the coldness of the climate and the people, so later on I moved back south to St. Tropez and started to work again as a waiter. I got tired of this kind of work and began to look for something different and that paid better. I found work in construction in Marseille. It paid more than being a waiter. I met my wife in Marseille and as jobs were getting scarce around here, we traveled to South America to work for a couple of years in the construction of a subway. I had heard that it was possible to make a lot of money in a short period of time working abroad. There was nothing here, so we packed up and left and sure enough managed to save up quite a bit of money.

I am now back with a wife and two kids and I am beginning to work on the land that was left to me. I have only 1.5 hectares of vines which I rented out while I was away. I also inherited the house that we are now living in. We have been using it as a vacation home and a kind of base while we have been away. We are now in the midst of restoring this old house which needs a lot of work before we can feel comfortable in it. I am working toward expanding the farm so I take on building jobs and my wife works as a tutor.

Cases of migrants returning to the village, such as Philippe, have prompted many to echo a comment made by Philippe's mother, Huguette, in a rather triumphal tone that: "Many of our young have gone up to Paris. They took a look around, hated what they saw. And now they've come back." Philippe harbored the hope, as did many owners of small parcels of land, to eventually become an independent smallholder. He subscribed to the ideology of land ownership that pervaded this agrarian context and his participation in the economic mainstream of the village fostered a sense of belonging in the community of Broussan.

While viticulture represented the main livelihood activity in Broussan, very few of the wine growers in the village worked exclusively on the farm. Indeed, the presence of a rural inhabitant who pursues a multiplicity of livelihood activities or is involved in pluriactivity is as pervasive in the village as it is in many other French and European contexts (see Holmes 1989, Blim 1990, Weber 1989).[8] Members of wine-growing households were involved simultaneously in very diverse forms of work and often in locations outside the village. Many women and men from wine-growing households commuted daily to Béziers and other towns and villages to work as wage earners in local factories, government offices, hospitals, as well as in shops and business as clerks and waiters. They set themselves up in local businesses as hairdressers, builders, and painters, baby sitters and cleaners in the village and often this is done in the informal economy. The involvement of women and men in a diverse array of livelihood earning activities is a phenomenon that was as prevalent in the distant past and it has been in recent decades. For example, J. H. Smith (1984) writes of smallholders in the late 1800s in the village of Cruzy, just west of Broussan, making a living through a "dual family" economy of wage and nonwage forms. Similarly, Frader (1991) notes in her study of Coursan in the Aude that women particularly were involved in bring cash in households through a multiplicity of means around the turn of the twentieth century. Despite the fact that a good number of women and men in Broussan were involved in an economy of pluriactivity, what often united them in terms of their interests and political inclinations was the commitment of their labor to farming. This unity encompassed independent cultivators who worked their own holdings, with the help of their kin and neighbors as well as agricultural laborers and tenants, who often operated small parcels of whole working land belonging to other larger farmers and estate owners.

Large and Small

Though the entire region of Lower Languedoc appears to be covered with one vast carpet of vineyards, vines are cultivated on relatively small farms. In Broussan, holdings can be arranged on a continuum of size that extends from less than 1 hectare to over a 100 hectares. The majority of holdings however would be clustered around the lower end of the continuum, from 1 to 30 hectares. Of a total of around 550 holdings, in fact, only four holdings exceeded 30 hectares. Even the largest holdings in the community were relatively small on a national scale, for example in comparison with the wheat farmers of the north whose holdings were often hundreds of hectares in size.

    The largest holding in Broussan was Château X, which consisted of 113 hectares jointly owned by a brother and sister team and their spouses. The chatelains, the S. and B. families, were considered the wealthiest members of the community. There was a drastic drop in size for the next largest holding which was also a château, but consisted of 55 hectares. This domain was owned by a corporation. Other large enterprises in the community were run by a local people and absentee owners who ran their operations either with a labor force supervised by stewards or using share tenancy arrangements. While such enterprises were considered the largest by regional standards, they occupied only about 10 percent of the land under cultivation. A situation of a high degree of land concentration did not exist and the predominant characteristic of land tenure was ownership of small, often minute, parcels of land that were often less that .25 hectares. The owners of the minutest parcels of land were in the main the elderly members of the community who kept a small parcel to produce wine for home consumption. While size of the holding is some indicator of the types of enterprises that were present in Broussan, two structural types could be distinguished that roughly correspond to a distinction between large and small operations—the family-run farm and the capitalist farm.

Two Types of Enterprises

The basic distinction between the family farm and the capitalist farm is that the former is run primarily using the unpaid labor of members of the household, that is, it uses unpaid or "noncommodified labor" (Friedmann 1980). The capitalist enterprise is run exclusively through the employment of a permanent force of paid laborers. Hence, the relations of production on the capitalist enterprise are "commodified."

Most of the viticultural operations in Broussan were family farms and 90 percent of the 500 or so farms were run using family labor. As a rule of thumb, it was held by growers that one person using one tractor could run a holding of about 8 hectares for the greater part of the year without the aid of extra labor. On family holdings larger than 8 hectares, additional labor was required and members of the household, when available, were recruited to help in the production process. According to one informant, the owner of a 7-hectare operation, an 8-hectare holding should generate at least 7,000 francs a month (i.e., roughly $2,000) which was approximately the minimum needed in order to sustain a household and to keep the farm in operation. The actual income generated from any individual holding apart from size will depend on a combination of factors such as location of the vineyards, fertility of the soil, the vine-plant varieties, age of the plant, and yearly weather conditions. A holding of 8 hectares was seen as generally sufficient to weather the fluctuations in the amount of income due to variations in average yields in any given year. While in theory, holdings of this size were generally considered sufficient for households to become established as independent smallholders, in fact, as I mentioned earlier, very few lived solely from revenues of their viticultural enterprises alone. The pressure exerted by what Bernstein has identified as the "simple commodity production squeeze" drove smallholders to seek supplementary sources of income, even among those with the minimum requirement for farm self-sufficiency.[9] On smaller holdings it was essential for the survival of the farm to obtain additional income from other sources. On many holdings then spouses, children, and often extended kin living in the household brought in additional income through a variety of types of employment. Members of smallholding households did this often in addition to working on the farm, when additional labor was required. If household labor was unavailable to be deployed to the fields, a variety of modes of gaining access to other sources of unpaid labor was put into effect. These involved reciprocal exchanges and many forms of mutual aid that drew on kin and friends from other households. The question of how the dynamics of the household economy and ways in which labor both from within the household and between households is deployed is discussed in Part 2.

Operations that were larger than 30 hectares could not be run but with a permanent force of wage laborers. Château X, for example, employed a permanent labor force consisting of three families, migrants from Spain, who made up the domestic labor force and three day-laborers who lived in the village. On holdings this size, owners seldom contributed their labor to working the land. Although no wine-growing enterprise that exceeded 30 hectares was run using family labor, on many holdings slightly smaller in size, owners often worked alongside laborers who were employed on both a permanent and part-time basis as well as seasonally and occasionally. Seasonal and occasional labor was hired during the very labor intensive periods of the agricultural cycle, such as pruning and during the harvest. Often a permanent and part-time labor was hired in due to the absence or insufficiency of family labor to run holdings that required more than one person and one tractor. So for example, many of the holdings between roughly 10 and 25 hectares consistently moved in and out of wage relations. While the presence or absence of wage relations was a truer indicator of the nature of an operation than the simple size of the holding, in Broussan qualitative and structural distinctions were difficult to maintain on many medium sized farms, because of this constant movement in and out of wage relations. Moreover, agricultural workers were themselves often also *petits propriétaries* (small owners) and they have labored alongside employers for well over a century. This merging of occupation and identities had distinctive implications for the kinds of political orientations and practices in the region (see chapters 2 and 3). Despite the difficulties in drawing distinctions between capitalist farms and family farm in that ambiguous middle-size range, operations located at extreme ends of the continuum can be contrasted in a significant number of ways.

Château X, a purely capitalist operation, for example, occupied the most fertile and flat land in the municipality, whereas, the holdings of the family farmers were often located on less fertile land on hill sides with difficult access. The vineyards of the domain were consolidated into one unit and concentrated around the château. This contrasts with small-scale family holdings, whose fields were usually scattered in small parcels throughout the canton. Equipped with the most advanced machinery, the production process was highly rationalized on the large capitalist estates. For example, individual vines on the Château have been planted in straight rows with enough space between them to allow various large and modern machines to pass through. On family-run farms, vines were often planted in very narrow rows, on small nonadjacent parcels of land dispersed through throughout several communes. Despite these contrasts, the operators of family farms and large capitalist operations, alike, positioned themselves immediately in the occupational universe as wine growers. What united smallholders and capitalist farmers in many of their interests and perceptions were landownership and their participation in the operation of a viticultural enterprise. Still, this shared occupational identity did not elide differences that existed in the ways in which operations were run, the size of holdings, and who committed their labor directly to the production of grapes and those who did not. The owners of capitalist farms were not engaged in the direct cultivation of the soil, while the owners of family enterprises operated their farms with the contribution of their physical labor. In other words, wine growers were highly differentiated and were divided by class. Large landowners and smallholders each had a very different relationship to the process of production. These similarities and differences as well and the ambiguities created by the commonality of *petits propriétaires* working as laborers alongside owners contributed to the intricate patterns of political practice and expressions of identity (see chapters 2 and 3).

Large Landowners: *"Les Propriétaires"*

The largest landowners in Broussan represented a pure landowning class who ran their operations strictly using wage labor. There were two categories of landowners, those who lived in or near the village or on the estate and those that were absentee. Absenteeism was a phenomenon that became accelerated in the late 1800s, when wine production on the Languedoc plain took on increasingly capitalist character. In that period, large landowners often removed themselves from their domains and the production process altogether, concentrating their efforts on keeping the accounts and on marketing, while residing in the centres of commerce. Authority on the estates was often delegated to stewards, a new position emerged on the estates with the transition to capitalist agriculture (J. H. Smith 1975).

In Broussan, for example, production on the 29-hectare holding owned by a businessperson who lived and worked in the town of Pézenas (a few kilometres east of Broussan), was supervised by steward who was roundly despised by workers. He was recruited from the village and once worked as an agricultural laborer on the same estate. When he rose to this position, many workers in the village became very wary of him, finding him untrustworthy as he now worked hand-in-glove with the bosses, *"les patrons."*

Altogether in Broussan there were about 30 landowners who ran their operations by hiring wage workers on a permanent basis, year round. Even landowners who lived in the village or on the estates were frequently absentee, preoccupied with the marketing and publicizing wines grown on the estates. One of the owners of Château X, for example, spent much of the agricultural year attending wine fairs nationally and internationally to publicize the estate wine. Much of his time was also spent negotiating deals with distributors and merchants, who have sold his wines to North American restaurants and liquor stores. His partners on the estate, who resided in Broussan year round assumed mainly a managerial role in the running of their operation. While pure landowners tended to run farms that were generally larger than 30 hectares, some among this class owned holdings that were much smaller. Many of these smaller owners ran businesses or were employed in the fairly lucrative professions of law, medicine, or dentistry. Such landowners acquired their vineyard properties either through inheritance or by purchasing land for the purposes of investment. For example, one holding in Broussan that consisted of about 24 hectares was owned by a doctor who lived near the village. He had inherited this property from an uncle who had no children of his own to take over the property. Another 22-hectare vineyard was owned by a lawyer who lived in Broussan while practising in Béziers. He had inherited a portion of the vineyard but also acquired more land as his practice became more and more successful. Moreover, a 20-hectare operation was owned by local businesspeople and worked by two laborers. By and large, this class of owners regarded their holdings in land as an investment, or a source of retirement income and seldom committed their own labor to the cultivation of vines on a sustained basis.

In the village there was another significant group of landowners who similarly did not make a direct contribution of their labor to the cultivation of vines but who derived revenues from wine holdings. They consisted of elderly residents of the community who were no longer able to work the land and who were widows or single women. For reasons of household composition or because of the constraints of the sexual division of labor (see chapter 5), they hired labor to run their holdings or rented out their property.

Direct Producers: *"Les Exploitants"*

On the family-run farms of Broussan, the owners of the enterprise tended to be engaged in the direct cultivation of grapes. However, like their predecessors in the eighteenth and early nineteenth century, most of the smallholders ran their farms combining farmwork with many other forms of work, including wage work and running businesses. The direct producers in Broussan operated holdings that varied greatly in size from very minute parcels (less than 1 hectare) to more substantial operations of more than 20 hectares. While by and large, members of smallholdings households worked in other sectors of the economy while running their farms, this did not necessarily imply that they owned marginal units of production that generated insufficient incomes. A number of the part-time growers, in fact, had very sizable holdings and through a variety of arrangements with family members and kin, operated their wine-growing farms while pursuing other livelihood concerns at the same time (see chapters 4 and 5). Many of members of the petty bourgeoisie in the village—the shopkeepers, the café owners and shop managers, then, ran sizable holdings in addition to running their own businesses. For example, the household that operated one of the village hardware stores ran one of the largest owner-operated holdings in the village (34 hectares). It was run by a father-and-son team with the help of a hired laborer. Still, such sizable units were by no means the rule among all businesspeople who operated farms.

Some members of the petty bourgeoisie actually operated very small agricultural enterprises in the village. For example, the family that owned and operated the small electrical appliances shop ran only a 4-hectare vineyard. Many other operators of small businesses and shopkeepers ran holdings of around this size. These observations having been made however, the possibilities for the expansion of farms owned by members of the petty bourgeoisie were greater than those for many family farmers and laborers. This group generally had access to larger capital resources. Furthermore, the ways in which labor was mobilized within and between households of the petty bourgeoisie and households of the smallholders marked very different trajectories of development in the overall process of reproduction.

Share Tenants: *"Les Fermiers"*

For the smallholding sector of the village population, one of the most common ways of gaining additional income from within agriculture was to take up a share tenancy contract.[10] The smallholders of the village both rented out parcels of land and took on tenancy contracts. There were two kinds of contracts in Broussan. One involved a division whereby the owner of the land received one-third of the income yielded from the harvest while the tenant received two-thirds. A second kind of contract, the Indemnité Viagère de Départ (IVD), involved the payment of an annuity by the tenant to the owner, who, on death relinquishes ownership of the land to the tenant. The payment of the annuity was made in addition to the regular payment division. Under both contracts, the tenant was expected to provide labor, equipment, and inputs. In the village, approximately 65 owners had rented out some portion of their land and in many cases, to several different tenants. For example, one retired grower, Etienne Bascoul, rented his entire holding consisting of 11.7 hectares to three different households. The Cros family rented about 4.5 hectares, while another individual, Marcel Mas, worked 6.7 hectares of Bascoul's land. The remaining 0.6 hectares were rented by the Vias household. All tenants were in fact owners of vine properties in their own right and they worked rented land in addition to their own holdings. Approximately 75 holdings in the village included rented land and inasmuch as one property was often worked by several tenants, tenants themselves often rented land from several owners. For example, holdings of the Vias household consisted of 11 hectares of vineyards. About 7.2 hectares of the holding consisted of land rented from three different owners. 1.6 hectares belonged to Julien Mas, 79, a retired wine grower who was also agricultural laborer and Marcel Mas's father. Another 5 hectares belonged to Jean Cot, a butcher in Béziers. The remaining 0.6 hectares belonged to Etienne Bascoul, mentioned above.

Roughly one-fourth of the contracts were IVD agreements. While the municipal records and the registers of the cooperative showed that only one-fourth of the growers were engaged in share-tenancy arrangements, in fact 40 percent worked as share tenants. The discrepancy in the statistics can be accounted for by the fact that many of these arrangements were made between households on an informal basis without formal, written contracts and thus they were not declared to official sources. Such arrangements existed between households also connected by kin ties, but not exclusively so.

A few landlords who were party to such agreements were in fact owners of the larger holdings in Broussan. However, for the most part, the majority owned fairly small units. A large proportion of landlords lived and worked outside the village but wished to retain ownership of land in the municipality. Philippe Dolques the returned migrant, we met earlier, was one example of this group. During his absence from the village his small holding was rented by Marcel Mas, a friend of the family.

Elderly and retired wine growers represented the second largest group of landlords, followed by widows and single, separated, or divorced women. For the majority of elderly landlords, income derived from renting out land supplemented their retirement benefits. In some cases, the elderly resorted to renting out vineyards since their children were reluctant to take up farming and have migrated out of the village. In other cases, the lack of heirs, forced some old folks into share tenancy. Many such landlords in fact lacked the necessary equipment to cultivate vines, hence share-tenancy arrangements were made with those who have access to such machinery and tools.

The majority of tenants were, in fact, owner-operators who wished to increase income derived from viticulture without expending large amounts of capital to buy additional parcels of vines. In many respects, in terms of livelihood strategies, it was the line of least resistance for wine growers. Share tenancy neither required the deployment of labor to tasks altogether different from vine cultivation nor capital expenditures on machinery. Many tenants also worked as agricultural laborers. In these cases, a considerable number of these agricultural laborers *cum* tenants were landless. Access to the equipment to work the vineyards was obtained in a variety of ways—through borrowing from kin and from employers and renting (see chapter 6). For many of the landless laborers in the village, share tenancy represented an intermediate step between landlessness and land ownership, especially for those who had succeeded in striking IVD contracts. Not all agricultural workers were landless, however, as the possibilities for mobility from a landless status to one of being landed were realized through a variety of means from multiplying income-obtaining strategies to mobilizing networks of kin and friends. This is discussed in the case studies in later chapters.

Agricultural Laborers

There were roughly 90 permanent agricultural laborers in Broussan and most were actually day laborers who lived in the village by night and traveled to work in the larger vineyards and estates on a daily basis. Day laborers generally put in an eight-hour day, returning to the village at 6 P.M., often to work on their own little holdings before the sun set. Over half of the permanent agricultural laborers owned land in the village running very small holdings that were generally from just less than 1 to 4 hectares.

At least three of the permanent laborers in the village were women who worked as members of the domestic workforce (*les domestiques*) at Château X. Two were married to the male domestic workers at the château and one was the unmarried daughter of one of the families of the estate workers. These women were generally responsible for the preparation of the meals for the estate workers and also worked in the fields occasionally. Workers resident on the estates did not own any land in the community.

On the large estates in Broussan, there was a division of labor between skilled and unskilled workers. The day laborers tended to perform the more skilled tasks, such as grafting, planting, pruning, and maintaining the equipment. Day laborers were usually the sons of wine growers or, very often, wine growers themselves and so were familiar with the specialized tasks in vine cultivation. The tasks requiring less skill were conferred to the domestic workers, mainly migrants from Spain, who usually lived on the estates with their families. There was also a hierarchy of wage rates that corresponded to skill levels. Day laborers earned about 3,500 to 4,000 francs a month, about 40 percent higher than the guaranteed minimum wage, which in the mid-1980s was about 2,500 francs a month, earned by the unskilled domestic workers. The costs of accommodation and food were taken into account in calculating the wages paid to the domestic labor force and as a consequence their earnings often fell below the minimum wage.

Before the capitalist transformation of Languedoc agriculture the workforce on the large estates of the region, such as Château X was largely undifferentiated. Day laborers and domestic workers worked side by side and performed similar operations on the estates. Where a division of labor existed, it involved a division by gender. The day labor force often included women (*jounalières*), who worked at tasks that were considered lighter and more delicate (see chapter 5).

The capitalist transformation Languedoc viticulture, however, brought on a more rigidly defined division of labor between skilled and unskilled work, between different labor forces and an arrangement of tasks on the estates based on a hierarchy of wages, responsibility, and power. A division of tasks came to prevail between the *journaliers* and *domestiques*, the domestic workforce also became divided according to task and differentiated in terms of power and authority as small retinues of supervisors emerged. For example, the *ramonet,* appeared and acted as foreman or the head of the domestic labor force executing orders given by the steward (*le régisseur*). While he held this post, and carried out his duties and tended to the horses, his wife, the *ramonette,* came to be in charge of the preparation of meals for the estate workers and supervised the wives of *domestiques*. As was mentioned earlier, the steward, a new type of employee, began to appear more frequently with the development of absenteeism. The steward was primarily responsible for the supervision and planning of work on the estates; the control of the labor force; the payment of salaries and payment for the supplies and provisions for the workers (Pech 1975, 375–78). As was noted earlier on a contemporary domain in Broussan, stewards were often recruited from among small farmers and estate workers. Many, though were simply men who had no experience in viticulture and had to be trained on the job. The great degree of familiarity with the workforce and the accounts of the estate made the position of steward fairly powerful and often loathed by workers.

A process of capitalist transformation on the estates held other implications for workers in the villages of Languedoc. The people of Broussan remarked that there was less and less work for agricultural laborers and as a result, over the years the number of laborers in the village has declined (Durandeu 1983). This decline can also be traced to the overall process of capitalist rationalization that has taken hold of the viticultural economy over the past century, first introduced on the large estates of the region. On the largest domains of the region, for example, techniques of production used came gradually to be more rationalized and capital intensive. Generally on local estates, work routines were altered, so that certain jobs could be done during the winter, a period of lower wages. New techniques were used to render wine production more efficient and cost-effective, which led to the displacement of skilled vine dressers who were comprised of day laborers from the village. Their methods of tending the vines were found to be outmoded and too slow. Landowners imposed a managed work system that relied almost entirely on unskilled laborers who could be paid less, supervised more closely by estate stewards, and who would work longer hours than day laborers. Through these means, then, economies of scale were achieved and estates became more economically efficient (Pech 1975, J. H. Smith 1975).

While jobs on the estate for day laborers began to diminish, temporary work and piecework appeared. Women day laborers were hired from time to time on the estates when there was a need for extra labor, for example, for pruning, collecting branches, and spraying. Since they were generally paid half the wage earned by male day laborers, the hiring of women represented a cost-effective measure. Moreover, migrant workers who traveled from area to area in search of work either as individuals or in groups were hired to perform piecework. Often the piece workers were paid salaries that were higher than those of day laborers and there was some degree of antagonism between the two types of workers. Moreover, day laborers blamed the presence of piece workers for the unemployment among day laborers.[11] The amount of work available and the nature of work done by agricultural laborers then was deeply contoured by the transformations brought on by the development of capitalism in agriculture in Languedoc and in Broussan. As employment as agricultural laborers was in decline other ways of making a living or getting by sustained the people of Broussan as much in the past as now.

Other Work

While women and men were preoccupied with many forms of work, providing services both inside and outside the village, other preoccupations were a very important part of the local and household economy. While producers were largely involved in the production of a commodity for sale on the market and not for domestic consumption, the major part of the household food supply came from the market. Still, a good proportion came from self-provisioning. Many families kept chickens in the cellar or garage to obtain a supply of fresh eggs and meat. In one case a goat was also kept to provide the household with milk. A large number of households kept a fruit and vegetable garden on small plots of land on the residential property or on garage rooftops. The activities in this economy were mostly undertaken for self-provisioning, in an effort to reduce consumption costs, but small surpluses were sometimes marketed. Eggs, for example, were sold to neighbors below the market price. Producers often placed a notice with the mayor's office that a certain product, such as artichokes, will be sold at the home of a particular grower. Local stores were also supplied with a variety of fruits and vegetables grown in home gardens. These products were sold to local retail outlets at prices below the wholesale prices. Often retailers took goods on consignment. As the market in wines is often uncertain and unpredictable, many growers tried to hedge their bets against a bad year by diversifying their enterprises by taking on market gardening on a scale more expanded than that required for autoconsumption.

Women were primarily responsible for maintaining the economy of autoprovisioning. Gardens were cultivated mainly by women and small animals were raised by women. Marketing of garden and home-grown products was also usually done by women who were often seen early in the morning in the center of the village driving small trucks and cars loaded with small quantities of asparagus, artichokes, cherries, peaches, eggs, lettuce, and other seasonal items to sell to local stores and regional markets.

One striking characteristic in Broussan was that among many households, a secondary house was maintained that tended to be fully equipped. These residences were used to house seasonal workers during the harvest, and more important, served as rental accommodation for tourists who flooded the area during the summer, especially since Languedoc has been designated a region for the development of tourism. These houses consisted of either a separate apartment in the same house or some separate dwelling units altogether. Women by and large tended to occupy themselves with the rental and maintenance of tourist accommodation and, as will be discussed in chapter 5, were pivotal in a village economy of pluriactivity.

Local Political Inclinations

Broussan is a communist village and has had a longstanding tradition of following left politics. For a period of at least 30 years the formal political structure of the villages has been dominated by members of the Communist party and its sympathizers. The mayors for the past few decades were members of the Communist party as were many of the people who served on the municipal council. The people who tended to occupy the seat of local government did not necessarily represent a power elite of the large landowners or wealthy professionals in Broussan. They tended to hail from a broad spectrum of occupational and class categories. The mayor of Broussan throughout the 1980s and into the early years of the 1990s, was himself a wine grower who worked as the mayor on a part-time basis. He had three deputy mayors. Over the years, his deputies have been teachers, laborers, and even pensioners. The members of the council have been made up of a railway employee, bank employees, postal workers, builders, housekeepers, as well as wine growers. The list of opposition candidates in the election that was held in 1983, for example, was similarly composed of a broad range of men and women. The person who was defeated as a mayoral candidate was a retired postmaster. The rest of the people on the list included an artisan, two retired wine growers, five wine growers, an accountant, the operator of the driving school, two housewives, a retired employee of the National Board of Education, a driver and engineer, a vine worker, a postal agent, and a hairdresser. Not only was there the participation of a broad range of people from a variety of occupations, but there appeared to be no interdiction against the participation of women in the formal political administration of the community.[12] Women as a matter of course put themselves up as candidates in the municipal elections, though men still make up the majority of the power holders in the village.

Over the recent decades and into the 1990s, the contest in every election campaign for mayor took place between the socialists and the communists in the village. The lines of cleavage between socialist and communist became most evident during election campaigns, but in everyday life, the general consensus was that there was little substantive difference between the two, either ideologically or in terms of policy. Many, like Marcel Mas, a former member of the municipal council and once president of the local cell of the Communist party of France, asserted that "Socialist or communist—we were all people of the left. After all we were the *midi rouge*. The only political differences are personality differences." The identity that many shared as people of the *midi rouge* was pivotal to their political commitments. Even as the left parties waned in the national political arena, villagers stubbornly adhered to their tradition of supporting parties that defended workers' interests and the interests of agricultural laborers. A long history of following left politics and struggling to defend a way of life has endowed wine growers with a strong sense of their identity, responsibilities, and entitlements and what must be done to preserve them. Struggling to defend their way of life and their interests has become as much a part of their lives as working in the vines. How these interests were defended through a wide repertoire of collective action is the subject of the next chapter.

CHAPTER 2

People and Politics in Rural Languedoc

La Marselhesa dels V inhairons
[The "Marseillaise" of the Wine Growers]

La Republica nos penchena
Al ras del col amb un rastel,
Los ministras son pas en pena,
Elis d'engraissan a vista d'elh!
(bis)
E tu poble de la campanha,
Del temps qu'elis manjan lo piot
E que coflan lo borsicot
Te cal crebar dins la caganha.

Armatz vos vinhairons!
Trapatz vostres fusilhs!
E anatz engranar
Totis aquelhs sadolhs!

[The Republic is hackling us
with a rake around our necks,
The Ministers are not worried,
They are obviously getting fat!
(repeat)
And you people of the country,
While they eat turkey
And fill up their coffers
You must die in misery.

To arms, wine growers!
Seize your rifles
And get rid of
All these scum!

A Song of the Revolt of 1907]

Napo, *Les Chansons de la Révolte*

Rural Resistance

In 1907, the massive "Revolt of the Midi" swept through four departments of Languedoc and neighboring Roussillon. Considered the largest mass movement in France since the French Revolution, it has captured the attention of historians, political scientists, and social theorists alike interested in questions of rural struggle and in developing an understanding the complexities of resistance itself. The sheer scale and intensity of this collective uprising which involved both smallholders and vine workers, has secured a place of prominence for the revolt in texts on the political history of Languedoc as well as in the popular memory of the people of the region.[1] To many people of the region, the year 1907 is a powerful symbol serving as a

45

reminder of the deep divisions that prevail in rural Languedoc (see chapter 3). Historians too have acknowledged its importance for rural people. Many have noted that the revolt has engendered the tradition of "furious action" that prevails among family farmers in Languedoc, who have been stirred from time to time to rise up en masse to contest the forces that throughout the course of the twentieth century have posed a threat to the continuity of their lives and their livelihood (Loubère 1995, J. H. Smith 1978).

Until very recently, such episodes of collective action initiated by rural people were often considered to epitomize peasant resistance and indeed resistance itself, not only in the European context but also elsewhere.[2] Resistance was understood as a form of political action that involved the masses, a collectivity that openly confronted the status quo and challenged the structures of domination. However, in several recent and highly influential works on the nature of agrarian struggle James Scott (1985 and 1986) has argued for a conceptual shift in current understandings of the term *resistance*. He suggested that definitions of resistance should move beyond the assumption of the primacy of collective action and mass movements to incorporate those acts of defiance not only initiated by individuals but also that occur in everyday life and that might be expressed as purely symbolic as well as motivated by self-interest (1986, 22). In a discussion of forms of peasant struggle then, he proposed that the objective of the great bulk of rural resistance is not to overthrow or transform a system of domination but rather to survive within it. Drawing on Hobsbawm (1973, 12), he further posited that the means of survival often implies adopting a strategy that involves the rural people in "working the system to their minimum disadvantage" (quoted in Scott [1986, 30]). In later work (1994 and 1990), Scott extended his perspective by drawing attention to the "hidden transcripts" of resistance that involve behaviors, practices, speech, and gestures that are used as part of the "survival skills" of subordinate groups in situations of domination and typically occur offstage (Scott 1994, 58). Analyzing and decoding such hidden transcripts was a means of assessing the impact of domination.

Several writers have taken Scott to task for a series of conceptual confusions as well as for failing to adequately address a central political problem that people confront in their efforts to actually mobilize small-scale farmers and others to engage in forms of collective action. This problem concerns the ways in which those acts of everyday struggle or hidden forms of defiance may transcend the clandestine realm and become collective and open guided by the objective of transforming structures of domination and not merely surviving within them (see, e.g., Smith 1989, Sider 1996). The shortcomings identified in his work, notwithstanding, Scott's interventions have contributed much to a reorientation of studies of resistance by urging scholars to rethink the realm of the political to incorporate realms of action and activity that have seldom been acknowledged as politically meaningful. In so doing, what has emerged is not only a broadened spectrum of expressive acts that are counted as forms of resistance, but hitherto unacknowledged actors, such as women as well as the most dominated among the powerless are constructed as political actors, acting and interacting in a political field that has been expanded to include the mundane, the private, and the clandestine. A problem, building on the critique of Scott's work mentioned above is not only to determine the conditions in which one form of resistance became transformed into another, but why certain actors, particularly women, under particular historical conditions may be confined to certain spheres while others cross the boundary between the private and public realms of political activity in a routine and sustained fashion. This issue is explored in chapter 5. In this chapter, however, I use Scott's insights to explore the nature of resistance among the petty producers of Broussan and I examine the broad spectrum of acts of resistance in which they were engaged.

Repertoires of Resistance

The small farmers of Lower Languedoc participated in broad "repertoire" of forms of political action (Tilly 1986). To assert their interests and to defend their livelihoods, they pursued a diversity of means of struggle that involved acting in concert both en masse and in small groups. Small family farmers also engaged in forms of resistance as individuals who practised a variety of means of expressing and acting on sentiments of defiance both in open confrontation with the powerful and in very hidden spheres of social life. The forms of resistance in which petty producers were engaged can in fact be classed into two categories—those that followed due political process and those that lay outside the domain of due political process.

Actions pursued through due political process were seldom a part of the hidden repertoire of resistance. In fact they often involved in making inroads into the institutional framework of government and included such practices involved in the pursuit of interests, making demands and pressing claims through political parties, unions, organizations, and various interest groups that are incorporated into the state bureaucracy or officially sanctioned.

Forms of collective action that occurred in a realm outside due political process, by contrast, involved more openly oppositional kinds of political practice. They covered the spectrum of forms from both organized and spontaneous protests to guerrilla-like campaigns and assaults initiated by individuals as well as small groups. Forms of resistance that occurred in the domain outside due political process tended toward secrecy and surreptitiousness. Through such acts more explicit challenges to the status quo were initiated in contrast to those pursued within the realm of due political process where actors made the attempt to merely negotiating better terms within the existing order.[3]

The participation of the family farmers of Lower Languedoc in diverse forms of contestation within the parameters of the two categories of political action reflects the ambivalent relationship that has evolved between the family farmers and the state (see also chapters 3 and 7). On the one hand, family wine producers of the region have become increasingly dependent on the state to defend their position in the national and international market. Various forms of aid from the state have been extended to support efforts made by growers to sustain themselves and safeguard their position in the market under various crises that have plagued the viticultural economy since the transformation of Languedoc viticulture to commercial monocrop production. However, on the other hand, the implementation of many such programs had the effect of hastening the differentiation of the agrarian population and promoting their absorption into the modernizing projects of the state, while increasing their subordination to the market. What has evolved in this relationship is that growers have developed an acute dependency on the very policies that encourage their demise as family farmers.

The contradictory effects of state policy and much legislation was as much in evidence in the past as it is in the present. For example, in the early 1900s, as the Languedoc wine-growing economy was wracked by crises due to over production and slumps in the market, laws were enacted to lower taxes and eliminate the *octroi* (concession) duties on wine. Intended to give growers a larger share of wine revenues, the elimination of these duties actually brought about an increase in the number of intermediaries who would claim a larger share of the product with the emancipation of the wine production from acting as a source of state revenue.[4] More recently, the very explicit demise of small-scale family-based farming has been promoted in the agenda of modernizing agriculture through a series of what has been termed Malthusian interventions (see Averyt 1977).

Malthusian Modernization

The main thrust of agricultural policy developed since World War II, has been to modernize French farming through structural reform. The legislation and aid packages extended to growers to achieve the objective of modernisation were Malthusian in their orientation. Structural reform was to be accomplished in fact by encouraging the smallest most unproductive farms to disappear, while promoting the consolidation of large-scale, commercially viable agriculture. In this way, agricultural policy since the 1950s consistently favored the development of a capitalist class of farmers. Noncapitalist farms have been constantly dismissed as hindering the path of the development of an efficient profitable agriculture and through many policies and legislation, was encouraged to disappear.[5]

The means by which such Malthusian goals were to be realized were many and varied. However, according to many analysts,[6] the most significant agricultural legislation to be passed since the war was the Orientation Law of 1960 and the Complementary Law of 1962. To foster the growth of the capitalist sector, these laws made provisions and introduced a series of subsidies for the creation of Société d'Aménagement Foncier et d'Etablissement Rural (SAFER), a network of rural agencies—land banks, essentially—which would be authorized to buy up land that became available on the market. The purpose of the land banks was first to consolidate "unviable" microfundia into what government legislation defined as "viable" farms. SAFER lands would then be upgraded and sold to those who conformed to what the legislation determined as "qualified" family farmers. This in fact meant the relatively prosperous and progressive sector of the farming population, which had assimilated the modernizing imperatives of the state, especially those young farmers who had been trained in degree and diploma programs sponsored by the state (see chapter 4). Structural reform through SAFER then favored the development of large-scale farming as only relatively wealthy farmers, those with already large and profitable farms, could afford to buy and maintain upgraded land according to the strict guidelines imposed by the state.

A system of subsidies that was put into place equally reflected the Malthusian intent of state intervention into agriculture. For example, Under the Complementary Law, a Social Action Fund for the Amelioration of Agricultural Structures was empowered to grant a special subsidy—the IVD—to those elderly farmers who would agree to an early retirement and render their land available for redistribution. This was designed to hasten the process of structural reform by freeing land held by elderly farmers, whose old-age benefits were an inadequate means of retirement income. These tracts of land would be regrouped into larger more workable farms under SAFER. Still, other subsidies were to be made available to foster occupational conversion, promote a rural exodus through migration, and further other many other processes which would free up land. Later, the Mansholt Plan and the Vedel Report made more explicit the state's goals in French Agricultural policy of eliminating farms that were deemed "unviable." The Mansholt Plan, for example, published in December of 1968 as a "Memorandum on the Reform of Agriculture in the EEC" stated that 80 percent of French farms were unviable and would be slated for elimination. The more radical Vedel Report of July 1969 presented by the Ministry of Agriculture maintained that one of the long-term goals of French agricultural policy was the elimination of five out six farms (Keeler 1979 and 1981, Wright 1964).

While the general intent of this legislation was clear, the legislation was unclear over the definition of "small" farms, "large" farms, and "medium-" size farms and which of these would be fall into the category of "unviable" farms and what was meant by "inefficient." Uncertainties followed, therefore, over which farms could be modernized in order to become truly competitive and which farms would be eventually eliminated or merged with larger operations. While such confusions persisted, the fact was that political expediency, in the end, dictated the definitions of such key terms as *viability* and *efficiency*. Therefore, in order to realize the goals of the state's modernizing imperative, there was a need to recognize the existence of "two agricultures" or "three agricultures" depending on the legislation in France.[7]

Agricultural policies then determined that there were, in France "large capitalist agriculture, small artisan farms and medium-size farms left behind by progress but capable of meeting competition if modernized" (Averyt 1977, 28). The combined effect of the confusion in the policies and how to achieve certain objectives allowed small growers in Lower Languedoc to take advantage of certain provisions of the legislation while rejecting those that were seen to be detrimental and overtly discriminatory against small farmers. While the specifics of such legislation and plans were ambiguous and ill defined, it was nonetheless clear that the policies that govern the production of wine were part of the drive by the state to oversee, monitor and direct the course modernization of farming in France.

The legacy of introducing measures and programs that appeared to protect growers' interests while in fact they have detrimental effects then have been a consistent feature of programs that have been initiated to restructure agriculture. Not only did they often increase their subjection to commercial forces but they also increase their subjection to the state. Through its programs, governments in France have continuously increased the means and multiplied the mechanisms to monitor and control the production of wines both to safeguard it as a source of government revenue as well as to realize a larger agenda of modernization.[8]

Such measures then have resulted in a paradoxical process in which growers simultaneously accommodated and resisted the incursion of the state into their lives. In accommodating the state, growers participated in the state's drive for modernization. They accepted state subsidies and became involved in the state's plans to "improve" viticulture. Moreover, growers have participated in a process of agrarian transformation by negotiating with the state over the terms and condition of change. Certain segments of the rural population have pursued their interests and made their claims through due political process and political parties and farm organizations sponsored and recognized by the state have been formed and they serve as the legitimate conduit for the presentation of the demands of family farmers. They provide a means through which small-scale producers can participate in the formulation of agricultural development schemes and plans to extend protective measures in aid to farmers. However, because of what I have describe here and discuss in more detail later as essentially the "double-edged sword" of state aid, many growers have also continuously contested the implementation of the measures that are ostensibly in place to protect them.

Because of the dimorphic effects of policies developed in a process of "state making" (Tilly 1986) in which the state must ap-
pease different groups competing for state resources, state
intervention has been regularly greeted with considerable opposition by family farmers. Moreover, since the state seldom autonomously defends the interests of the powerless groups against
the powerful, state sanctioned organizations and bureaucracy
tended to rarely represent the interests of the small family farmers of Lower Languedoc. Being cognizant of this "double edge"
and of the multifarious character of the state in mind, many of
the small farmers actually inserted themselves into what has
been called a "two-pronged" (Keeler 1979) strategy of collective
action, which involved negotiation through due political process,
as well as contestation through a series of diverse means to
challenge what are in effect attempts by the state to realize its
Malthusian ends. Certain segments of the farming population in
rural Languedoc then tended to accommodate this imperative by
participating in programs and allowing the state to provide the
institutional means for representing farmers interests and
adopted a corporatist strategy while others followed an "antimodernization" strategy.

Corporatism and Collusion

Scott (1986, 28) pointed out that the parameters of resistance
are often set in part by the institutions of repression. In France,
while the state played a major role in the formulation of agricultural legislation, government ministries and agencies collaborated with agricultural organizations who directly determined
the content of agricultural policy. The agricultural policies of the
1960s then were, in fact, drafted in league with the major agricultural organization in France, Fédération Nationale des
Syndicats d'Exploitations Agricoles (FNSEA) and its youth branch
the Centre National des Jeunes Agricultures (CNJA). While claiming to represent all agricultural interests, in reality FNSEA
supported the interests of only the large-scale farmers concentrated mainly in the northern regions of France and the terms
of the policies directly reflected capitalist agricultural interests.
    Founded in 1946, the FNSEA is the general federation that
claims to be the "intransigent" defender of the "legitimate interests" of all French farmers, small as well as large. It has adopted

a strategy of defense for farmers based on what Keeler (1979) has called "corporatist modernization through concertation"—that is modernization of French agriculture through intimate cooperation with the government. FNSEA, or more accurately its youth wing, participated in the formulation and implementation of virtually all aspects of agricultural policy and so state programs directly reflect the programs of the FNSEA itself.[9]

The most important features of these programs were that FNSEA accepted the continued decline in the agricultural population and it supported structural reform, or modernization, which was overtly "discriminatory" toward small farmers. Thus this strategy of corporatist modernization came to be rejected by small farmers and support for an alternative organization, Movement Pour la Défense de l'Exploitation Familiale (MODEF), a movement for the defense of family farms grew.

Antimodernization

Founded in 1959 by Socialists and Communists, MODEF offered an alternative strategy of "antimodernization" for the defense of small-family farmers, who in fact made up the majority of farmers in France. It repudiated the Malthusian assault on small farms and rejected official distinctions between "viable" and "nonviable" as arbitrary. In directly opposing the measures that discriminated against small farms, MODEF called for the implementation of policies that would strengthen the position of the small farmer. For example, it proposed that the state should issue loans for 30 years at 1 percent interest to small farmers, while lowering taxes on small farmers. MODEF demanded a reduction to the cost agricultural equipment by limiting industrial profits and raising agricultural prices, while indexing them to industrial prices. Virtually all small farmers supported MODEF, though its dominance by the Communist party has caused it to be avoided by some.[10]

In dealing with the state, MODEF adopted a two-pronged strategy. Participation in due political processes is practised, on the one hand, while on the other hand, other types of actions are undertaken outside the political mainstream. In following a strategy of pressing claims through due political process, MODEF pursued a course of making inroads into the state apparatus by presenting candidates for election to the Chamber of Agriculture, an organization that represents the local interests of agricultural professions for the state to consult. It accomplished this, despite the lack of infrastructural support and state subsidies enjoyed by its rival FNSEA.[11]

MODEF then was the institutional voice of the small-family farmer in France and it became the primary officially recognized vehicle through which petty producers and agricultural laborers articulated their demands to the state and negotiated the terms agricultural policies. At its inception, however, its status as a representative union of family farmers was not recognized by the state and the actions taken by MODEF to defend family farmers were pursued outside due political process. MODEF often organized mass protests and demonstrations against the state and vocally denounced state policy in its union newspaper. Indeed, until very recently, the state has not only refused to endorse MODEF but it has employed a variety of repressive means in dealing with unions rivaling FNSEA. These measures included the denial of the right to hold union meetings in public places; the deployment of riot police to deal with demonstrations organized by MODEF, and interference with their attempts to exercise power in the Chamber of Agriculture (Keeler 1981). However, in 1983, under the socialist government the state granted it legal union status and accorded to it subsidies, council seats, and access to state officials, formerly unavailable under an official policy of discrimination against alternative unions. The reluctance of previous governments to acknowledge MODEF resulted from the stance of opposition to the state adopted by a union that threatened the hegemony of the state's ally, FNSEA. While MODEF continued to organize mass protests, it became a means of pursuing small-farms interests within the structures of the government.

Due Political Process in Broussan

There were very few supporters of FNSEA among small farmers in Broussan while support for MODEF was strong. As there has been an established tradition in Broussan of supporting parties of the left, there was little difficulty in accepting a union that was backed by the Communist party. For several decades, Broussan consistently favored the Communist Party of France (PCF) and its members dominated the municipal council. In the 1980s, many members of MODEF in the community were also members of the Communist Party.

As members of MODEF, many of the family farmers of Broussan then followed a political strategy of legal political pressure, pressing their demands within the political system, as an interest group. The process followed is one in which interest groups such as MODEF transmit "pragmatic specific" demands to political parties; parties aggregate these demands, mobilize support for them, and under ideal circumstances, parliaments and bureaucracies enact them as policies and laws and implement them (Berger 1981, 9). Members of the village consistently gave their electoral support to MODEF's candidates in the Chamber of Agriculture and participated in the meetings and demonstrations organized by a coalition of agricultural organizations, including MODEF (see below). While there appeared to be much grass-roots support for MODEF among small farmers, because of its overtly critical stance to state policy, and as many of the demands made by MODEF came into dramatic conflict with the modernizing agenda set by the state, MODEF has been less successful than FNSEA in capturing the sympathies of ministers and state power holders.

Because the ear of the government is seldom turned toward MODEF, the strategy of interest-group action and negotiation through due political process represented a limited means for asserting the claims and demands of small growers. This strategy was, in fact, pursued alongside demonstrations of protest against state policy organized by MODEF and other local unions such as Comité d'Action Viticole (the Committee for Viticultural Action) (CAV), the organization that directs the viticultural movement. This reflected the peripheral status of MODEF within the institutional structure of the state and its consistent oppositional stance vis-à-vis government.

Mass protest and large-scale demonstrations reflected the relationship of conflict that has prevailed between the wine growers and the state since the development of wine as a commercial crop. Indeed, in the repertoires of collective action followed by small growers, demonstrations and protests, both large and small in scale have punctuated the entire history of wine production in Languedoc. They have involved both localized forms of action as well as large-scale regionwide forms of mobilization. Moreover, many localized small-scale protests that originated outside due political process gathered momentum and spawned larger regional-wide protests. This process of mobilizing from the locality to the region characterized the processes that led up to the Revolt of the Wine Growers of the Midi in 1907.

Mobilizing Then

1907: A Legacy of Mass Resistance

In the early 1900s, a series of riots, strikes, rallies, demonstrations, and violent protests erupted in the wine-growing areas of Mediterranean Languedoc. In 1901, the French wine market became saturated and the process dropped. In 1903, the price rose and workers, many of whom had recently established trade unions, demanded higher wages. When employers refused, strikes and work stoppages broke out throughout the region. Though they were settled in 1904, the renewal of the wine slump and its intensification in 1905 and 1906, resulted in systematic layoffs and wage cults. In 1907 villages throughout the Hérault, Gard, Aude, and the Pyrénées-Orientales, smallholders and vine workers rose up en masse to protest against wage cuts, falling prices, layoffs, and foreclosures, as a deep crisis gripped the wine economy. On large domains, wine cellars were ransacked, vines set alight, landowners and their families received threats from vine workers whose ire was aroused by the deteriorating conditions of estate work.

Smallholders and agricultural workers looked to the state for protection against the vicissitudes of an erratic economy that saw wine prices plummet as the market became satiated. The government of Georges Clemenceau responded by introducing legislation to remedy the causes of the slump but their efforts were seen to be slow and halfhearted. So the riots escalated. Tax payments were suspended. Municipal councils and mayors resigned, effectively cutting off the region's ties to Paris. The government intervened with military force and troops were dispatched to occupy the south to attempt to quell the revolt. This repression spawned more riots and acts of sedition. Government buildings were sacked by marauding groups of militants and soldiers attacked in violent confrontations in city streets. The agitation of the wine growers lasted over a period of three months and finally faded at least for the moment, after the introduction of the Law of the 19 June 1907, to suppress fraud, thought to be the main culprit in the crisis.[12]

The struggles of the vine workers for the "right to work in the vineyards" was broadened by Marcelin Albert, the leader of the 1907 movement, in the mass meetings of 1907 to become a generalized "right to live from the vine" as a basis to appeal to all wine producers. It became apparent to the vine workers that the strikes of 1904–6 failed ultimately to defend the economic position of the vine worker, while the slump persisted. The strikes thus did not provide a satisfactory basis for the economic defense of workers who were, in fact, both wage laborers and petty producers. Thus, a tactical reorientation was undertaken, in which vine workers emphasized their interests as petty producers, not wage laborers, and villagers turned to the state to demand protection from the economic forces of commercial capitalism, rather than seeking solutions, as in the earlier years, outside state intervention.

The basic issue, as the growers saw it was that the slump was produced by a large illegal industry in adulterated wines flooding the market. It was precisely over this issue of adulterated wines that the theme of class emerged in the struggles of 1907. Growers were firstly suspicious that wine merchants and large landowners were manufacturing and selling adulterated wines. Small growers had neither the stocks nor the equipment of produce-adulterated wines, and so class antagonisms developed as small growers came to see merchant and landowners as having caused the crisis. Moreover, the revolt of 1907 took on a regional character. Villagers suspected northern industrial interests as having a hand in creating the crisis, for they stood to profit from the sale of commodities used in adulterating wines (sugar, chemicals, and industrial alcohols). This reinforced the seeds of regionalism and regional antagonisms between the north and the south that were sown as early as the thirteenth century.

In 1907, then, the struggles of petty producers and agricultural laborers reached an unprecedented scale and intensity so much so that the Revolt of the Midi has been described as the most violent, as well as the largest, disorder that France had known since the French Revolution (Wright 1964, 27). Mass meetings spread throughout Lower Languedoc with an estimated 500,000 participants from over 450 towns and villages (J. H. Smith 1978, 118). Moreover, the memory of that moment in history was a constant point of reference in the struggles of contemporary wine growers. That period of strikes and demonstrations of the early 1900s have left an indelible mark on the history of Languedoc. The symbols that evoke that era encode the experiences of the past, the themes of past struggles into the present through memory (Lüdtke 1995, 207). While, the tumultuous event of 1907 are key in the tradition of furious action, stories that recall the events, the issues and who the actors were in many smaller scale confrontations serve as a blueprint which defines the forces of opposition as well as the various ways through which opposition is enacted. Memories tend also to revolve around such events as the smaller scale strikes and forms of contestation that occurred regularly throughout the 1900s.

Small-Scale Legacies

While the scale and intensity of the 1907 revolt has not had its parallel in the political history of Languedoc, instances of open and collective forms of confrontation were repeated in the course of the twentieth century as the economy of wine growing slumped and boomed. In these occurrences, as well as in the insurrection of 1907, the measures taken by the state to diffuse rural resistance over the course has fostered the sense that the state, in the last instance would align itself with political and economic elites against the small farming masses. Over and over again petty producers, who often worked as estate laborers found themselves pitted not only against landowners and merchants, but also troops and the gendarmerie as women as well as men undertook to defend their livelihoods through a variety of political acts.

In 1911, for example, when a group of about 200 strikers in the village of Lunel, rallied to march toward one of the village estates to protest low wage rates, they were greeted by a group of soldiers. Wreaking havoc en route to the estate, by overturning and destroying the equipment of small owners who would not join in their march, they arrived at the estates to be greeted by a small force of military who were called in by the estate owner to maintain calm. Once the soldiers saw the size of the group of strikers they left the estate to find reinforcements. While they were gone, the strikers set up a barricade on the road to impede the movements of the soldiers. When the soldiers returned they found that not only were they cut off from the estate but that they had to contend with women and children as protesters as well as men. Women and children had positioned themselves on the tops of the barricade. Women jeered at the soldiers and thrust out their chests deliberated provoking the soldiers into an offensive. Angered by this kind of contempt, a lieutenant unsheathed his saber and ordered his troops to attack. However, one of the officers of the gendarmerie countered this order and the troops were made to retreat.

That the state and its agents rose to protect the interests of large landowners and the elite was evident again in the winter of 1912 as estate workers engaged in a multiplicity of means of defending their livelihood from taking up strike action to initiated a series of acts of sabotage. In Thézan-lès-Béziers, a village located a few kilometers south of Broussan a confrontation between large owners and workers began with a lock out of workers on the village estates. Estate workers had rejected the terms of a contract offered to them by local owners. Owners of various estates responded to this refusal by convening a meeting and voting unanimously on taking up a course of action that involved a lock out the estate workers. Workers retaliated not only with the declaration of a general strike, but they launched an all out offensive on village estates by undertaking a campaign of sabotage. Vines on the large estates of Thézan-lès-Béziers were torn up. On one of the estates a bomb was installed and detonated setting fire to the vines and destroying a good part of one vineyard. Not only was property attacked, but estate owners and managers became subjected to intimidation. Stewards on the estates began to fear for their lives as they received letters threatening death. These tactics prompted estate owners to call for police protection. On many of the estates, armed police and guards were posted to protect the property of the estate owners. What provoked small growers to move beyond fairly peaceful means of protest to more violent acts of sedition was that estate owners attempted to import strike breakers to keep their operations running. In Thézan-lès-Béziers, an entrepreneur who saw an opportunity to profit from the disturbances in village, which from beginning to end, lasted for a period of 18 months, set off to recruit workers from for estate owners. As workers arrived, an arrangement was made with the gendarmerie to escort the recruits to village estates. Strikers greeted each attempt to bring in strike breakers by setting up road blocks and human barricades to prevent the recruited workers from working on the domains.

While vine production on the estates was crippled, the small holdings of in the village carried on vine cultivation as usual. Many of the strikers were also small owners, who managed to keep their farms going with the help of their families. Over the duration of the strike, women and men were arrested and sentenced to various prison terms for committing acts of sabotage and interfering with the police. In one incident a simple denunciation made by one estate owner against a 54-year-old worker with two children was sufficient to result in the arrest of the worker and a sentence of six months imprisonment.[13]

In these instances of contention and conflict, the forces of the state rallied to defend property owners and members of local elites. While many of these conflicts often ended peacefully, a half century later, however, one such confrontation between government troops and petty producers resulted in considerable violence and death. In 1976, in the demonstrations at Montredon-des-Corbières, near Narbonne, wine growers protested en masse over the imports of foreign wine into France. Riots broke out and the protests ended with the shooting of a wine grower by the police. In retaliation, wine growers shot an officer in the police force deployed to put an end to the protest. To the wine growers, the killing of a protester demonstrated once more the Machiavellian measures that the state would use to deal with the wine growers (Cazes, Castéra, et al., 1976, 10). The events of Montredon serve as a cautionary tale outlining the lengths to which the state would go to diffuse rural protest.

The legacy of these forms of resistance has meant that the family farmers of Broussan, like their predecessors in the many villages of Languedoc continued to rally to the call to participate in mass protests and open confrontations with the state organized by MODEF in league with the CGV and the CAV.

Mobilizing Now: The Masses Protest

One of the largest mass demonstration since the protests at Montredon in 1976 occurred on May 20, 1983 (see de Sède 1982). Wine growers throughout the Midi, were called on to leave their vineyards for a day, to protest against the entry of Spain into the EEC, and to negotiate better terms of trade for the wine producers of the south.[14]

During the entire week of May 20, 1983, in the local newspapers, the regional committees of the CAV had been calling on their colleagues in the departments of the Aude, the Gard, the Pyrénées-Orientales and the Hérault to demonstrate their opposition to the proposed expansion of the EEC and to participate in a show of force to impress on the state and the public that the entry of Spanish wine would mean certain death to southern viticulture. All agricultural unions—the CNJA, FNSEA, and MODEF—in the region had been calling for their members to take part on this day of protest. Even the association of wine growers with private cellars had called on their adherents to take part in the demonstration.

In Broussan, the administrators of the cooperative were charged with organizing protesters from the community and disseminating tactical information. Two days before the day of the demonstration, the cooperative received its first set of marching orders from the regional CAV. The orders were kept secret until just before the demonstration was to take place out of a concern that the state and its police force would somehow thwart the plans. Orders were relayed only in part at this point as a further safeguard against preventative action. The protestors from Broussan, were to assemble at the soccer stadium in Béziers where they were to be dispatched to one of the main points of entry into the city.

The objective of this demonstration was present a show of force and strength to the government and to publicise the issue that threaten family wine production as widely as possible. The main tactic was to set up road blocks made up of burning tires and trucks parked at right angles on roads. Growers wanted to disrupt as much as possible the daily order of things in the region to demonstrate that they were a force with which the government needed to reckon. All the main arteries in the wine growing region Languedoc were blocked and even small roads into the regional towns were also blocked. Only ambulances and cars with elderly, sick people, and children were allowed through the barricades of people, burning tires, and wine growers' cars. Some cars that tried to run the barricades were stopped by the growers who surrounded the vehicles and rocked them with the drivers inside and then, they were simply released, usually driving in the opposite direction. Cars with Italian or Spanish license plates were especially selected out for this kind of treatment. Drivers of such cars shouted out after they were released words to the effect that these wine growers were a bunch of lunatics to attack the cars of innocent foreigners. The flow of traffic to and from Spain was stopped on all highways. Transport trucks carrying agricultural products especially from Spain were to be stopped, emptied out, and the contents destroyed.

While calls to take action were made by every group claiming to represent some part of the population of wine growers, those who immediately responded in the case of Broussan were largely the men of the viticultural community who operated family-based holdings. Some agricultural workers who also operated farms were also present. The participants from the community, all men, were a mixture of those who could collaborated in exchange networks, such as Roger and his mates (see chapter 1), members of MODEF, the Communist Party, as well as those who claimed to belong to no union. The mayor and members of his municipal council participated in the demonstration. Members of the Socialist party in Broussan were also present. The presence of participants from different parties and village factions seemed to corroborate Marcel Mas's suggestion in chapter 1. Local political differences were cast aside in a united effort to take over an issue which affected all family wine growers. As those who participated in such social actions did so with the overriding objective of securing personal survival, following correct party lines seemed low on the priority scale, at least in so far as differences between the followers of Socialist or Communist parties prevailed (see also Lüdtke 1995).

The gendarmerie was also present at the demonstration but maintained a respectful distance from the growers. The riot police were nowhere to be seen to the wine growers' relief and the demonstration was carried out relatively peacefully, with very few incidents of violence. Although quite a few growers anticipated that violence would break out, as it did during 1976 in Montredon-des-Corbières (see de Sède 1982).

There were however several notable absences. Large landowners of the community did not seem to heed the call. By and large, like the owner of Château X, they tended to pursue their own individualist strategies for survival, eschewing the tactics of what many large landowners believe to acts that laid outside the bounds of reasonable, civilized behavior (see chapter 7). Another notable absence was women.

In contemporary Languedoc, by and large, only a very few women tended to participate in the spectacle of mass protest. The absence of women from this stage, and many other particularly public of forums of protest, contrasts strikingly to an earlier era, when women routinely attended political meetings and participated in strikes and riots. Now, many rural women, at least in the context of Broussan confined themselves to playing a subsidiary political role, often off the stage of public protest. Women in the village tended to participate in political struggles and campaigns largely through such activities as relaying information concerning the organization of a demonstration or act of protest. They also participated by manufacturing the banners and painting the icons of grapes, the Occitan cross, and the names of places and events that conjured up significant moments of local political history. There was in a sense a division of political labor based on gender and this in many ways corresponded to the contemporary division of labor in viticulture, in which women tended to become progressively alienated from the process of vine cultivation (see chapter 5).

Regionwide mass mobilization campaigns, such as 1907, were often the culmination of many smaller-scale actions that took place in a spontaneous fashion often in a hidden arena of local life. It is evident that such mass campaigns and even smaller localized forms of collective resistance can only take place periodically. As a form of collective action it involved a large investment of time and energy as well as a vanguard completely dedicated to organizing and mounting such mass protests. Growers in Broussan were convinced that forms of collective and public protests were highly effective in reminding the state of an extant and powerful opposition to its policies and agendas. Still, however effective such mass protests were as a form of collective action, they could neither be sustained on a regular nor continuous basis, since frequent mobilizations seriously disrupted the participants' efforts at a daily livelihood. At the local level and outside the parameters of due political process, a more constant campaign of struggle and small-scale acts of resistance was, however, sustained. While a good part of these more sustained acts of opposition occurred in a clandestine realm, whenever they entered into the public eye, they were no less effective in conveying their opposition to agents of domination. Occasionally, these small-scale collective acts were staged in response to calls by farmers' unions and organization, which disseminated information on targets to strike and events that merited a call to action for growers. The small growers of Broussan, for example, were often mobilized by the Comité d'Action Viticole (CAV), for example, to picket local supermarkets that stocked imported wines. From time to time, the CAV also recruited small groups of growers to stage demonstrations at Sète, the main port of entry for imports of foreign wine, when tankers carrying wine from Italy pulled into dock. In all these public demonstrations, large and small scale, banners with the Occitan Cross and the red flag of Occitania were waved about along with placards denouncing the state and the EEC, while posters of grapes withering on the vine symbolized the plight of the wine grower. However, many acts of defiance at the local level were organized spontaneously without the leadership of unions and organizations. These actions were small in scale, they occurred both offstage as part of the hidden transcript of defiance but also they very quickly translated into public transcripts in striking a very calculated blow to power holders and state authorities. Beyond the purview of power, nonetheless, the political practices of the small grower also included a diversity of forms of collective action that ranged in method and scope, from strategies of noncompliance to maintaining the clandestine economy.

Clandestine Forms of Collective Action

In the surreptitious realm, the wine growers of Broussan participated in a spectacular array of forms of collective action that range from boycotts of state programs, to participation in an underground economy and to organizing commando-style attacks on specific targets. Such acts to some extent conform to Scott's (1986) definition of everyday forms of resistance, insofar as they often required little or no coordination or planning. Furthermore, in pursuing these actions, while growers may strike a blow to the system they were unlikely to do more than marginally affect the systems of domination in place (1986, 6).[15] While the ultimate objectives of such acts of resistance or defiance may not necessarily be to overturn the existing system of domination, the continual participation of smallholders in clandestine acts of defiance has visible effects on the state. This was evident in the what has emerged as a strategy of partial compliance to agricultural policy.

Partial Compliance

In Broussan all state agricultural programs were channeled through the cooperative and implemented by its administrators who work closely with state agencies responsible for various programs. The provisions of the laws aimed at the modernization of French agriculture through structural reform were implemented through the cooperative. The transfer and upgrading of land through SAFER were both accomplished through the cooperative. IVD arrangements were made through the cooperative. Measures to improve the quality of grapes produced were likewise executed through the cooperative. So the cooperative effects and implements the plans for the modernization of viticulture (see chapter 7).

Many of the petty producers of Broussan boycotted such programs and only a small minority participate in these government schemes for structural reform. Among some growers an attitude prevailed in which growers cautiously took advantage of certain aspects of state-sponsored programs, all the while refraining from fully accepting state aid and subsidies mindful of the proverbial double-edged sword of "gifts" from the state. It is widely acknowledged that the system of grants and subsidies put into place were calculated to eliminate the smaller enterprises that made up the majority of operations in Broussan. Moreover, these long-term objectives were also openly expounded by policy makers in the Ministry of Agriculture. So, many of the growers boycotted such schemes, seeing all too clearly the two sides of state aid. Growers adopted survival strategies in working the system to their minimum disadvantage and this is apparent, for example, in the practices that follow on initiatives to improve the quality of grape production.

Although penalties are imposed that discourage the continued cultivation of high-yielding varieties of grapes, growers continued to replace old vines with the high-yielding varieties. Many growers preferred to pay the fines and refused to participate in such schemes declaring that *"Nobody has ever proved that quality pays."* This was a constant refrain in informants' discussions about the cooperative, the state and its programs. While this strategy of boycott and noncompliance was the sentiment that prevailed among those who overtly refused to take any subsidies given by the state, other growers adopted a strategy of partial compliance with government policies.

Among petty producers who partially complied with programs advocated improving vine stocks, subsidies for tearing up old stocks were cautiously accepted and applied in different ways. Since after twenty or so years or so some vines tended to become less productive and needed to be replaced with new stocks, subsidies were accepted and used to uproot only those aged high-yielding varieties that were at the end of their productive years. Some growers, then took subsidies for replantation and only replanted a portion of their uprooted vineyards with approved stocks, slowly experimenting with new stocks to see how they fared. Still others use the replantation subsidy to plant the old, high-yielding varieties that the state had been attempting to suppress. In this instance, they surreptitiously subverted the state's directives while taking advantage of its programs.

Many of the growers then rejected the insinuation of the state, through its policies in the local economy. This was also reflected in the kind of reception that SAFER and IVD have had locally in Broussan. Among the family sector of wine producers, growers have tended resist both selling or buying land from SAFER. Many growers felt not only that the purchase of land from the land banks would be expensive, but that they could not comply with the stringent regulations for maintaining a parcel of SAFER land. The purchase of a piece of this upgraded land was only the first in a cycle of expenditures, for the costs of production would increase dramatically as planting with approved stocks, using approved products and techniques were all requisite under the program. The reasons often given for not selling land to SAFER were more ideological in nature, as many growers saw it as surrendering the control over the fate of a piece of land and a livelihood to an anonymous and impersonal agency that favored the disappearance of the small farmer. Selling land to the land bank was also associated with failure of the farm and the family (see chapter 4) and those who did turn land over to SAFER, often did so as a last resort, largely by farmers on the edge of bankruptcy and by those who failed to find successors to take over the unit of production.

Despite the prevalence of boycotts, non- and partial compliance, some of the larger household enterprises have launched themselves fully into state programs. These tended to be the relatively prosperous households that were members of the rural petty bourgeoisie and those on a developmental trajectory of expanding the scale of production. In general, those households with larger financial resources at their disposal were able to take advantage of government schemes.

Boycotts of such government schemes, as well as a strategy of non- or partial compliance, were among the means by which the people of Broussan resisted the thorough subordination by the state. While, growers who practised these forms of resistance openly expressed their opposition to such programs in declarations and statements to the public and to the state, such acts of defiance were practised in a clandestine sphere beyond the purview of state authorities. Clandestine acts of defiance were also manifested through other practices, such as maintaining the hidden economy.

Maintaining the Hidden Economy

One of the most prevalent forms of clandestine resistance to the state was manifested in the participation of almost the entire community of petty wine growers in the informal economy. Often a conspiracy of silence shrouds the informal economy. Intricate mechanisms of cooperation through a system of checks and balances bind officials, employers, and employees in this conspiracy, ultimately protecting the hidden economy from detection by the authorities. The maintenance of exchanges of goods and labor outside the sphere of state regulation may be seen to represent a strategy of collective action in two respects. On the one hand, such practices effectively deprived the state of a source of revenue. On the other hand, it served as a means for defining the limits of state control. Thus men and women exchanged goods and labor at costs below the official market price of the commodity. Women worked as housekeepers, baby sitters, clerks, and seamstresses without formally declaring their wages to the authorities. Men worked as laborers in the vineyards, operated building, and contracting businesses, as well as provided a whole array of services, again without formally declaring their earnings. Men, women, and children worked in the harvest of grapes and other fruits in the few orchards planted with cherries and peaches in Broussan. Women cultivated gardens and sold their products to local shops or marketed their products individually at their homes and in roadside stalls without formally declaring the returns (see also chapter 6).

It was generally acknowledged that everybody took part in it and nobody violated the village norm of silence by reporting incidents of informal work to the authorities. Indeed, there was a tacit contract of maintaining the invisibility of this economy between the local representatives of the state and the ordinary citizens of the community.

The informal economy was accepted and indeed condoned by the municipal authorities. In the public transcript, the existence of the flourishing informal economy was recognized as problematic by the local and national authorities and often gestures were made to see to its eradication. The municipal council of Broussan, for example, declared several campaigns to uncover cases of illegal work. However, these campaigns involved more rhetoric than practice. Anthony Giraud, who worked full-time as an undeclared day laborer commented on the nature of informal work and hypocrisy of municipal politicians:

> The monthly wage of a worker is 1500 francs. After the state takes its share only one-half was left. How can you live on this? It was much better both for the worker and the employer to black leg, even if it was illegal. Besides the municipal government doesn't care. A little while ago the municipal

councillors did say that they were going to try to get rid of this cheating, but the funny thing was that the members of the municipal council were all taking part in this illegal work.

Indeed, the municipality often served as the intermediary between employers and employees in the informal labor market. Each month the *mairie*, posted a list of the unemployed people living in Broussan. Any wine grower who needed to secure extra labor simply contacted one of the individuals on that list. This practice was pursued with the full knowledge of the officials in the municipal office. The state and its officers at the local level, therefore clearly colluded in maintaining the informal economy as a sphere of interaction beyond the reach of higher officialdom and state regulation and a protective shell was formed around it by its participants. A tacit understanding was forged that kept the state at bay, guaranteeing access to employment for workers, and minimum costs to employers.

This conspiracy was based on a strong antistate sentiment and it was commonly asserted that not only was the state responsible for the economic ills suffered by growers, but the state only made laws to serve its own interests. Petty commodity producers then rejected definitions of legality on the issue of work. The state was also seen as the culprit that created a situation of high unemployment and low revenues for demanding exorbitant charges.

To call such actions acts of collective resistance may seem an idealization of what can be seen as self-interested acts, on the one hand, and exploitative acts, on the other. Clearly, those who hired labor in the informal economy minimized the cost of production on their enterprise, but also, the profit margins increase by depriving the state of its share of each transactions. For those who sold their labor in the informal village economy, the wage contract was struck that might not otherwise have been in the formal economy. This, however, placed them in a vulnerable position for not only did they sell their labor below the average market price, but they were susceptible to demands made by employers to work long hours, without the protection of laws against worker exploitation. Also, protection through social security benefits such as unemployment insurance, pension benefits, and medical insurance was precluded in informal work. Therefore, to dignify such practices in the informal sector with an explicit political purpose, as did many participants, obscured the potential for class exploitation in cost-minimization strategies.

The effect of such actions did nonetheless deprive the state of resources and so one of the effects of the perpetuation of informal economy was to maintain a sphere in which economic transactions were impermeable to the state. It also suggested that the limits of state power and control can be defined through various forms of collective action. While the self-interested element of these actions was undeniable, their political importance as an element in smallholders' general struggles cannot be easily cast aside. The terms of the struggle is clearly acknowledged in the popular consciousness of the members of the community who denounced the state as the main enemy of the large and small wine grower, alike and who roundly proclaimed that: *"Social insurance contributions were killing us!"* Agricultural workers also maintained that because of the large contribution that employers must make per laborer hired, jobs in the vineyards have become scarce, and many like Jacques Tourres in chapter 6, felt that they have lost their jobs because their employers could no longer afford to keep them and so the state is defined as the enemy.

Scott furthermore comments that it is important to understand the element of self-interest in rural resistance:

> It was precisely the fusion of self-interest and resistance that was the vital force animating the resistance of peasants and proletarians. When a peasant hides part of his crop to avoid paying taxes, he was both filling his stomach and depriving the state of grain. When a peasant soldier deserts the army because the food was bad and his crops at home were ripe, he was both looking after himself and denying the state cannon fodder. (1986, 26–27)

In this light he also suggests that class struggle is, first and foremost, a struggle over the appropriation of work, production, and taxes (1986, 27). Therefore, participants in the informal economy can be understood to be engaged in struggle over the appropriation of taxes and that share of their labor that was appropriated by the state. Moreover, as Lüdkte suggests, the objectives participants in forms of struggle are multilayered and involve grappling with constant anxiety about one's material means of existence among those other things and this is done in a variety of ways (1995, 206–7). The repertoire of clandestine forms of collective action were largely undetected in the public eye. They were undertaken by individuals and groups, with a mixture of both intended and unintended political purposes. Other forms of collective action adopted by wine growers, while occurring outside the sphere of due political process, were practised openly and required some effort of coordination and were calculated to strike a blow to the system by communicating an intended and explicit political message.

Guerrilla Tactics

Growers periodically engaged in a kind of guerrilla warfare employing "commando tactics" in pressing their claims. Through such practices as raids, spray-painting operations, and roadblocks, such tactics emphasized a direct approach to resolving certain issues. This often involved focusing their actions at particular local targets and disturbing the normal operation of local economy and society. As I have mentioned earlier, since the expansion of the common market to include Italy and Greece and now with the entry of Spain into the European Union, guerrilla tactics have been employed with a regularity as recorded in the local newspapers. One of the main actions undertaken by certain growers in Broussan was to conduct periodic raids of local supermarkets who stock wine imported from these countries.

Such raids usually involved small bands of men, usually no larger than six in number. First, they tended to notify the press, informing them of where and when a raid will take place. The actors felt very strongly that their actions were driven by a desire not only to convey their opposition to the actions of the state and merchants, but to compel the public at large to reflect on the implications of their actions as consumers of wine for the local people who produce it. Therefore, the presence of media to record, disseminate and preserve this event for the public and also for posterity was critical.

In one such operation then, a van was rented and driven into the supermarket parking lot. The men, who often disguised themselves by wearing handkerchiefs around their faces, leapt out of the parked van as it drove away. Rushing by the customers in the parking lot and into the supermarket, the men headed immediately for the shelves stocking the foreign wines, grabbing as many bottles as they could and immediately smashed them on the store floor, while the press photographers snapped away. They then charged past groups of astonished customers and supermarket employees out of the store, and ran into another rented van and drove away. This direct approach simply removed the competition from a store shelf as well as communicated a message to the authorities, importers, and the state that foreign wines will not be tolerated. This very localized act then carried a more far-reaching message. When this incident was reported in the local papers, the participants felt that they had registered their anger at the continued importation of foreign wines and the little mission was accomplished. The news photographs and articles recording such campaigns were usually kept in the family archives and were often proudly exhibited as a memento of a few minutes of anonymous infamy, while the story of each incident was told and retold to anyone willing to listen as I was (see Introduction).

The growers of Broussan have also participated in other autonomous and direct forms of action that have involved violent confrontations with those whom they have targeted in their offensives. Their attempts to sabotage the imports of foreign wine have brought groups of growers to the port of Sète. On hearing of the arrival of these tankers, small groups of men often arrived at the port at night, climbed onto the ship, and emptied the vessel of its cargo after having subdued the crew. The tanks were forced open and, the imported wine was allowed to flow into the Mediterranean. In other offensives, blockades of roads were set up in which tanker trucks carrying imported wine to bottlers in France, are often stopped and the contents of the tanks emptied on the roadside. Other actions have involved targeting the Talgo, the passenger train that travels between Barcelona and Paris for assault. The Talgo has been stopped a number of times and spray painted with the insignias of the land of Oc and the slogans of Occitan wine growers. The significance of using such slogans are discussed in chapter 3.

Many of these assaults were often initiated in a spontaneous fashion through barroom and street corner discussions but soon gathered momentum as a discourse of hostility and disenchantment comes to be translated into action, enlisting participants in local networks to organize and execute offensives. For example, one Occitan "guerrilla" related a story about how one operation was initiated:

> Me and a few of my buddies [camarades] were chatting in the bar one day, talking about how we were sick of the way the government was not doing its part to keep out foreign

wine. We were all good citizens. We pay our taxes and we keep the government happy and all the civil servants, the *"fonctionaires"* of the *north* supplied with fancy clothes and cars. "Look at us," I said, "We drive beaten up old cars and work like slaves." The more we talked about it the more we thought we had to do something, anything to make us feel better and to let the government know that we were angry. So we got hold of some cans of spray paint and very early one morning my buddies and I drove off to the ministry of agriculture buildings and spray painted *Oc* all over the walls and windows. In the newspapers the next day, we saw a photograph of our handiwork and we read that an angry official was denouncing this whole thing as an act of vandalism, violence and wantonness typical of people of the south.

This particular assault then began as an expression of antipathy through speech acts in an everyday forum but quickly transformed into a mobilization of friends to take up action. While discourses of enmity and such collective acts were executed clandestinely, the effects of such practices were meant for the public record. Through sustaining these many and varied forms of collective action, small-family farmers have attempted to resist being subordinated to a state in France that has seldom autonomously supported the interests of the small-scale family farmers.

Accommodating and Resisting the State

The state in France seldom acted autonomously or automatically to defend the interests of groups that were politically dominated or economically marginal except when other groups emerge to compete with the state in the appropriation of rural surpluses (Brenner 1985). There was often an economic rationale as well as a political expedient in the identification of the state with dominant classes. So, in their experience as family farmers, petty producers have felt that the French state has tended to represent the dominant classes in the agriculture, that is, the large-scale capitalist farms and commercial and trade interests in the countryside. I have argued, in this chapter that their experience of domination was premised on the being the objects of agricultural policies that drafted in league with organizations promoting capitalist interests. Since state policy under capitalism must ensure the reproduction and accumulation of capital, commercial interests have consistently received a favored status in state policies. This as I have argued was as much in evidence in the agricultural policies of the post–World War II period as it was in the early 1900s. That commercial interests benefit from policies designed ostensibly to aid small wine growers, was demonstrated again in the creation of vinification cooperatives. In effect, their creation promoted the development of commercial monopolies in the circuits of distribution of wine by centralizing the manufacturing and marketing processes (see chapter 7).

The specter of state aid looms so large in the lives of small farmer that many writers have argued that, the reproduction of family farming was entirely dependent on state support (see e.g., Warner 1960). But as I have been concerned to demonstrate here, the thrust of much state agricultural policy was drafted against the interests of small-scale agriculture. It was aimed in fact at the elimination of small-scale family farms rather than its preservation. Given such Malthusian conditions, it was not surprising that family farmers in Lower Languedoc continually complained about the state and consistently contested the conditions that imply their decimation.

Political practice in Broussan then often involved the mass mobilization of smallholders and workers in the vine and a variety of forms of collective action that directly and openly challenged and confronted agents of domination, on the one hand. On the other hand, it involved a series everyday forms of defiance and resistance that were lodged in the hidden transcripts of local life. Although periodic mass movements such as regional protests and demonstrations in Languedoc are often understood to exemplify the tradition of furious action of growers, they are often the culmination and open expression of rather more sustained forms of political activity that while taking place offstage, were no less an expression of the tradition of fury than the large organized coordinated protests. In the realm of everyday life, through a multiplicity of social postures, speech acts, behaviors, practices, and gestures often displayed outside the purview of power holders, defiance was often expressed, articulated, and encoded. In the clandestine social arena of private conversations between family, friends, and associates (and often in discussions with many interlocutors, such as the anthropologist, from outside the village), a range of antipathetic sentiments from anger to disaffection to hostility directed at the state, capitalism, transnational capital, landowners, politicians, local elites, and state officials were voiced. As many such gestures were made, postures assumed, and discourses expressed and articulated in those mundane forums of social life often secreted from agents of power, such acts of resistance seldom reached the power holders and the objects of protest tended to escape attack. At the same time, however, in the very acts of exploring and ventilating sentiments of antipathy, a momentum was often built setting into motion a process of transformation in which such hidden acts of defiance became translated into forms of action undertaken by individuals and groups that led to direct confrontations with superordinates and power holders.

Throughout the twentieth century then, the smallholders of Languedoc have been engaged in a collective effort to work the system to their minimum disadvantage and resist the claims made on them by the political and economic elite. Rural resistance in Lower Languedoc then has involved confrontations between the peasant and landlords, the state, and merchants. On the one hand, they attempt to mitigate or repudiate the claims of rent, taxes, or deference made on them. On the other hand, petty producers have also been involved in advancing their own claims and interests of maintaining its share of the market, ensuring fair prices, and wages through such acts of resistance.

In this chapter, then my purpose was not only to apprehend the array of forms of political struggle, but to suggest through specific examples how political practice may begin as one form of resistance, located in the hidden transcript, and end as another form lodged very much in the arena of open confrontation. Part of the solution to this problem rests in understanding the nature of the forces with which growers must contend and here some discussion of the nature of the state and its policies was broached. However, in order to fully appreciated peculiar nature of political practice among the wine growers of Broussan requires an understanding not only of the forms that resistance takes but also an exploration of who becomes engaged in actions initiated to defend the means of making a living. Tilly (1986) has argued that the political actions of the people are often ordered in the routines in everyday life and therefore the specification of the matrix of relationships in the everyday life of working people in Broussan provides the key to understanding which groups of people become mobilized into taking up repertoires of action. The nature of relations in work and everyday life are the subject of later chapters. However, in the next chapter, I begin to explore the question of who the participants in the multiplicity of acts of resistance are, by focusing on the question of identity. I discuss how that tradition of furious action has contoured the collective identity of small growers, conferring to them a specific subjectivity that locates subject in time and place, in terms of their relationships to each other and to agents of domination.

CHAPTER 3

Cultures of Class and Region: Collective Identity and Its Configurations

The revolt of 1907 profoundly marked and continues to mark all Midi viticulture. . . . It is necessary to understand that the lessons drawn from 1907 have guided all the policies of our organisation and that those events themselves are lodged in our memories. In each large demonstration, 1907 is evoked, people come with the flags or placards of that era, town halls have faithfully preserved the souvenirs of that era. . . . 1907 then is our own history, our collective memory, a piece of the map of identity of each wine grower.

—Manifesto of the *Comité d'Action Viticole*

It is often argued that with the constant rapid and permanent changes that define modern society, individuals and groups of people often have no unified, stable, or permanent identity, but many that are different, shifting, and often contradictory. Moreover, it is frequently asserted that no "master identity" can serve to unite people who subscribe to disparate identities into groups of unified political actors and this assertion has often been made to demonstrate the irrelevance of class as a focus for collective consciousness, identity, and action.[1] There seems then to be a great preoccupation with the phenomenon of multiplicity, difference, and division in modern societies and polities in contemporary western intellectual discourses about identity, subjectivity, and political inclinations. This, to some extent has been influenced by the emergence nationalism and the conflicts between "nations" in Europe and elsewhere in recent years. But while the sentiments attached to nationalism divide one group from another, they also act as a force that is as unifying as it is divisive, especially in the field of political practice. To this extent, it seems that the recent tide of nationalist sentiment and nationalist struggle in Europe and elsewhere, belies any assertion that no "master" identity can serve as a force that binds different groups of people into a coalition of unified political actors. Indeed,

contemporary nationalist politics and struggles seem to perform
this role. Moreover, it is often thought that when it serves as the
primary locus of identity, it in fact supplants "class." In this
regard it achieves a mastery over class. In many recent discussions on nationalism, for example, it has been has suggested
that nationalist sentiments and solidarities in fact transcend
class distinctions. In this view, class is declared irrelevant both
as a solidifying force and also as an explanatory principle in
understanding the contemporary world in which nationalisms
are salient and nation-states are declining (Anderson 1983). Other
interventions have sought to problematize, rather than simply
jettison the notion of class both as an organizing and explanatory principle, specifically addressing its relationship to nationalism. Many, in fact have emphasized, the integral connection
that exists between class and nationalism in understanding the
ways in which states have been formed and exploring the processes that lead to the disintegration of states. Hobsbawm (1990
and 1983), for example, stresses the ways in which states were
historically formed around the nationalist visions of elites. He
also problematizes, in the wake of the demise of states, the
question of the role of class and its relationship to the resurgence of nationalisms. What these very different views on the
nature of collective identity as well as the relationship between
class and nationalism suggest is that where subjects define themselves in a multiplicity of ways, not only must the diversity of
their subjective positions be explored but the relations between
them must also be interrogated. This is especially true in cases
where their praxis is contoured by distinctive subjectivities that
are not only diverse, but appear to be contradictory and incoher-
ent. This is indeed the case among the smallholder of Broussan,
who while negotiating their subjectivity through a multiplicity of
identities, themselves, privilege both a class and minority national consciousness, simultaneously.

In Broussan no single identity encapsulates the subjectivity
of smallholders, who variously refer to themselves as "peasants,"
"farmers," "smallholders," "workers," "people of Broussan,"
"Languedoc people," "people of Occitania," and "Frenchmen and
-women." The subjects of this study subscribed to a multiplicity
of different identities and they expressed this diversity through
a variety of means and in a variety of different contexts. Yet in
self-definitional statements and discourses about the past, particular identities tended to be privileged above others. These
identities achieved their prominence precisely because they en-

capsulated the material conditions of peoples' lives, in the first place and they also served to coalesce people into groups of actors, unified in their political activities and commitments. Although, smallholders positioned themselves in a social and cultural order in many and diverse ways, two realms of self-consciousness were particularly salient. Within one realm, the small farmers of Broussan embraced a distinctive cultural consciousness and this emphasized the specificity and particularism of being members of Occitan culture living within the cultural and territorial boundaries of Occitania. This prevailed alongside a realm of class consciousness in which the universalism and generality of being members of the working class and citizens of France was emphasized. While these realms of consciousness appeared to be mutually exclusive and diametrically opposed in their orientations, among the family farmers of Lower Languedoc, they were in fact, interpenetrating and intertwined. So small farmers defined themselves specifically as Occitan growers engaged in minority nationalist struggles, but this was combined with an identity as French citizens and members of the national working class. Specific regional identities then were combined with national identities and cultural identities combined with class.

Among the petty producers of Broussan, therefore, the boundaries between class and cultural identities were fluid and overlapping. This was not only strikingly evident in everyday talk, stories narrated, and political discourses, but also in political and cultural practice. This chapter therefore focuses on narratives and self-definitional statements, through which smallholders recounted their experiences of work, of daily life, and political struggle both in the past and in the present. It attempts to decode the multivalency of words, metaphors, and rhetorical conventions that are used by the smallholders of Broussan in Lower Languedoc to position themselves in a cultural and social universe. Another purpose here is also to attempt to apprehend the ways in which economic and political processes have been captured as experience. The chapter then also directs attention to the ways in which small farmers expounded on the social relationships of domination and exploitation that they experience in their work lives as they toiled within the vicissitudes of capitalism and the modernizing state. I am concerned particularly with how that experience enlivened and informed political identity and praxis. Since identity expresses and defines relationships (Weeks 1987, 48–49), deciphering the multivalency of expressive forms used in self-reflexive narratives will shed light on changes in relations of the locality to the state and people to economy in a changing political economy.

Occitania: History, Territory, and Identity

While earlier, I located Broussan in space as situated within the region of Languedoc, the meaning of that geographic space has resonances beyond mere physical territory. The region of Languedoc is the heartland of a larger, more amorphous entity called "Occitania."[2] Occitania refers to the southern half of France, a territory in which the Occitan language was once spoken. Occitan, unlike other regional languages such as Breton, Basque, and Catalan, is rarely used today as a language of everyday interaction. Yet in many rural areas of Languedoc it is used in some fairly circumscribed spheres. For example, many elderly rural people were often heard to converse in what they themselves referred to as "patois." In some settlements in the mountainous zones of Upper Languedoc, Occitan continues to be spoken, at least with a greater degree of frequency than on the plain. One informant, a man in his sixties and a migrant to the plain from the hills, spoke of how many migrants automatically switched into speaking Occitan after crossing a conceptual frontier when visiting their home in the hills. Nevertheless, the decline of Occitan as a spoken language is relatively high despite the efforts made by regional intellectuals to preserve popular culture and regional distinctiveness.[3] Still, one of the outcomes of the conflict between regional activists and the state has been that the Occitan language and history has come to be taught in schools and universities to offset the Francization of the regional population.[4] Moreover, regional activists have been highly successful in ensuring that Occitan identity has been firmly embedded in the popular consciousness of Occitan people. Regional activists have been involved in a variety of consciousness-raising efforts to disseminate Occitan history, culture, and language. They have been engaged in the dissemination of Occitan history through television programming, magazines, lectures, books, and pamphlets distributed to the regional population through village councils and tourist offices. In these ways, images of the Occitan past enter into the popular imagination. There is a great degree of variation in the forms that Occitanism may take ranging from the cultural and linguistic nationalism advanced by intellectuals to the commercial forms adopted by local tourist boards and entrepreneurs, as well as the protests initiated by local farmers. Nevertheless, one of the defining elements of all forms of Occitanism from commercial cultural promotion to Occitan political struggles[5] and what, in particular, gives struggles their impetus are references to a specific history. This is the history that tells the story of a "lost" country or a "nation," that might have been formed (Roach 1997). It is a narrative that relates the historical erosion of regional autonomy that accompanied the incipient processes of forging the French nation state initiated in the thirteenth century.

In discussions of local history with villagers, women and men frequently began their accounts of the past with a version of the story about the absorption of Languedoc into the French polity. Accounts invariably recall Pope Innocent the Third's crusade against the Albigensian heresy in the thirteenth century. In this story, villagers often emphasized the invasion in 1209 of the south by the armies of the north after the Pope preached against the Cathars. The story concludes with the Northern conquest of Occitania and the end of the political autonomy of Languedoc, and how the region came to be subjected to the power of the French crown. It is also often stressed in these accounts that the last stake was driven into any vestige of the political independence of the south some 500 years later, after the French Revolution, with the abolition of provincial jurisdictions and the old estates which had previously taxed southern France. These facts of history have become part of the shared knowledge of the past in rural villages and many of the inhabitants of Broussan repeated a rendition of this story to me, when I asked about local history. Despite the fact that this story ends with the defeat of the south by the north, the shared memory of this past kept alive through the act of retelling this history arouses the sense of a nation, recalling what might have been and what was, while fuelling the lingering hope for what still can be.

The Midi Rouge

So Occitan history, so far, may reveal that the administrative autonomy of Languedoc has been eroded over the centuries with the building of the nation-state. However, the process of French unification has not completely suppressed the political and cultural distinctiveness of the people of Occitania. This was most vividly captured in the expression *"midi rouge"* or "the red south," which is often used by national and regional newspapers as well as rural women and men to refer to the southernmost area of France. For example, one elderly woman in the village, Louise, encapsulated her explanation to me of the differences between politics practised in northern France and those followed in southern France by saying simply, *"Nous sommes le midi rouge!"* [We are the red south!] *"Midi rouge"* underlines the distinctiveness of the people of the south in two senses. In the first place, they are known as people who have historically espoused left politics and perhaps more importantly practised political radicalism.[6] In the second place, Languedoc people are known to engage in what people of the north, especially in Paris, saw as idiosyncratic and extreme forms of political expression. They burn tires in the road, they spray paint the Paris to Barcelona train. They smash bottles of wine on supermarket floors. They block traffic and conduct almost guerrilla-like attacks on designated targets. Such practices are seen as idiosyncratic, not necessarily because they are tactics of protest unique to Languedoc people, but because they are forms of political expression that are thought to lie beyond the bounds of due political process, sound reason, and rational action. This point is taken up later.

Assertions of such distinctiveness in the subjective positioning of the small farmers surfaced repeatedly in the discussions rural men and women had with me (as an outsider), among each other and also, most vividly, in their (more public) contemporary political events. This distinctiveness was expressed through many keywords—to use Raymond Williams's (1983) expression—which served as referents for class and cultural specificity. These keywords were *les ouvriers* (workers), *l'exploitation* (exploitation in many senses and in the sense of a farm), *Occitanie* (southern France), *le nord, le sud* (the north, the south). *L'ouvrier* and *l'exploitation*, were quite evidently referents for class and class relations. The referents of *l'Occitanie* and the distinction made between people of the north and the south offered a lens through which to view local relations, local consciousness, or local culture. In political action, in political discourses, and in everyday life, the referents for class and those for culture were at certain times used in a dissociated fashion. At other times, they were interconnected, interlocking, mutually resonating, reciprocally transforming, and reinforcing. In Languedoc daily discourse and political performance then, the referents of *exploitation* and *locality* occupied a preeminent position in the self-reflexive exegeses of rural women and men. Cultural referents will be examined later. First, I will look at the nature of class referents.

Class Claims

Among the small farmers of Broussan, class consciousness was expressed explicitly through the referent of *"exploitation."* Through this term, associations with the working class were frequently made in comments made to me during informal chats and formal interviews about work, making a living, and surviving. Many male smallholders who described the nature of their work drew analogies between themselves and the working class claiming that they worked like an exploited worker. One such farmer, Christian, who operated a smallholding of 8 hectares stated: "In wine-growing, you earn the lowest income, just like an exploited worker (*un ouvrier exploité*) in the factory. In fact, you can earn a better income working in a factory." This analogy was reiterated constantly by women and men whose experience of work encompassed wage work as well as farming.

In recounting their daily experiences of work, farmers identified themselves as members of the working class, that is as *"ouvriers"* (workers) who are *"exploités"* (exploited) and who exploit themselves in the work context, not only in the sense that they brought in low incomes but also because they habitually work long hard hours, under unhealthy conditions, often performing dull and monotonous tasks. Given such perceived similarities in the conditions of work, another farmer, Marcel Mas, proclaimed to me that when one thought about the conditions of work in which family farmers and workers find themselves: "There is no difference between us and the worker." When I questioned another farmer Cyril on the validity of these claims, he reinforced the identification with the working class by outlining the similarities in income levels earned by small farmers and workers in order to explain how he felt exploited:

> I earn what amounts to 3,500 francs (roughly $700) a month. This is what a worker earns after putting in an 8-hour day and a 39-hour week. I, in fact work well into the evening and on week-ends. I work overtime and after paying all my expenses, for taxes, fertilizer, replacing equipment, replanting, and so on, there isn't much left. But even though I work

such long hard hours, I don't seem to bring in much. We
small wine growers are forced to *exploit* ourselves and our
families to make a basic living.

Indeed, in Broussan, many of the smallholdings are kept in
operation through the use of the unpaid labor of women and
children and other members of the family and household both in
the fields and in the domestic arena (see chapter 4).

In their testimonials to me and often to each other, the
identification with the working class was a recurrent motif in
discussions of farmers' daily lives. Still, while smallholders often
conceded that they did not work in factories, they nonetheless
maintained that there was little difference between the smallholder and the worker. For example, Madeleine Dissane, wife of
a smallholder in the village, explained to me that while farmers
do own parcels of land, they are usually very small, especially in
relation to the capitalist farms in Languedoc and as a consequence, small farmers tend to make a marginal living off the
land. Mathieu, Madeleine's husband, went on to say that they,
therefore, consider themselves among the marginalized people
in France—the *smicards de la vigne*, the minimum wage earners
in viticulture. *Salaire minimum interprofessionel de croissance*
(SMIC)[7] refers to the minimum wage in France and as an acro-
nym, converted to a noun, *smicard* is a term that usually refers
to wage workers in an urban industrial setting. As the *smicards
de la vigne*, smallholders considered that for all intents and
purposes, they had the same earning potential and buying power
as workers. Also, like workers, they are intensely vulnerable to
the shifts and movements of the market as their source of livelihood was threatened through lay offs and firings as a result of
market conditions. The term *smicard* had become highly charged
in the context of struggles of the small farmers in Lower
Languedoc. By making the connection between workers and farmers explicit *smicard* entered into the language of struggle among
the small farmers in Lower Languedoc as another highly evocative keyword.

Class Traditions

It can well be argued that the adoption of the vocabulary of
working-class struggle by the smallholders was, in effect, a act
of strategic appropriation, by a group who are not bona fide or

"authentic" members of the working class. The use of analogy in discourses on class simply underlines the inauthenticity of class claims. Pursuing this line of reasoning, it may also be argued that the use of language of workers struggles was the most efficacious strategy for presenting and representing the grievances and claims of a dominated class. For in the social and political context of France, the language of working class struggle is one that is understood by the powerful and the powerless. Moreover, in the years of a socialist hegemony in France, left discourses were particularly privileged and legitimated. Thus the self-conscious adoption of the conventional vocabulary of workers' protest most effectively expressed the concerns, demands, and claims of small farmers as members of a powerless class.[8]

While certain conjunctural moments privilege certain discourses and silence others, it must be emphasized that the working-class identity that smallholders of Languedoc expounded and embraced is not merely a metaphorical claim in self-reflexive discourse with little foundation in life experiences and history. This identification is, in fact, firmly grounded in the historical and contemporary work experiences of rural women and men. Both in the past and in the present, women and men of smallholder households have earned a living not only by working as farmers but also by working as laborers on local estates, as well as wage earners in local industries. The work histories and life stories in Part 2 vividly capture the "real" experiences of wage work in an agrarian context.

Historically, smallholders, in fact, put together a livelihood through an economy of pluriactivity or what was earlier referred to as a "dual family economy" of a wage and forms of nonwage work. As members of the peasantry, smallholders maintained their farms growing wheat, olives, grapes, and rearing animals, while also journeying to the local estates in the region to make up part of the agricultural proletariat on the Languedoc domains. So the peasantry in Lower Languedoc, in fact, straddled class divisions through land ownership, on the one hand and through selling their labor for a wage, on the other hand (see Smith 1978 and Frader 1991).

In the contemporary context, the identity between the working class and the smallholder has been reinforced by the forms of pluriactive work pursued by both women and men. Many of the life histories of the smallholders revealed that farmers often worked as agricultural laborers or as factory workers in their

youth before acquiring small parcels of land either through purchase or inheritance. While not all contemporary smallholders of
Lower Languedoc have had the direct experience of wage or
factory work as individuals, they were often, nonetheless the
progeny of men and women who labored on the agricultural
estates in the early twentieth century and who participated in
the labor protests in that period of history. This contemporary
and historical work experience has contributed toward building
a tradition of self-positioning as members of the working class.
Therefore, such an identity was not merely factitious, nor simply
an ad hoc political tactic in a climate that gave license to working-
class ideologies.

Because of this work experience, the statements made are
straightforward. By using the language of struggle of the working class, in making such claims as "like the working classes,
we are exploited," farmers were locating themselves within a
precise set of social relations, that is within the relations of
class and they were drawing the lines between contending
groups in conflict. The use of the words of workers' struggles
served to succinctly define the fundamental characteristic of
these relations while it also defined the parameters of the conflict
in which they are engaged. In other words, these terms synthe-
sized and encapsulated the complex dynamics of class relations
and the inherent conflict that arises from an inextricable connection between a class of producers and a class of nonproducers.
For these small producers, then, as for workers, it is a conflict
which arises from a relationship between producers and
nonproducers over the distribution of resources. Under capitalism this relationship is crucially mediated by control over valued resources. Direct producers produce these valued resources
while certain nonproducers use their control over these resources
to extract surpluses. This nonreciprocated extractive relationship is *exploitation*.

Yet not only is conflict a defining feature of these relations,
but the relations themselves are also based on a condition of
mutual dependence. Because an owner of a resource does not
produce directly, he or she is *dependent* on a laborer; and likewise, a laborer, being deprived of one or more valued resource,
is *dependent* on the owner to make that labor productive. Conflicts
then arise over the carving up of the surplus—between bigger
profits on the one hand, and better wages on the other hand—
hence, disputes over wages and profits, working hours, and
conditions.

Such a formula serves to emphasize what is critical in the relationship between workers *as a class* and capitalists *as a class*: that they are locked into this relationship of dependency and conflict and that it is precisely the *inextricability* of this nexus which gives rise to confrontation. Such relationships are captured and encoded in such keywords as *ouvrier, smicard,* and *exploitation*. Through the repetition of these linguistic conventions individuals established their communion with others whose experiences are encompassed by the "imagined community" (Anderson 1983) of the working class. Working class identity can be thus propounded by rural women and men who may not have direct experience of factory or wage work as experience is often extended through time and place through imagination. Moreover, in Broussan, such a self-positioning is not based exclusively on the work activities of the men of the household, but it crucially factors in women's work activities in the wage sector of the economy. Class identity is not strictly and necessarily defined in terms of the male head of the household.

But the French term *exploiter* and *exploitation* allow for a far wider set of resonances than simply class relations. While in English, many of these resonances of the term *exploitation* are also retained, what is noteworthy is that in Lower Languedoc, these meanings are by no means archaic. *Exploiter* means of course to exploit in the sense of taking advantage of somebody. But it is equally often said by informants to mean "to exploit the soil" hence specifically "to work the land" and then more broadly as a substitute for "work" in general.

The meaning of the word then has come full circle: *"exploiter"* means "to exploit" (that is to say—to exploit a worker) and "to work" (and hence to be exploited). Readers of Chayanov will not be surprised by this, for it is the local reference to his famous "self-exploiting" peasant. The term creates a necessary elision between owner and direct-producer for smallholders who own land and who identify themselves as working class. In fact, the term *"paysans"* is often juxtaposed with *exploités* in local discourse and further effaces the distinction between owner and direct producer, while at the same time encoding more of the central tensions in rural France.

Sedentarism and Sedition

As the farmers use the term *l'exploitation,* it narrowly refers to the exploitative relationship earlier associated with class. But it also refers to the farm, the *l'exploitation agricole*. As such, the term is inseparable from the condition of being tied to a plot of land that is the *sine qua non* of farming. That is to say, farmers make a living from the land and this renders them immobile. Some aspects of this condition—where mobility is low—inclines people toward a sense of localness and a sense of intimacy in peoples' relations to each other and the language and the symbols that are used in everyday talk and political practice, resonate with the associations of locality, local history, and local understandings. Part of this localness includes not only systems of shared meaning but also common experiences of local social relations and history in the context of community, kinship, and neighborhood. The cultural referents in discursive practices then express sentiments of distinctiveness and local relations.[9] One of the most significant and distinctive qualities of the local life of farmers was that they shared the experience of being tied to the land. They were committed to the farm, the *"exploitation"* and therefore to place. The condition of immobility offers clues to the interconnectedness and the interlocked relations between the referents of *exploitation* and *locality* and in this context, *exploitation* becomes tied to *locality*.

In this respect then, class is tied to culture. A precise and restricted use of the term *exploitation* effectively relates the farmers of Lower Languedoc to a universal relationship of *class*. Simultaneously, we have a general and more embracing usage of the terms embeds Languedoc small farmers in a particularistic and local set of restricted relationships. Yet, these distinctions, which are as clear to the listener as to the interlocutor, are blended, run over and played with so that the multiple resonances effectively make the word serve for a whole battery of sentiments. For slippage in the meanings of *exploiter* and *l'exploitation* allow for, and express, a crucial interlacing of universalistic class referents and localized cultural referents in the ongoing constitution and reconstitution of collective identity. Specifically this means the working out of a linkage between the evocation of the oppression of a universal working class—as we saw in the earlier testimonials—and another form of identity that has to do with locality, on the one hand, and the nation-state, on the other, since the referent *l'exploitation* was also evocative of the historic role played by the French state, simultaneously, as the protector and the exploiter of the peasantry.

Brenner (1985) has argued that the relationship between the French state and the peasantry is precisely marked by a kind of ambivalence bred into the contradictory role it has played in the economy and society of small-scale cultivators. For historically in France, unlike Britain, the state—first in the form of the monarchy, later in the form of the republic—has sought to extract revenues directly from the peasantry. As the absolutist state emerged at the expense of the aristocracy, so it has become the case in France, that the state has been seen, as much as, if not more, as the extractor of surplus—the exploiter—than the local landlords (Anderson 1974). But for this extraction to be effective, the state had to protect its interests, which in effect meant protecting the peasantry, at least in part from the forces that threatened it, that is to say from other extractors of surplus—landlords and the aristocracy. As the state consolidated itself as a multifarious entity after 1789, however, smallholders' interests represented but one of a variety of interests within the polity that the state must uphold. It therefore played an ambivalent role and introduced interventions into Languedoc viticulture that in fact acted as a double-edged sword, providing certain subsidies and enacting legislation that had contradictory effects. These contradictions combined with its complicit role in promoting the conditions that contributed to the increasing subordination of smallholders to the capitalist market have stirred Languedoc women and men to the riots and rebellions that punctuate Languedoc history since the beginning of the twentieth century. Petty producers and the state, like the capitalist and the worker, were thus also locked into a relationship characterized by dependency and conflict. As was suggested earlier, it is precisely this relationship that has inherent conflict and confrontation built into it. The sense that the state acts as the preeminent exploiter of the smallholder in the localities has fueled a wide variety of confrontations and has a long historical pedigree. It is precisely in *this* regard that the ideas of exploitation and locality are blended in the struggles of Languedoc family farmers.

Cultural Distinctions

As discussed in the previous chapter, smallholders of Broussan publicly expressed their antipathy toward the state through demonstrations and protests. In this sense the smallholders both associated and *dis*sociated themselves with workers in their everyday talk. Hence the juxtaposition of *les paysans* with *exploités* appears often in local discourse. Individuals also made distinctions in talking about the kinds of political action that are practised. One smallholder, Pierre Gourou outlined the difference in a remark about acts of protest: "We have to defend our future, the same way workers defend their rights by having strikes. We don't go on strike as wine growers. We protest. We march on governments." Workers go on strike, while farmers demonstrate and protest.

In June and July of 1992, however, when farmers took to the streets again, a certain kind of collusion arose between two groups of protestors. The protest activities of small farmers of the south became extended to a wider area within France. Their attempts in the north to block the autoroutes around Paris with tractors and other farm equipment initially failed. In areas of the south, however, sporadic blockades sprung up around cities and towns, effectively choking up the major arteries to Toulouse, Albi, Montpellier, and Béziers. This tactic was very quickly taken up by striking truck drivers who extended the tactic to the entire "hexagon" of the French autoroute network. While in the north, the truckers operated alone, in the area around Montpellier, and Béziers, farmers aided the truckers' protests by blacking out, removing, or redirecting road signs on rural routes, thereby tying up the traffic seeking to avoid the truckers' barrages. A common feature of the conditions facing northern and southern groups of farmers and workers was the government's attempt to *regulate* elements of worker's livelihoods alongside a stunning ignorance of the conditions of production in ever harsher economic conditions.[10] The actual form political expression takes must be understood by being firmly contextualized within tradition and local cultural production. Among the small farmers of Lower Languedoc, the particular *form* political expression took in the demonstrations did not in any way resemble the well-organized strikes or the across-the-desk negotiations of political specialists working in the industrial and urban arenas. As such the referents used in political expression are not precise and sharply instrumental but were evocative and multivocal. In political expression, a whole range of referents are deployed that exhibited the polysemic characteristics that have been stressed for "*exploitation.*"

In confrontations between the state and the smallholders, the most potent, evocative idioms of mass protest were those which expressed a sense of local identity preeminently in terms of the cultural referents of Occitania. Thus, in the rhetorical conventions of the oppositional politics of the family wine growers of Languedoc revendicationalist themes were pronounced. Slogans are chanted and displayed, not in French, the language of the state, the bureaucracy and the dominant culture, but in the Occitan language, the language of the south. Proclamations such as—"*Volem Viure al Païs*" (We want to live in our land) and "*Volem Viure y Trabahar al Païs*" (We want to live and work in our land)—are repeated in mass demonstrations evoking the sentiments of people's aspirations, hopes, and demands for making a living in a land that they called their own, Languedoc. The emblems of Occitania have been brandished in mass protests. The red-and-gold Occitan cross was prominently displayed on flags, posters, and placards, often juxtaposed with a bunch of withered grapes.

Expressions, themes and slogans such as these underline the fact that Occitania more than merely a *cultural* construct is thoroughly invested with political significance. Occitan symbols, idioms, representations, and historical referents have become politically charged with the sentiments of opposition, resistance, and challenge to exploitation and domination by the state.

What informants expressed in a whole battery of arguments among themselves, to me and to other outsiders was that one kind of *exploitation*—through taxes—requires the simultaneous defense of another kind of exploitation, the *exploitation agricole*, the farm enterprise. It was felt that the state had abdicated its historic role as defender of small farmers with its collusion with the forces of capitalist modernization and its acceptance of the entry of Spain and Portugal into the European Economic Community. It is the injustice of a failed reciprocity that fueled the indignation of farmers and inspired them to engage not only in public mass resistance but also a whole battery of clandestine acts of protest and sabotage discussed earlier. Indeed these acts are often denounced by public officials as irrational acts of violence that reaffirm their perception of how the farmers from the south are morally and politically beyond the pale.

Participation in these acts of protest and the use of the Occitan language in making claims and demands, both serve to embarrass the opposition—the state—and to define it as the opposition while simultaneously, serving to draw the participants on one side of the struggle together. They are an embarrassment to the state as these forms of resistance served as a reminder of the failure of the state to create national unity through its efforts to impose a homogenous culture and language and to foster a docile rural population that assimilates the modernizing imperative of the state. The use of Occitan symbols therefore had oppositional value because it highlighted a failed, inefficient, and incomplete hegemony. So, for example, graffiti in Occitan are often concentrated in two areas—physical objects representing the state—that is, road signs, government buildings, and schools, one of the main purveyors of the dominant culture; and buildings representing large-scale French or international capital such as Mammouth supermarkets or factory walls. So such practices as spray painting "Oc" as graffiti were effective as long as the state responds in terms of frustration, describing these actions as diametrically opposite to the sound reason and bureaucratic rationality of the French. In these respects, Occitan symbols served to draw lines of distinction between contending groups in the politics of opposition. Marcel Mas commented on the differences between other regions and the midi by focusing on the attitude of the state toward southern viticulture:

> Those people up there (in Paris) don't care about us down here. They only care about the rich farmers of the north who have the power and the money and so they gear their policies to make them happy. The state buys their votes. Do you know what the Minister of Agriculture once said about us, down here in the midi. Let viticulture die! (*Que la viticulture crève!*) So now do you see why we Occitan wine growers are against the state?

Moreover, regional division of interest are underscored by the widespread belief that laws made by the government apply differently to different regions. So for example, Christian Rey, a wine grower remarked to me during the demonstration in May 1984, that after the introduction of the Law of 1907, which regulated the use of the sugar in the making of wine, that fraud is still the culprit responsible for problems facing the smallholder in the market:

> Fraud is the main reason that our wine doesn't sell. Even if you have a law, it is not easy to enforce it. There is no way of figuring out who is cheating and who isn't. All the information about the size of harvest and the amount of land you own that you have to report to the government is all made up. Who is going to bother checking up on you. There is a law against this, but it only applies to us growers down here in the south. Wine growers everywhere else in France are allowed to add sugar to wine. There is one law for the north and one law for the south.

Occitan symbols then articulate sentiments of opposition to the north and to the state. It also draws participants together as users of a metonymic weapon that figuratively assails state hegemony. Occitan symbols then evoke a whole shared history of state domination that has become embedded in local consciousness through the retelling of events of the past in daily discourse.

In retelling tradition, everyday talk as I mentioned earlier then was often replete with allusions to events that extend from as far back as the thirteenth century to the more recent history of local and regional struggles at the turn of the century and also to the contemporary moments of resistance against forces from the north, the center of state control and cultural domination. In many conversations with me, rural women and men recollected and retold stories about the Albigensian crusades in the thirteenth century. The act of recounting to me and to each other served often to reignite hopes for the once-lived reality of political autonomy and freedom from northern domination. As discussed in chapter 2, one of the events often alluded to is the revolt of the Midi in 1907, which fires the indignation of smallholders. Informants also discuss the events in Larzac a small farming community in the highlands of Languedoc, in 1974, in which government troops killed several protestors who were protesting the expropriation of farm land to install a military base. While historically, the struggles of the people of Languedoc ended in defeat, and part of that defeat is exemplified by the near extinction of the Occitan language,[11] these narratives, nonetheless, serve as a reminder of the possibilities for taking up collective action. They form part of the political dream life of smallholders and fuel a vision of freedom and autonomy which converges with their ideals of independence in work (see chapter 4). The residual and highly politicized phrases in Occitan retained and deployed as struggle concepts, served also to buttress their image as contentious people to themselves and to outsiders.

Carnaval

The lines of opposition and the ties that bind people together are not only reinforced in the realm of collective political practice; they are also galvanized by social and cultural practices in everyday community life. For example, these ties are reinforced in such activities as reciprocal networks of exchange in work; participation in the sport and leisure associations in villages and also in cultural events and local festivals. One such local festival, *Carnaval*, an annual event can be seen to reflect feelings of association and dissociation. *Carnaval* is thought of as a means through which local life is publicly validated serving to draw people together. Many comments made to me during a *Carnaval* parade conveyed these precise sentiments. For example, one person claimed to speak on behalf of many villagers when explaining to me the function of *Carnaval*: "*Carnaval* is an event through which we rediscover each other (*On se retrouve*). We feel part of something very alive and it makes us feel good about living here."

Carnaval is also an event that had become highly politicized. In *Carnaval*, representations of outsiders, of noncommunity figures and politicians are taken and used as the subject of carnivalesque antics.

During *Carnaval* in February of 1983, for example, a crowd gathered in the main square of Broussan. Being dragged into the square was a huge *paper mâché* figure of a gorilla in a characteristic apish pose, baring its huge teeth at the crowd. Next, several costumed and masked men ignited the figure with torches. The gorilla burst into flames and the crowd cheered and screamed with delight. Two bystanders laughingly argued, one saying that the gorilla looked remarkably like the village mayor, the other saying it represented the bureaucrats in the minister of agriculture office. I was told that in *Carnaval*, the practice of burning politicians in effigy in protest against various agricultural policies and political practice is a common occurrence in many villages of the area. Various ministers of agriculture have been burned in protest against agricultural policy and Valéry Giscard d'Estaing was also burned in effigy during *Carnaval* in one year to protest against the propensity of a right-wing government to ally itself with capitalist interests and northern agriculture. The *paper mâché* figure was an icon of all the ill fortune of the year gone by and it became by and large de rigeur during *Carnaval* to burn political figures in effigy.

The cultural practice of *Carnaval*, however, is not *just* about local matters, juxtaposed against the outside. It does not simply evoke the local life of *exploiting* the soil, it has come increasingly to reflect other aspects of *exploitation*. As such, it brings the alien state into the arena of daily discourse but only to underscore local opposition to state power. In this regard, culture and cultural practices combine and express ties people develop in local contexts while also expressing ties of unequal appropriation that within and beyond the boundaries of the local (Sider 1984).

North and South

One further working out of the slippage between class and cultural referents and how they merge in daily discourse is related to the regional and class division in French agriculture. When the small farmers spoke of themselves as people of the *"midi rouge,"* followers of left, regional, and particularly radical politics at the same time, this was an explicit referent to the fact that they set themselves against capitalist systems of production. But in France there is also a regional specificity to the class structure in agriculture. Regional divisions to a large degree correspond with class divisions in the agriculture of France. Large-scale, highly mechanized, and capital-intensive agriculture is located largely in the north. Small-scale, labor intensive agriculture is located mainly in the south. Because of the distinction between the agriculture of the "north" and the agriculture of the "south," the modernization policies of the state in agriculture are seen to favor the development of the north, at the expense of the south. It is in this respect, that the notion of exploitation takes on a further local referent. The state and the north and hence, the state and capitalism dominates the south. The class identity of the smallholders, then, converged with the cultural referent of a specifically Occitan identity. In this way, the Occitan idea served to cohere a potentially disparate group of farmers, both large and small, who felt that people of the locality are exploited.

While the Occitan idea unites farmers of the south, there is a flaw in the image that *all the people* of the rural south are exploited both by the state and capitalism. Large wine-growing domains—that is, capitalist farms—are not only located in the northern regions of France but they are also found *within* the Lower Languedoc region. Occitan people then include a highly differentiated population of capitalist farmers as well as petty commodity producers. In overt political demonstrations, everyday talk and political action local smallholders were able to distinguish themselves *against* large-scale, capitalist estate owners both as a class and culturally. In the first instance, large owners seldom participated in demonstrations and protests alongside small owners. Nor did they participate in clandestine acts of sabotage. In the realm of praxis then, large owners were set apart from small owners of the region.

Large landowners also colluded in identifying themselves against smallholders. The owner of a local château, for example, maintained the distinction between himself and the small farmers in a rather candid commentary to me about his estate and the farms operated by small growers:

> Apart from working as common laborers and producing inferior wine, my small neighbors are incapable of doing any other kind of work. As a result they may all go bankrupt. They may lose their little farms, but my kind of farm and my estate will survive and flourish.

Large owners, then, tend to dissociate themselves from the smallholders, seldom taking an active part in local life, and this dissociation with locality is built into the condition of bourgeois life. Bourdieu encapsulates this dynamic in his comments on the nature of the existence of those who live by the accumulation of capital:

> The accumulation of economic capital merges with the accumulation of symbolic capital, that is, with the acquisition of a reputation for competence and an image of respectability and honourability that are easily converted into political positions as a local or national *notable*. It is therefore understandable that they should identify with the established (moral) order. (1984, 291)

In Lower Languedoc, then large landowners tended to maintain a social, physical, and moral space between themselves and what they see as a disreputable and uncultured mass.

Once again, historical experience plays a key role in this process, for in the past large landowners tended to identify themselves less with the locality and more with the national bourgeoisie and this was symbolized not only in lifestyles but language used.

Marcelle Pigassou, who worked as a laborer on the estates between the two wars commented on the worlds of difference between her and her employers:

> My employers wore the finest clothes and had lots of very expensive things. They hardly ever spoke patois because they thought it was vulgar and French was more refined. French was really the language of the rich. All of us work-

ers, however, spoke patois because this is what we grew up speaking and many of us don't even speak French properly because we didn't finish school.

Historically, the estate owners tended to speak French, seen by many elderly smallholders who worked on the estates as the language of the rich and leisured classes. By contrast, Occitan was the language of work, spoken among laborers and smallholders.

In maintaining a distinction between the north and the south, nevertheless, the way smallholders dealt with this apparent contradiction to their view of the world in which injustice emanates from the north and not locally is to treat it as the exception that proves the rule.[12]

These examples of everyday talk and cultural practice emphasize that decoding the meanings of cultural and especially expression requires some understanding of how they have been configured by political and economic processes and transformations. Through this lens it becomes apparent that there is nothing idiosyncratic nor particularistic nor irrational about Languedoc political events—as northerners in France and journalists would have us believe. Rather, what they reflect and express is the wide range of evocations that can be produced in political practice.

Petty Producers, Politics, and Collective Identities

Much interest in the rural population of Europe has been centred on the question of how collective identity has been shaped under the modernizing impulses of the nation-state and economy and how identity itself has shaped political allegiances and practices.[13] In historical treatises on rural France, for example, contrasting images have been produced in which the French small farmer has been represented alternately as the politically contentious heirs to a tradition of nineteenth-century rural radicalism (Frader 1991, Judt 1979, Loubère 1974, Agulhon 1982) or as the politically quiescent heirs to a tradition of rural conservatism (Weber 1976 and 1982, Jones 1985). In both representations, it is often held that the processes of modernization and nation building have begotten a population of family farmers whose orientation has transcended the locality, in as much as collective identities are no longer configured by local ideologies but by those of national groups. The identity and interests of

rural radicals, so it is argued, have become increasingly conso-
nant with those of the national working class (Margadant 1979).
For those who represent petty producers as conservatives, modernization has brought about the disintegration of what are considered inert and anachronistic local and regional cultures, as
petty producers have acquiesced to the universalizing forces of
national integration and cultural homogenization (Weber 1976,
Mendras 1970). This forceful image of the peasant, transfigured
as "Frenchman," has contoured the expectations of anthropologists who have ventured into rural settings. For example,
influenced by Weber, Rogers (1991) writes of anticipating a rural
setting in which cultural differences had been eroded giving way
to a homogenized French citizen. Yet, she encountered rural people
in the Aveyron who participated in a local culture that was
infinitely dynamic in its ability to reformulate national political
discourses. However, this cultural dynamism did not translate
into overt political action, at least in contributing to the construction of a politically active and engaged subject that publicly contested the hegemony of French national identity. For Rogers, then,
people are publicly "French" and only privately "Aveyronnais" and
still quiescent in the noisy world of national politics (1991, 197).

Such representations as this are found in ethnographic texts
about sites as far apart as Scotland and Northeastern Italy, so
that the same kind of introspection in the face of the state's
failure to deliver the goods that modernization promises and the
nation to serve as a social and psychological repository of identity was noted by Cohen (1987), for the rural north of Great
Britain. And Holmes (1989), whose study of Friuli was explicitly
focused on the intersection between "peasants" and "workers"—
rural people who found themselves engaged in livelihoods tied
both to the farm and to sojourns in factories—nevertheless found
that experience of the factory did not produce a form of class
consciousness geared to contentiousness. To the contrary, Holmes
argues that the liminal situation of people who straddle the
enchanted world of tradition and the disenchanted world of contracts has tended to reinforce a sense of fatefulness and individual, rather than collective, resourcefulness.[14]

Such varying images of rural people experiencing modernization in the most advanced of capitalist societies can be partly
explained by differences in regional histories and traditions.[15]
Moreover, what dominates in many studies is the insistence on
maintaining a series of radical separations in the representation
of the collective identity of rural people, each positing an image

of the small-scale farmer that is supposedly fixed and eternal.[16] A tradition-bound, locally oriented peasantry is counterposed to a small-scale farmer that has shed the weight of custom to embrace national culture and the ideologies of political groups and classes; or a line is drawn between the radical, contentious rural inhabitant and a small farmer that practices a politics that affirms the political and cultural status quo as imposed by the hegemonic state. Such radical separations often belie the ephemeral quality of identity and the intricacies of the ways in which collective identities may be produced in local rural settings.

In Broussan and the larger context of Lower Languedoc, the small farmers who have consistently voted socialist or communist at the local level, appear to embrace some characteristics of the nineteenth-century radicals noted by Judt, Agulhon, Margadant, and Loubère, by subscribing to the ideology of France's working class. Yet many saw their commitments as neither entirely subsumed by a proletarian ideology, nor indeed the ideology of any other national group. In maintaining these distinctions, the small farmers exhibited the introspection and the alienation from national society and culture, noted by Holmes, Rogers, and Cohen. However, such alienation from the national level did not imply a withdrawal into an enchanted world of tradition and passivity, but a world in which tradition was enlivened by class consciousness and local cultural consciousness and continually "invented" to give authority to contemporary actions and to the selection of certain identities over a host of others (Hobsbawn and Ranger 1983). The small cultivators of Lower Languedoc have assumed a collective identity that evokes, in turns, elements of *local cultural* participation and elements of a universalistic, class participation as members of the French working class and this has configured political praxis in ways that forcefully challenge state hegemony.

Conclusion

Drawing radical distinctions between locally oriented rural people who may be politically quiescent and those who are politically vigorous in contesting the established hegemonies often masks the intricate processes involved in the construction of collective identities. Such processes may involve combining and synthesizing different identities and forms of consciousness that are seemingly opposed in their orientations. I have argued, following from this, that class and cultural consciousness under specific conditions are not antagonistic and mutually exclusive forms of identity. Particularisms or "primordial" loyalties can be linked to universalistic forms of identification and minority nationalistic sentiments can be combined with the sentiments of belonging to a subaltern class, when the nation is seen as an entity that is class divided. Moreover, these divisions can coincide with territory or involve contests over territory. Among the petty producers of Lower Languedoc, everyday talk and political practice is inscribed with class and cultural referents. I used a very formal definition of class to explicate the nuances of the class referents that are wielded among the smallholders of Broussan. The term *culture* was also used very specifically as the product of historical and daily practice. In this sense, culture is a system of meanings, understandings, dispositions, and practices that is produced, created, made, and remade by people in their social relations with other people. While this conceptualization is hardly new,[17] it nonetheless suggests that there is an immediate connection between the production of culture and the economic and political forces involved in the reproduction of social life. These interconnections are apparent in the forms of expressions used by the small farmers of Broussan as they negotiate a political subjectivity under the vicissitudes of capitalist development and a nation state determined to enact its modernity project.

I have been particularly concerned then with the connection between the subjective positioning of small cultivators as "Occitan people" and the expressive forms this identity took in practice. As this chapter has also been devoted to apprehending the potency of emotive terms in discourse, I have argued that this can only be accomplished through exploring the ways in which social, economic, and political transformations have injected specific meanings into expressive forms. In examining the self-reflexive narratives and political discourses of the Lower Languedoc small farmers, decoding the polysemy of words, metaphors, and other cultural signifiers perforce involved exploring shared and local knowledge of the specifics of regional history and the variety of ways in which rural people have been exploited in their relationships in the contemporary economy and society.

Anthropologists and other scholars readily acknowledge that the determination of the nature of "consciousness," "praxis," and "identity" is a difficult task. Yet the urgency of this project is especially warranted in order to grasp the meaning of the political expressions that have arisen in response to the conditions of contemporary political and economic crisis in which capitalist and transitional capitalist societies are embedded. So, if the notion of "class" has become obsolete as people's consciousness and praxis appears less to be expressed by reference to it, then the lens of cultural analysis may go some way toward illuminating the dynamics of identity construction. But where expressions of class maintain a potency in political practice, cultural analysis alone fails to penetrate to the heart of social identity and praxis. Moreover, studies of nationalism and regional nationalism, must, at minimum, problematize the question of class, for it illuminates the ways in which certain visions of nationalism come to the fore, under what circumstances they achieve the status of hegemony, as well as the ways in which other visions become occluded. It also contributes toward an understanding of the relationships that might prevail between forces competing for the loyalties and attachments of people in the history of changing political economies. So, in rural Languedoc, and in other contexts, where people continue to negotiate their subject positions by reference to history and social relations, the lens of class continues to offer clues into collective identity and praxis and culture must also be understood to reflect history and social relations. In the chapters that follow, then, I explore the dynamics of those social relations and the organization that orders political action, which until now have been presented as representations in the discursive practices of the smallholders.

PART 2
WORK, SOCIAL RELATIONS, AND EVERYDAY LIFE

Only in the local network of labor and recreation can one grasp how, within a grid of social-economic constraints, . . . [everyday] pursuits unfailingly establish relational tactics (a struggle for life), artistic creations (an aesthetic), and autonomous initiatives (an ethic). The characteristically subtle logic of the "ordinary" activities comes to light only in the details.

—Michel de Certeau (1984)
The Practice of Everyday Life

Authorities and thoughtless historians commonly describe popular contention as disorderly.[. . .] But the more closely we look at the same contention, the more we discover order. We discover order created by the rooting of collective action in the routines and organization of everyday social life and by its involvement in a continuous process of signalling, negotiation and struggle with other parties whose interests the collective action touches.

—Charles Tilly (1986)
The Contentious French

CHAPTER 4

Negotiating Consensus: Production, Reproduction, and Power in the Domestic Realm

It is through their commitment to the concept of the family that people are recruited into the material relations of households. Because people accept the meaningfulness of the family, they enter into relations of production, reproduction and consumption with one another—they marry, beget children, work to support dependents, transmit and inherit cultural and material resources.

—Rapp and Ross, "Examining Family History"

The language of kinship is concerned with generosity and sharing; this is only one side of the story. Kinship is also a language of hierarchy and dependency, of authority and obedience.

—Harris, "Households and their Boundaries"

Contention and political practice pivot around relations in everyday life. Struggles in the political field are rooted in very direct ways by struggles in everyday life undertaken to make a living and the relationships into which people enter in order to ensure the continuity of a way of life and their livelihoods. This, as de Certeau posits, establishes "relational tactics" and an "ethic." In order to comprehend how political action, "autonomous initiatives" and collective identities are anchored to, reflect, reinforce, and inform social relations, we need to investigate the dynamics of the relations into which people enter in order to engage in their "struggle for life." In this chapter, then, I begin to unravel the dynamics of everyday social relations by focusing on how people become recruited into the material relations of the household in Broussan.

Petty Commodity Production

Theories of petty commodity production are often used to explain how family farms and agrarian enterprises, such as those found in Broussan persist under a series of changing conditions in the political economy of both developed and developing countries. Observing that a variety of forms of petty commodity production have endured under a series of different economic and political regimes in many different historical periods, led a number of scholars in the 1980s to pursue a rigorous examination of organizational principles in the process of production in petty commodity enterprises. For example, Friedmann (1980 and 1987), Bernstein (1987), and among many others, focused their attention on isolating the structural properties of petty commodity production in an effort to understand how a form of production not entirely subsumed by the logic of capitalism managed to sustain itself under capitalism. In the rich dialogue that emerged, a series of debates erupted over a number of questions included the characteristics of and the actual role played by labor in production the nature of surplus generation on family-based farms.[1] Views diverged considerably around this issue and from the debates, three positions on the nature of labor emerged. In one view, it was emphasized that relations outside the household in petty commodity production were commodified locked into circuits of exchange through buying, selling, and competition, while relations in the domestic sphere were not commodified and exchanges were embedded in the interpersonal ties of familial cooperation and reciprocity. Exchanges of labor outside the household involved the payment of wages, while in the household, labor was unpaid. In a seminal work on petty commodity production, Friedmann (1980 and 1987) suggested that the reproduction of the petty commodity enterprise and its persistence in a variety of social formation was attributed to the the use of unpaid family labor. The mobilization of the labor of household members that is unpaid eliminates the need to generate a profit. Therefore, the petty commodity enterprise is able to maintain itself in the face of competition from capitalist enterprises that must rely on wage labor. In fact, the distinction between commodified relations and noncommodified relations marked a the boundary that separated the "private" households from of the larger "public" sphere. In another intervention on this issue, Chevalier (1982a and 1982b) argued that all social relations within and external to the domestic sphere are commodified, valorized or potentially valorizable. Therefore, the distinctions made in Friedmann's view cannot be upheld. In yet another view again questioning the distinctions and conceptual divisions made by Friedmann, it is argued that while the domestic domain in many contexts of petty commodity production is free of the process of commodification, social relations outside the domestic arena are often not thoroughly subjected to market forces even under the conditions of highly developed capitalist economy (C. Smith 1984). While views and conceptualizations vary and despite the disagreements that emerged in what became an intricate and very rarefied debate, all the interlocutors seemed to acknowledge that the understanding the nature of labor, particularly family labor, somehow lay at the heart of petty commodity production's capacity to persist under many circumstances that threaten its demise (Scott 1986, 6). Efforts to define the nature of social relations in petty commodity production are therefore critical, not only as a matter of theoretical interest, but also, as I discuss later, as a matter of practical concern in terms of strategies of development.

In the discussion that follows then, I build on the insights offered by theorists of petty commodity production not only to illuminate the characteristics of labor in the petty commodity households in Broussan, but also to isolate the mechanisms through which the labor of the members of households becomes mobilized to guarantee farm continuity. My overall argument in this chapter is that while much attention had been devoted to isolating the structural dynamics of petty commodity production, particularly to the issue of whether labor is or is not commodified, less attention has been directed toward how family labor is in fact mobilized. In order to address this question, I argue that the issue of ideology and the cultural factors that influence the ways in which labor, paid or unpaid, is mobilized must be analyzed and subjected to inspection. Moreover, it is by pursuing the problem of how ideological factors intersect and interact with structural features of family farming that a clearer sense of the dynamics of production and reproduction of family-based enterprises may be achieved.

From studies of petty commodity production, we understand that the household is often a sphere that is not only isolated but insulated from market relations. The labor of family members is embedded in the social relations of family and therefore located in a "familistic" ethic where the values such as reciprocity and generosity govern interactions and exchanges and not market calculation. Labor goods and services therefore are exchanged among family members without payment. In the case of the family wine growers of Broussan, the deployment of the unpaid labor of members of the household is indeed a consistent feature of their daily struggles to make a living. Family members commit themselves and their unpaid labor to what I refer to as the "common family project" of ensuring farm continuity. Wives, sons, and daughters who work collectively to keep the family farm in operation appear to do so through an established consensus and the general acceptance of the meaningfulness of the idea of the family and the common family project, as Rapp, and Ross in the epigraph of this chapter suggest. What is often omitted from analyses of petty commodity production, irrespective of the position held on the characteristics of labor, both inside and outside the household, is an understanding of how the acquiescence to surrender family labor has been achieved. In other words, the processes through which an acceptance of the meaningfulness of the idea of the family is seldom explained.[2]

In many instances, then what the life histories of many villagers reveal is that family labor is neither routinely nor often very spontaneously surrendered to a common family project. Indeed, the "commonness" of the common family project is often contested. Conflicts and crises regularly arise as farmers attempt to secure labor for the reproduction of the enterprise both over the short and long term. These conflicts are intensified in the context of Languedoc by the facility with which labor that is "unfree" can be transformed into "free" labor in a highly developed market context. In this respect, a kind of market determination has intruded into the "private" world of domestic life. Various forms of capitalist calculation contour arrangements, negotiations, and strategies not only used to restrict the mobility of labor securing it to the farm, but also to allow it to be freed but only within the constraints of commitment to the common family project. The limits to mobility are imposed often through the deployment of an arsenal of ideological weapons defining people's modes of conduct while enforcing values to compel family members to commit themselves to farmwork and the common family project. In this way, market relations have indeed intruded into the domestic sphere, for while the labor that is often mobilized on family farms is unpaid, its potential market value has influenced the strategies for the mobilization and deployment of labor. Under these conditions, it becomes evident that the domestic sphere and relations within that sphere are not wholly governed by the principles and precepts of kinship and family.

The dynamics of conflict, struggle, and negotiation, as Harris suggests in the epigraph of this chapter, illustrates that the household is in fact a multidimensional entity. While the ethic of reciprocity and generosity is meant to prevail among family members, implying that the household is a site of consensus, the household is also the site of profound and intense conflict. Moreover, while the bonds of kinship may invoke sentiments of mutuality and generosity, they also summon up obligation, duty, and responsibility that is enforced by the exercise of power, by the powerful over the powerless. The household therefore is also an institution based on hierarchy and dependency where members are differentiated in terms of their access to power and control over material resources.

In this chapter, then, I attempt to isolate the dynamics of power and the exercise of patriarchal authority in the households of Broussan, by focusing on the ways in which the labor of members of the household is deployed both on a daily basis and over the longer term. To focus the discussion, I direct attention particularly to the issue of inheritance and discuss the attempts made by family farmers to resolve crises of succession. For it is in those moments when crises of continuity over the short and long term arise, that the multiple dimensions of the household as a site of conflict, hierarchy, and dependence as well as cooperation and consensus are most vividly exposed. The crises of succession, as I later argue, are particularly acute in the context of a highly developed market in land and especially labor. The conditions prevail for high degree of labor mobility in the economy of Lower Languedoc and France, where a variety of forms of wage work coexist with family-based enterprises. The facility with which the noncommodified labor of family members can be converted to wage labor and escape the binds of family has intensified the efforts of farmers, particularly parents to secure the labor of succeeding generations. Many of the examples, therefore, capture the conflicts that arise between parents and children over the question of succession as well as the negotiations and the means of manipulation used by parents to guarantee the continuity of the farm. It is during these moments of crises and conflict that the ideological prescriptions of the family are invoked and wielded as a weapon of compulsion to bind labor to households. The discussion then centers on the ideological dynamics of petty commodity production and through the households of Broussan, I attempt to shed light on the role that ideology plays not only in the material reproduction of the farm but also in the symbolic reproduction of the family.[3]

The Intrusion of Market Relations

The domestic arena in Broussan then is not a site that is free of market principles and relations. While social relations between household members are embedded in ties of family, they are often also embedded in the market in the sense that they are subjected to a kind of "commodification effect" (Lem 1988). The commodification effect results from the fact that in many contexts, capitalist development is essentially an uneven and in many ways far from a totalizing process. In the context of Lower Languedoc, it implies that market calculations prevail in many spheres of social and economic life, though the commodification of social relations may not actually occur. Within the farming households of Broussan, the unevenness of capitalist penetration means that the market has intruded into domestic life and while social relations household members are embedded in ideologies of family and kinship, on the one hand, they are, on the other hand, often also governed by the *principles* of market calculation. This does not imply however, that the *practice* of market calculation and that instrumental rationality necessarily rules. In practice, labor is exchanged between household members without buying and selling, as this takes place in a context in which people are ever cognizant of the value of labor as a commodity. The pervasiveness of the market influences strategies, structures social relations and individual decisions on how a struggle for life will be played out. Ideas surrounding the value of labor power, wages, and wage equivalence have penetrated to the heart of the domestic sphere and this then gives social relations within the household their characteristic as being, in a sense, symbolically commodified, while economic commodification has not occurred. Because commodity penetration is uneven, social relations then are governed both by market calculation and distinctive cultural principles.

Examples outlining the dynamics of household production stress that the presence of a market in labor power and that the potential valorization of domestic labor produces a central tension within the household. In a highly developed market context, conditions that favor labor mobility are pitted against the strictures of kinship, which in fact function to render labor immobile for the purposes of reproduction of the enterprise. As household members can readily evade their commitments to the common family project by seeking to realize the price of their labor in a highly developed and accessible labor market, the task of securing labor to work on the farm is paramount and it is often at the center of conflicts between members of the household in Broussan. Yet despite the presence of forces that threaten to dissolve the continuity of farms and families, the production of commodities in Broussan continues to be organized around the household. Before examining the household economy, some discussion of the forms of the household that prevail in the village is in order.

The Household as a Domestic Formation

In Broussan, the household is a domestic grouping that is based on the coresidence of people tied together by affinity and descent. Two dominant forms of the household can be distinguished in the village—nuclear households and extended household, both of which varied in size and composition according to demographic cycle, as well as class. Both the size and the form of the household affected the organization of labor in important ways.

As a domestic group, the household was usually formed upon marriage. After marrying, children were generally expected to establish a residence, physically separated from the parental home. The size and composition of households depends on the demographic cycle. Newly formed household tended to expand in size while at a later point in the demographic cycle, households tended to decrease in size, consisting for the most part of elderly couples, whose children have married and left the parental home. A significant number of households in Broussan were also made up of single individuals, including widows, widowers, divorced individuals, and bachelors.[4]

While new households tended to be created upon marriage, many domestic groupings contained two and occasionally three generations of people in extended arrangements. Grandparents, their children, and grandchildren frequently lived together in many of the larger houses of the village. Such extended arrangements greatly facilitated access to labor as often members of three generations made a contribution both to running the household and the farm. These very large households were more common among the large landowning families who lived the grand houses located on the outer perimeter of the village. The larger landowners tended to have the resources to support three or more generations of cohabiting kin. Moreover, in the larger landowning families, land was often passed down to one heir, usually the oldest male, in order to prevent fragmentation of the landholding. He and his family tended to live in the natal home, along with parents while other children, who received compensatory sums of cash or other property, usually left the parental home to take up work in other occupations, either in business or in the liberal professions. While large extended households tended to prevail more among the wealthier members of the village, many smallholder families were often organized into extended arrangements, also with male heirs living in their natal home, being groomed for succession. This domestic configuration generally resembles the "stem family" arrangement studied by demographers and historians of Europe.[5] Though households are defined by separate physical spaces, kin and family relations extended well beyond the boundaries of individual households and often the functions of production and consumption were shared among members of different domestic units tied together by collateral or affinal links (see also chapter 6).

Amongst both smallholders and large landowners, the preferred marriage partners were people who owned land. Parents often encouraged their children, especially their sons to marry individuals with vine holdings. While marriage to a landless person was not prohibited, it was frequently frowned on and when such unions occurred, they were the focus of much strife, especially among the upwardly mobile, entrepreneurial group of wine growers. For example, shortly before my arrival in the village, a marriage between a relatively prosperous man and a landless woman took place. The groom's family ran a local business and operated one of the larger holdings in the village. The bride was a landless woman, a Spanish migrant worker, who came to the village to work during the harvest. It was common knowledge among the villagers that the mother disapproved of the marriage and tyrannized the new daughter-in-law. The hostility that was directed at the daughter-in-law was explained by many people as "racism." But others in the village denied this, explaining simply that this was a gloss for the fact that the mother had hoped for a marriage to someone who would bring land into family. Nevertheless the tensions in this union were the focus of much speculation among the villagers.

The Household as an Economic Formation

Though the household is in one sense a domestic formation that functions to fulfils the requirements for the symbolic reproduction of its members, it is also an economic formation that fulfils the function of material reproduction. In this sense, it is centred around the production, consumption, redistribution, inheritance, and reproduction. As an economic unit, the household in Broussan is rooted in the production of use-values through domestic labor as well as exchange-values in the production of items to be exchanged on the market (see also Mackintosh 1988). Irrespective of variations in form, in Broussan, the household represents the basic unit of production and as is the case for all family farmers, domestic relations can imply work relations (Rogers and Salamon 1983, 534). Differences in the demographic characteristics of the household imply differences in the organization of labor (see also Chayanov 1966).

In the discussion that follows the ways that labor was organized within different household will be illustrated. To facilitate the discussion of illustrations, I will focus on the household as an livelihood seeking unit and differentiate between them on the basis of the types of work activities undertaken to generated incomes. Along this axis, two general kinds of households can be distinguished among the petty commodity producers—those that derive an income from work in agriculture exclusively, that is, independent cultivators, and those whose incomes derive from work in a series of economic activities, that is, pluriactive households. Within the last category, several types of households can be further distinguished. First, there were households that made a living from a "dual-family" economy that combined farmwork with wage work. Second were those households that combined farmwork with the operation of a business as members of Broussan's petty bourgeoisie. Also, included among pluriactive households are those that combined farmwork with income from other sources such as, retirement benefits, or rent. I wish to stress that this classification is not meant to serve as a typology of households or to present ideal types in any way. It is used here mainly as a means for highlighting several facets of making a living in Broussan—the organization of the household economy; how the market and ideologies influence labor recruitment and reproductive strategies within households; the nature of pluriactivity; ideological strictures of the family; and gender and generational relations.

Independent Cultivators

Both nuclear and extended households, with stem family arrangements, existed among the independent cultivators of

Broussan. Independent cultivators relied exclusively on the cultivation of vines for sustaining the household and reproducing the enterprise. The average size of the holdings run by independent cultivators was 12 hectares (excluding rented land) and they occupied roughly 21 percent of the land under cultivation. Few holdings fell below the 8-hectare minimum considered necessary to sustain full-time farming. While, historically and in the contemporary context, many wine growers aspired to become independent smallholders, in fact, relatively few households lived off farm revenues alone. In Broussan, of the total of 300 farming households only 25 or so actually sustained themselves from farming alone. Actually, then only a very small proportion, about 7 percent of the wine-growing households could be identified as independent cultivators. True independent small ownership seemed to represent more the exception than the rule. Nonetheless, since the appeal of independent small ownership was so pervasive to wine-growers, it is worth examining the household economy of independent cultivators, the nature of the "common family project" and the ways in which it evokes commitments to farm and to family.

The Common Family Project

By and large, households of independent cultivators were organized around a core of a couple and their unmarried children. For example, the Barthes household consisted of three members of the household, Eric, Jeannette, and their son Gérard, who together worked their 15.5 hectares of land. Eric and Jeannette also had three married daughters, who lived in separate households nearby in the village. Among independent cultivators, men tended to work in the vineyard while women said that they "helped out," irrespective of how frequently they went to the fields (see also chapter 5). Sons were expected to help their fathers on the farm after school and from a very young age were required to familiarize themselves with all the tasks necessary in wine growing. This fulfilled the purposes of symbolic and material reproduction. On the one hand, fathers played a key role in transmitting both the values and the practices of vine cultivation that prepared sons for their eventual take over of the enterprise. On the other hand, the "help" given by sons and wives also contributed toward getting the tasks done on the farm. The work contributed by members of the household was not remunerated, at least in the form of wages. Because the total product of their respective labor inputs tended to be consumed by members of the household unit and used up in the reproduction of the enterprise, independent cultivators tended merely to reproduce the conditions that allowed them to maintain their enterprises without a rapid expansion of the size of the holding or the scale of production. That is to say, living off farm revenues alone, they tended toward simple reproduction.[6] Nevertheless, expansion of the holdings can take place through other means.

Virtually all farmers interviewed had secured bank loans both for the purchase of land and equipment. However, a preferred means for gaining access to land and to increase farm revenues was to take up share-tenancy contracts. Share tenancy allowed the expansion of the unit of production but without incurring debts and without large outlays of capital. As noted in chapter 1, the amount of land rented varied from enterprise to enterprise, as did the number of share-tenancy contracts. A household may take on one or several such contracts and the size of a holding may grow appreciably with the addition of rented land. For example, of the 10.5 hectares worked by the Barthes family, only 5.5 hectares were owned outright by the family and an additional 10 hectares was rented from two retired wine growers in the village.

The Barthes household illustrates the ways in which independent cultivators put together a living, in a capitalist context. While the labor of household members is exchanged without remuneration and household resources are shared and pooled, market calculation nonetheless entered into every facet of the strategies used for mobilizing labor and reproducing the household. Calculations of the value of labor took place constantly. This kind of calculation was summarized by Jeannette as she discussed her own and her son's work:

> Were it not for our son and my contribution to working in the vineyards, we would have to hire a worker to keep the farm running and this we cannot afford to do. Because when you run such a small holding and you hire help, you end up paying out more than you get back.

The Barthes enterprise then was a product of the delicate balance that must be maintained between the labor demands of the farm and the household's ability to meet them. In Jeannette's words the importance of the unpaid labor of household members was underscored by juxtaposing it against wage labor. Without the contribution of the unpaid work of Jeannette or Gérard in production, it would be impossible to operate a farm of 10.5 hectares without hired help. Hiring help, according to Jeannette, would upset the delicate balance, since any competitive edge achieved through the flexibility of using family labor would be lost in the need to generate a profit. Thus cooperation prevailed in the household based on a common commitment to sustaining the family farm both on a daily basis and over the longer term but this form of cooperation was premised on market calculation.

One of the most serious problems that farmers must confront is the issue of who will run the farm after retirement is taken or once death approaches.[7] The various ways in which crises of succession are managed and resolved reveals some of the central tensions and conflicts that govern enterprises that rely on the mobilization of family labor. In the case of the Barthes family, it was resolved fairly smoothly. It was accepted by all members of the family that Gérard would be the heir as the only son in a family of four children. Reciting the oft-repeated values of smallhold farming, he stated:

> My parents are country folks *"paysans"* and I am the son of a *paysan*. Naturally, I love working in the fields. I love it because you are free. There's no boss looking over your shoulders, giving you orders and pushing you around. You are really working for yourself and for your family.

The apparent facility with which it was resolved in the case of the Barthes illustrates again how deeply Gérard assimilated the ethic of a common family project. Gérard accepted his role as heir without question and proclaimed that it was in his own words, only "natural" that he did so. In his declarations of the naturalness of his chosen path, the values of liberty and attachment to the soil reinforced a commitment to the ensuring the continuity of the family's means of making a living. While such values were often repeated, they were also rehearsed and reinforced through various forms of action and strategies pursued to ensure farm continuity. For example, Gérard was following a course of study in viticulture at the Ministry of Agriculture in Montpellier. Such programs were offered by the state to encourage the creation of a generation of not only of modern farmers versed in the latest techniques of farming, but ones who also assimilated to the ideas and ethics of a country that had embarked on a path of capitalist modernization with the creation of a modern progressive farmer. The process of establishing a hegemony, where the ideas of modernity and modernization became accepted as common sense, involved offering not only programs in education, but also a system of material rewards. Participation in these state programs had its material benefits. While Gérard maintained that the course provided good training in modern methods of cultivation, one of the most important advantages of having a diploma was that it guaranteed access to loans at low interest rates. Eric and Jeannette encouraged Gérard to enrol in this course since they saw it as a way of securing credit for land purchases at low interest rates. Moreover, this diploma will serve Gérard well, especially after the four-way division of the holding that will take place at Eric and Jeannette's retirement. Though Gérard will get the larger share of the land, having made an important contribution of labor to the farm, this division will result in a small share. Nonetheless, Gérard will later be in a good position to add land to his holding by the relative ease with which he would be able to obtain loans.

Because Gérard was enrolled in the diploma course in viticulture, he was viewed by his parents as a household asset. Gérard would be a member of a new generation of progressive farmers with the knowledge and also the resources to remain competitive in viticulture. Moreover, because his diploma guaranteed loans at low interest rates, Eric and Jeannette were anxiously awaiting their son's graduation so that they would able to buy more land through Gérard. His abilities could be thus converted into a monetary form and his diploma acted as a financial guarantee. In this particular way, the Barthes household harnessed the market to serve family interests, in calculating the value added to Gérard's labor on completion of his course of study. It must be noted that while many sons in wine-growing households were enrolled in this program, no daughters pursued this course of study. As few households could afford to support a child in this program, only sons were encouraged to enroll since wine growing was considered an occupation suitable for men. Such state-sponsored programs then tended, by and large, to be focused on men reinforcing a gender-based division of labor in rural context, while encouraging male ownership and control of property (see chapter 5). The state, then, reinforced the masculinization of viticulture, a process which accompanied the modernization of viticulture and established it as a hegemonic practice.

From the example of the Barthes family, it can be seen that monetary calculations then entered into many facets of domestic life. Unpaid family labor was measured against wage labor and the value of the labor of sons can be strategically augmented and easily converted to a monetary form. In these ways, the commodification effect influenced the ways in which the labor of household members was deployed in households of independent cultivators. Nonetheless, in the Barthes household, the day-to-day operations were carried out in a smooth fashion, and the members of the domestic unit were organically linked on the basis of sharing and pooling resources. However, in many instances, the organic quality of households is often the phenomenal form that such unit assume, once various domestic crises have found resolution.

Succession Struggles: Gifts and Power

In family farming, an inextricable connection exists between securing labor for the daily production and the reproduction of the farm over a generation. In many households, the crisis of succession involves complex maneuvers and negotiations that revealed that the domestic sphere as a site of intense conflict in which the exercise of power and relations of domination became manifest. Sons and daughters often resisted their family duty to help keep the farm in operation and intergenerational conflicts focused on the question of succession were as common as smooth farm transfers. What was accepted by some as the "natural" order of things was challenged by others who sought to abdicate their responsibilities to the family.

In situations in which filial duty is challenged, parents employ a variety of means to compel children to devote themselves to what is defined as the common family project. Bribes were offered, threats made, gifts given, and exhortations were wielded to compel children to assume that was defined often by parents as their familial responsibilities. The effectiveness of these tactics, was based on the fact that in the context of family farming, parents—usually fathers—monopolized both the ideological and material means for the domination of children who rely on them for their material sustenance. The withdrawal of the material means for the sustenance of dependent children, whether actually carried out or implied, served to reinforce the power that fathers can exercise to reign in recalcitrant members of the household. Conflicts between parents and children were often resolved then through the exercise of patriarchal power.

The dynamics of struggle and negotiation as well as the exercise of a form of patriarchal domination assured the reproduction of the Martinez enterprise. The Martinez household, for example, is another unit of production and consumption, which appears organically tied together on the basis of pooling and sharing resources. As independent cultivators, the Martinez family lived entirely off the revenues from their wine holding of 11 hectares, of which 5.5 was rented. The household consisted of a family of three, Albert, his wife Sylvie, and their son Daniel. Albert worked full-time in the vines, while Sylvie and Daniel worked in the fields from time to time on those occasions when extra labor was needed. Daniel was 19-year-old student in Béziers. Sylvie described herself as a housewife by profession though she was often found accompanying her husband to the fields. Daniel was also recruited to help on the family farm during periods when he was not occupied with his studies. Such complementarity in work and organic solidarity in the households in Broussan, though, often masked family history of conflict. The Martinez enterprise was the product of a negotiated settlement that took place between Albert, his brother, and his father, over who would take over the farm.

Albert's father was an agricultural laborer who had managed to acquire 6 hectares of land by the end of his working days. He ran his holding with the help of his two sons. Both Albert and his brother Marcel were taken out of school at the age of 13, to help on the farm, while their sister Marie continued in school. Marcel had always resented being forced to quit school for work on the farm and continually announced that he would quit farming as soon a he could.

In 1972, Albert's father died and the entire family holding was divided up between the three children. In the same year, Marcel cut his ties to the land by selling his share of his inheritance to Albert and moved off to Lyons to work as a mechanic. Marie also lived in Lyons and worked in a nursery school. She had left the village much earlier and rented her land out to Albert.

Having given up on Marcel after many long bitter battles that often ended with the exchange of blows, Albert's father started to exert pressure on Albert, whom he thought was the last hope for the survival of the family vineyards. He recounted how his father managed to persuade him to stay on the farm:

When I turned 18, in 1958, my father gave me a "gift" of 1.6 hectares of vines and he said that from that point onward I was a wine grower, in my own right, no longer just a helper to him. This gift was really part of my inheritance. It was given to me early, before my father retired, as a way of keeping me interested in farming. Because, my brother had always said that he would leave farming if anything else came along and because I was the younger son and I didn't have such strong feelings, my father saw me as insurance against the farm failing.

I hesitated for a while over whether to accept this gift, for I knew that accepting it meant that I would be tying myself to the farm and to the land and that I would not be able to do something else with my life. For a while I did want to follow in my older brother's footsteps and leave this life of drudgery and uncertainty. But, I couldn't face the prospect of endless fights with my father, seeing how he and my brother were always going at each other. So in the end, I accepted the gift and gave into to my parents' pressure for me to stay on the land.

By capitulating to parental pressure, Albert felt that he had committed himself to a way of life that rife with crises and that this had led to hardship and economic insecurity. He and Sylvie claimed to have been on the brink of bankruptcy several times, but managed somehow to recover. As a result of these experiences, they were adamant that similar sorts of pressure would not be brought to bear on their son. They encouraged him to carry on with his studies at school. Still, despite their professed disaffection with viticulture, they had never seriously entertained the possibility of selling the holding. When they retire, they planned to rent out their land, if their son chooses not to take over the farm.

The possibility of selling the family holding was not entertained for several reasons. Like Albert's parents, the Martinez household had committed so many years of their lives to farming that the sale of the family vineyards in many ways implied the sale of a lifetime of work. There were also other reasons for this attachment to the land. In the milieu in which the Martinez lived, the sale of farm lands had a very strong association with bankruptcy and failure. And among family farmers, where there is a strong sense of identity between the family and the farm, the failure of the production unit implies failure as a family unit. It implies a personal deficiency, in the sense that parents have failed in carrying out their responsibilities to ensure the successful transfer of skills and values associated with farming (see also Rogers and Salamon 1983, 535). Still other reasons existed for keeping the farm despite the possibility that their son may not take it over. The perpetual hope of rises in the wine prices was often given as a reason for not selling vineyards. Moreover, the hopes that land prices would also rise, make the Martinez's feel that the future might hold a more opportune moment for selling land.

"Who knows," was uttered by both husband and wife on the question of selling the vineyards. Given, the variety of factors that acted as prohibitions against selling land and the noncommittal replies over the future of the Martinez farm, it was likely that another intergenerational struggle would recur. As the retirement age approaches and the question of inheritance arises, Daniel will be forced to choose between maintaining the farm and or moving away from it to work in the industrial and commercial sector of the economy.

The reluctance of children to take up farming was reinforced by several factors. In the light of the state of permanent crises in which viticulture seems embedded, many children equivocate and outrightly refuse to commit themselves to farming, a way of life beset by economic hardship. Moreover, the presence of a highly developed market for their labor provides an easy means of escape, since, in principle, employment in industry is readily available. In practice, however, the availability of employment has varied in according to economic developments in certain historical periods. For example, in the immediate post–World War II period, a situation of high labor mobility was stimulated by the development policies of the state in as mentioned chapter 2, which promoted the demise of small-scale farming, on the one hand, while favoring the development of an industrial proletariat, on the other hand. However, the economic downswings of the "Post-Fordist" decades of 1980s and 1990s have reduced the possibilities of employment in industry (see Lem 1996).

Familism and Farming

These examples show that the members of households in Broussan were acutely aware of the wage potential of labor power. This awareness guided and influenced decisions and choices made in the act of transferring skills and resources from one generation to the next and also how to secure labor. Such calculations were embedded in a long history of participation in an extensive commodity economy, in which human labor and material resources have a determinable market price.

In this context where there is a keen awareness of the wage that labor power can command on the open market, the forces of the market were often pitted against the ideological strictures of kin relations. Given the indispensability of unpaid household labor for the reproduction of the petty commodity units of production, the means through which family labor was mobilized became very important in the calculus of the social costs of production. Labor was embedded in a "familistic" morality, in which members of the family often accepted their obligations to commit wholly to the collective family project of maintaining the farm. In the case of the Martinez household, the powerful ideology of the continuity of the family was invoked by the father and all the values and obligations attached to this was symbolized in a "gift" of land. The acceptance of this "gift" by a son concretizes a promise for the farm's future. The labor of that son was thus effectively bound to the family farm. Albert's commitment to his family, and in Rapp's (1979) terms, to the ideology of the family and hence, to the family enterprise, forestalled his entry into the labor market. However, some, like Albert's brother, did manage to escape the grip of this ideology, but only by finally removing himself after the death of the patriarch from the community and out of the range of family constraints and communal sanction. The effect of his brother's escape was to bring more pressure to bear on Albert.

The effectiveness of this familistic morality to some extent depended on consent. Children accepted the rightfulness of family obligation and their assimilation to the precepts of family life is largely determined since the meaningfulness of the family often exists as part of the "common sense" view of individuals who have been immersed in a context in which such values are propounded and transmitted. Nevertheless, the inevitability of this "common sense" is challenged in the face the emergence of alternative cultural fields in which other values legitimate pursuing other forms of work. Among the petty commodity producers of Broussan, the highly developed market in labor presented itself as such a field and calculations were made by all members of the household about the value of labor and the virtues of taking up forms of work outside farming. Thus, the labor market can exert powerful pressures that can threaten the continuity of the household and the enterprise and undermine patriarchal authority experienced and exercised in these cases as the rule of parents, usually the father, over children. Nonetheless, patriarchal authority acted as a very powerful mechanism and often enterprises were held together and sustained by flexing the patriarchal muscle. The case of Sébastien Cabanel illustrates how fathers exercised their power to restrict their children's access to those alternative cultural fields. Sébastien, a widower, who operated a vineyard while running one of the local garages, recounted how his father, a day laborer with a few parcels of land, plucked him out of school the day after his thirteenth birthday much against his objections:

> From the age of about ten, I had missed so many days of school because my father held me back from classes to help out in the fields. Many of my lessons were also interrupted midstream because he used to always come to the school to fetch me when help was needed in the vineyards. It was a bit humiliating, but it did happen to other boys as well.
>
> I never wanted to work on the family farm and I liked being in school, but because I was so young, I had to do what my father wanted. Finally, I turned 13, and my father withdrew me from school altogether and my father said it was time I learned how to become a wine grower.
>
> I worked with my father in the fields and sometimes on my own when he went to work on one of the local estates. I also had to look for some other kind of work to help keep the farm going. For a few years our family holding was too small and my father wanted to buy more land. I said to him that I did not want to take up any job that I could find, but I wanted to learn a trade. I refused to work as an agricultural laborer, which was what most sons of wine growers did at the time because I did not want to be pushed around by some large landowner. My father agreed that it would not be a bad idea to learn a skilled trade outside agriculture. It would bring in a bit of money and give me way of earning a living if the farm failed. So in 1931, when I was 14, I started to work as an apprentice to a mechanic in Béziers. After the War, I borrowed some money to buy myself a garage and I continued to work on the family farm. With some of the money I made as a mechanic, I increased the size of my farm and when my father died in 1957, I inherited 4.5 hectares. I also inherited some land from my uncle who had no children.

In looking into Sébastien's life history, it was evident that as a son, he was compelled to defer to this father's wishes of maintaining the continuity of the farm. As a youth of 13, thoroughly dependent on his parents for his own sustenance, Sébastien had little choice but to yield to his father's authority and to what his father defined as the family imperative, that is, maintaining a viable unit of agricultural production.

The presence of a highly developed market in labor promotes labor mobility in a context in which labor immobility offers some assurance to family farm continuity. However, the mobility of labor also offers advantages to the family farm. Various members of the household can be deployed to work in the wage sector of the economy and in a context in which members of the household accept their obligations to maintain the family farm. Under these circumstances, the diversification of the work activities of the household contributed toward the viability of the enterprise. The reproduction of the petty commodity enterprise involved the unpaid work of family members, on the farm, but it also frequently involved the paid work of household members who earned wages through work in other sectors of the economy.

To be an independent cultivator, working on an individual holding and living exclusively from farming as I said earlier was more an ideal than an existential reality. In the experiences of most farmers, making a livelihood involved pluriactivity, as household members pursued work strategies that involved wage work in factories and earning income through petty trade, offering services and running businesses. In households that pursued a multiplicity of forms of work, ideologies of family, kinship, and indeed familism were also pervasive. Similar tensions and conflicts over issues of succession also occurred. The embeddedness of social relations in market principles in these cases were not simply metaphorical, merely inscribed into the consciousness of household members as a mental calculation, but it corresponded to the life and work experiences of women and men who inserted themselves into wage earning economy, while trying to run a farm and struggling often to attain the ideal of independent ownership.

Work in Its Diversity: Wage Work and Farmwork

In the many households that pursued a multiplicity of forms of work, both women and men participated in a series of wage-earning activities while running the farm. Men of the household often held down several jobs and worked on their holdings on a part-time basis. In these cases, women of the households were often also involved in several wage-earning activities, but often left the farmwork to men. Growers within this group tended to operate very marginal holdings that seldom exceeded 4 hectares. Of the total of 70 households in this group, only 16 operated holdings larger than 4 hectares. Roughly 36 percent of all wine-growing households fell into this category and as a total, their holdings occupied about 16 percent of the cultivated land surface.

Viticulture played a subsidiary role in the household economy of this group and, to some extent, they resembled Lenin's "allotment holders"—rural proletarians who were not a class of pure wage laborers (1974, 177). However, they differed from Lenin's allotment holders in that their plots of land were not allocated to them by their employers. While the women of these households worked in many of the same types of jobs as the wives and daughters of households with more substantial holdings, many of the men were employed as agricultural laborers for the large landowners of the village or nearby villages and on the local industrial wineries, like Château Y. Men also were employed in a variety of jobs in the nonagricultural sector of the economy. They were employed as construction workers, road maintenance workers, local store managers, clerks, tradesmen and mechanics.

In many cases, women used some of the household earnings to buy machinery in order to undertake homework. One woman bought a sewing machine and started to make clothes for a local manufacturing company. Another woman, reported using some of the household income to buy a washing machine to take in laundry. Many men reported using some earnings from agriculture to buy tools to do occasional handiwork, carpentry, and so on. The Tolinos household, for example, illustrates how a pluriactive household put together a living from a diversity of sources.

Paul Tolinos worked as an agricultural mechanic at Château X. Francine, his wife, worked as a cleaning woman for one of the village butchers. She was also employed as a housekeeper in the village. They had one son Robin, who was 16 and a student in Béziers. The case of the Tolinos family not only illustrates how smallholders often put together a living through a variety of means as a collectivity of individuals, but also that the life time of one individual is contoured by diverse work experiences. Paul outlined his highly fragmented work history:

I worked in many different jobs before going to the château. I took up an apprenticeship as a mechanic at the age of 13 and after getting my certification, I began to work in Béziers. After a few years, I changed jobs and took up work as a plumber and I went into the army at the age of 20. At 22, I left the army and worked as a plumber again. I saved enough money from this job to pay for a tractor and I set myself up as a contractor, ploughing the land for those who did not own machinery. I hoped that this would eventually lead to full-time contracting work in the village. I did this at a time when there were still few tractors in the village, though people were starting to buy tractors. A few years after this, I bought 1 hectare of land with a bank loan and some of my wife's earnings. She worked as a cleaner in the village. For a number of years I worked as a truck driver while running my contracting business on a part-time basis. In 1969, at the age of 27, I began to work more or less full time as a contractor, while working part time as a truck driver. At 34, I started to work as a mechanic at the château. At 38, I inherited 1 hectare of vines, from my father who had been an agricultural laborer.

Well over half the pluriactive households (i.e., 45 out of a total of 70) who put together a living through a multiplicity of means, combined their activities with agricultural wage work. Most of the households of day laborers tended to operate very small vineyards. Paul, for example, operated a very small holding of only 2 hectares. He claimed that it was difficult to expand the size of his holding. Nevertheless, agricultural laborers were often driven to pursue a multiplicity of income-obtaining sources, since they aspired to full ownership. Because of the very small scale of their agricultural operations and limited resources, many of these households seldom made large expenditures for the purchase of capital equipment. Equipment was often obtained through loans and reciprocal exchanges (see chapter 4). Hence, depreciation, maintenance, and input costs were kept low. Combined with the fact that such small holdings seldom warrant the full-time work, adult members of the household were free to pursue a variety of other means for obtaining incomes. These factors allowed for the possibility of saving cash. Also a number of these households have made land purchases through obtaining bank loans. Despite certain advantages of the small scale of these enterprises, among this group, there was a tendency to sell off parcels of land as individual households were unable to maintain a viable holding, even through pursuing a multiplicity of income-earning strategies. However, this was only done as a last resort as earning income from an agricultural source confers a sense of security and allows laborers to channel funds into the other ways of making a living. The Tolinos family intended to add as many parcels of vines to their holding as they could, that the purchase of even very small pieces of land by workers was difficult with the low incomes they earn as agricultural laborers. Also, agricultural laborers found it difficult for them to negotiate bank loans for land purchases, caught in a vicious circle, where land was required as collateral for loans to purchase land. The trajectory of development experienced by many such smallholders who supplement their incomes through wage work contrasts with that of the households of the village petty bourgeoisie.

The Petty Bourgeoisie

Households of the Petty Bourgeoisie derive earnings from the ownership and operation of a business, in addition to vine cultivation. In Broussan, there were several examples of such households—garage owners, store owners, hotel keepers, bakery owners, dry cleaners, and florists. In these households, women often ran the family business and worked in the shop with the help of various kin, while men worked in the family vineyards. Men often took over the shop from the women at the end of the day, when women set off to prepare the evening meal.

Many households within this group represented the relatively well-to-do members of the community, operating relatively large holdings. Though they comprised only 10 percent of the total households, or roughly 35 households, their holdings occupied 25 percent of all arable land in the canton.

There was a greater possibility of expanding the unit of agricultural production as profits from business could be used toward the purchase of land and capital equipment. Having greater amounts of capital and easier access to credit, than pluriactive households that combined farm and wage work, they were in a better position to make such purchases. Thus, for example, the Fages family ran the local hardware store and owned 35 hectares of land. Only a total of 8 hectares of that land came to the family as an inheritance. Over a period of 15 years, a total of 27 hectares were added to the Fages's holding. By contrast, the Sion family, an example of a pluriactive household that combined wage and farmwork, inherited 6 hectares of land in 1952. Over a period of 25 years, the household operated a holding of only 10 hectares, with an additional 4 hectares of rented land.

The purchase of land with revenues from business thus represented a rational investment for local businesspeople living in a community in which the mainstay of the economy was viticulture. Participation in wine growing meant taking part in the mainstream of village life. Wine growing thus represented the economic and, as will be discussed in later chapters, the social and cultural essence of the village and so commerce was seen only as a means of supplying commodities to the local wine growing population. While this was the case, the sector of the population involved in commerce seldom abandoned their business pursuits in favor of becoming independent cultivators, thus hedging their bets against the uncertainties in wine growing and maintaining a competitive edge. The shop owners of the village—the hardware stores owners, butchers, garage owners, and bakers—all also maintain their businesses as a safety valve against the ever-present threat of crises and natural disasters that plagues the viticultural economy.

Living Alone

One further kind of household may be distinguished. Households consisting of single people were usually made up of retirees, or widows and widowers. The elderly are often included in statistical representations in the category of the economically "inactive," since it is assumed that retirement means the withdrawal of their labor from the economy. However, a large number of the elderly in the village still maintained and cultivated some vineyards. Still, for the most part, they relied on social security for support. While they are included here under the category of pluriactive households who derive revenues from a multiplicity of work activities, they actually belong to a residual category in terms of our classification since they secure their means of support not though their current work activities but largely from an entitlement from having once worked. Nevertheless, they are discussed here because in Broussan, such households represented a numerically significant group, making up roughly 27 percent of all households enterprises. Still, in total, their holdings amounted only to a mere 7 percent of the cultivated surface. Moreover, their farms rarely exceeded 4 hectares and most holdings were in fact microparcels of land, usually no larger than 1 hectare. Larger properties once held by the elderly were transferred to sons and daughters or sold as growers reached retirement age. Many of these households were engaged in the divestment of their properties and the maintenance of remaining vineyard properties was largely to ensure an adequate consumption levels both in the provision of wine for home consumption and to provide a supplementary source of income.

One of the ways in which a supplementary source of income was secured by the elderly was through renting out land under share-tenancy arrangements. Parcels of land were often rented out to various kin, as well as nonkin members of the community. This was the case for Lucien Millau, a 70-year-old widower who lived on his own. Lucien's case illustrates not only the ways in which retired members of the village put together a living, but the difficulties of succession and running a holding with limited labor resources even before retirement. Moreover, his life history illustrates how individuals combine and move through different class positions as a function of their place in the demographic cycle. Lucien focused on the issue of succession and several familiar themes run through this segment of his narrative:

> At the age of 16, I was pressured by my father to leave school to work as a day laborer at Château X, as well as to help out on the family holding which then consisted of about 4 hectares. My father kept saying to me over and again that the survival of our little holding depended entirely on my ability to earn some money and to help out more on the farm. Going to school, my father said, would not help the farm succeed and so I obeyed my father's wishes, quit school, and took on what I saw was my duty to help keep the farm working.
>
> I married at the age of 22 and we had two girls, Laura and Christine. Laura is 50 years old and lives in Narbonne. She works as a nurse's aid. Christine is 45 and lives in a nearby village. She is married to a builder.
>
> My father and father-in-law died within a year of each other in the early 1950s. I was the sole heir to the family vineyards and my wife was also the sole heir to her family's. So we had a holding of 7.5 hectares. When my father died, I went to work as a full-time grower quitting my job as a day laborer. I worked my small holding on my own until I retired in 1977. In that year I sold just over 4 hectares to another household in the village as I was unable to persuade

> either of my daughters or their husbands to work on the
> family holding. I also rented out 2.5 hectares of land. I work
> the remaining 1 hectare mainly on my own, now that my
> wife has died. My daughters return to the village every year
> to help me in the harvest.

Lucien's main income source was his pension. He also supplemented his pension with some income from his vineyard and received a rent. In the different phases of his life he put together a living as a laborer and a smallholder and then as a landlord. Lucien maintained that he would not sell the rest of his vineyards as he hoped that his daughter and their husbands would eventually take over the land. "Still," he said, "once I have gone, the vineyards will be theirs to do as they please. But maybe if it is in their hands, they will feel a bit stronger about being growers."

Lucien's case highlighted some of the difficulties encountered by the households with limited labor resources for viticulture. It resulted in the sale of part of his property. He had never exerted a great deal of pressure on his daughters to commit themselves to running the family farm. Lucien explained that they were women, after all, and their interests did not lie in doing farmwork, but elsewhere in pursuing occupations more fitting for women. "Also," Lucien said, " they're all I have left now and I don't want them to hate me for forcing them to do what they don't want to do." Lucien's case again underlines the importance of securing domestic labor for the reproduction of the enterprise and the implication of failure in securing that labor within the strictures of a gender-based division of labor. I explore questions of gender and the division of labor in chapter 5.

Households, Hegemony, and Resistance

These illustrations, segments of work histories, and life stories shed light on how the embeddedness of social relations in markets principles, on the one hand, and family ideologies, on the other, contributes to a considerable degree of ambiguity in the household. In one light, the household was an entity whose member were united in pursuing common interests. Relations within the household were governed by the familial attitudes of mutuality, reciprocity, rights, and obligations. Husbands, wives, parents, and children exchanged their labor and the products of their labor for the reproduction of the household as a domestic and economic formation. The ideology of the family prescribed cooperation, mutuality, and reciprocity in committing one's labor to the common the family project. Where there was a shared acceptance of the common family project and the ideological prescriptions of family ties, the household appeared as democratic institution, in which there was consensus and participation in decisions, as well as sharing and pooling of resources.

From some of the stories recorded above, many household members willingly devoted themselves to the common family project of ensuring farm continuity. In this respect a form of hegemony was established in the household in which members unquestioningly assimilated to the ideology of the family and accepted its obligations.[8] Resources obtained by various household members from farming and from a series of pluriactive pursuits were automatically contributed toward the regeneration of farms, families, and enterprises. The nonmonetary exchange of labor were devoted to the renewal of the household as a home, on the one hand, and the household as an family enterprise, on the other. Within the parameters of such sharing and pooling, then the household could be seen as a domain that was, in fact, insulated from commodified social relations and an instrumental rationality tended to govern modern life. It was a realm in which the language of kinship was used to imply generosity, close collaboration and the absence of strict calculation. In this respect relations amongst kin within the household was the antithesis of the commodity relations based on exchange-value (Harris 1982, 146–50).[9]

The household, in another light, however, is hierarchical in character. It is the site of power differentials, calculation, and conflict in which the powerful impose their will on those with less power. In several of the cases discussed, the hierarchical character of the household was revealed in the conflicts that arose over the issues of inheritance. Because the identity of the family is so bound up with the farm, farm continuity depended on the successful intergenerational transfers of family resources as well as the values associated with family farming. Moreover, often an elision occurs between the idea of the farm and the idea of the family, in which an intimate and almost indistinguishable identity tends to be forged between the family, the farm, and also the male head of the household. Much along the same lines as Louis XIV, declared *"L'état, c'est moi!"* [I am the state!], such a blurring of boundaries suggests that the declaration *"l'exploitation, c'est moi!"* [I am the farm!] from male household heads would reflect such an intimate connection. Such conceptual elisions were further reinforced by the fact that both social practices and juropolitical forces discussed earlier, vested control of land in the hands of the patriarch and fathers tended to control the material as well as the ideological means for domination of the other members of the household (see chapter 5).[10]

In Broussan, several forms of family sanction prevail. As children were the legal dependants of the oldest male in the household and since, by and large, fathers legally controlled of the means of production, the power exercised by fathers was sanctioned by threats of material deprivation, on the one hand, and social deprivation, on the other. Threats of cutting off children without a penny and never allowing a child to set foot in the family home again have been used as powerful means to compel children to yield to the will of fathers. Whether such threats were made explicit and carried out, they existed implicitly. The effort to bind children to the farm, as described, has taken the form of threats, bribes, exhortations, and pleas to compel family members to carry on the household enterprise. Very often, gifts of land were given, and as Bailey (1971) reminds us, once accepted they poison one's independence. In intergenerational struggles, then, fathers are identified as the main adversaries with whom daughters and sons must contend in struggles and negotiations over inheritance.

The hierarchical character of the household is further reinforced by the saturation of social context in the market. A highly developed and ever-present market in labor provoked *resistance* to familial duty and obligation and posed limits on the effectiveness the processes of hegemony. The forces of the market intrude on domestic life in ways that potentially shattered the unity of the family and farm. This serves as a means for achieving individualistic ends, as members abdicated their commitments to the common family project by seeking alternative forms of work on a highly accessible labor market. The highly erratic economy of wine production, as well as the state development plans often promoted this kind of labor mobility. The ways in which patriarchs dealt with the persistent threat of this kind of resistance, also throws into the stark relief the hierarchical character of the household. Fathers have recourse to a whole arsenal of ideological weapons and economic sanctions to secure help on the farm on a daily basis and over the longer term. Fathers called on the obligations of children, indeed the debt owed to parents, to compel them to continue the family farm. The force of the strictures of kinship and its obligations often compel reluctant children to relent to their fathers wishes in the end. Women and men often recounted with great bitterness the tales of struggle that often ended in their resistance being broken through bribes, threats, exhortations, and humiliation as their fathers tried to resolve the imperative of succession.

Therefore, while the household can be constituted in one light as a democratic institution, it can be seen also as an institution in which dictatorial powers were exercised. So it is the site of considerable struggle, negotiations, compromise, and uneasy consensus struck between unequals. Battles were fought between those who monopolize both the symbolic and the material means for domination and those who were dependent on the powerful.

Conclusion

In all examples, the continuity of the petty commodity enterprise was critically linked to the mobilization of the labor of household members both over the short and long term. I have tried to illustrate in this chapter that the mobilization of domestic labor was not the simple expression of the structural properties of the family farm, as some theorists have suggested,[11] but involves some understanding of the ideological and political dynamics of the labor process in the domestic and also, as I later discuss, the larger social sphere. I have further tried to illustrate that while the viability of individual households is linked to its structural properties, its potential for resistance is also tied to the practice of pluriactivity. I have also argued that in these respects the household is not insulated against highly developed market in labor power. While, the exchanges of labor between members of the household were not mediated by the market, its potential valorization leads at least to a "partial" commodification of relations within the household and this influences strategies for reproduction. Members of wine-growing households generally acknowledge that a unit of labor has a market price, irrespective of whether the price was realized in a wage form. This subjectivity then informs decisions that are made on how labor is deployed in production and whether wage labor can be hired, even on a temporary basis and how much that labor can be paid. In these respects, I have tried to show how the market has intruded into the "private" sphere of domestic life in petty commodity production.

The discussion presented here suggests some modification of theories of petty commodity production that speculate on how family farms and agrarian enterprises, such as those found in Broussan persist under a series of changing conditions in the political economy of both developed and developing countries. While it has been established, historically and theoretically, that such persistence belies the assumptions made by early scholars of agrarian society, such as Lenin and Kautsky, that such forms were transitory and would eventually be replaced by capitalist farms using wage labor, the question of why such forms persists still remains open. In this chapter, I have attempted to provide some insight into this question as it applies to domestic labor, ideology, and forms of work in the context of advanced capitalism. Historically, the pervasiveness of small-scale family-based enterprises under contemporary capitalism not only challenged the assumptions of early agrarian scholars, but it, perforce, initiated a reconsideration of the larger question of the nature of capitalist transformation itself. The viability of petty commodity production stimulated the interest not only of theorists of agrarian change, but of development planners and politicians also keen to understand the mechanisms at work in a form of production that promised an alternative to the "old orthodoxy" of large-scale capitalists forms of organization (Kitching 1982). Rural populists, albeit of various political inclinations, focused on the efficiency of the small-scale and argued that they should be the objective of development programs.[12] This argument was further buttressed by the observation that various forms of petty commodity production endured in the face of national crises engender by transitions from colonialism to capitalism; from capitalism to socialism; and in the 1980s and 1990s, from state-led to market-driven economies.[13] I have tried to show that reproduction of the family farm often involves a patriarchal dynamic that is supported by ideological as well as material forces. The presence of generational and gender in petty commodity forms of production casts doubts on the virtues of establishing small-scale enterprises in capitalist economies. While development planners and rural populists see small-scale family enterprises as an alternative to capitalist forms of production, circumventing forms of capitalist domination, their promotion as the objects of policy would result in the reinforcement of the dynamics of patriarchal domination in the household and in the larger society. I have examined the dynamics of patriarchal power in the relationship between parents and children. In the chapter that follows, attention is turned to the nature of patriarchy, power, and gender relations in rural households.

CHAPTER 5

Engendered Practices:
The Politics of Wine, Women, and Work

In an annual general meeting of the cooperative in Broussan held in March of 1989, one of the few women present, Josette Bonnefoy, a wine grower, was the first to respond to the announcement of yet another intervention by the state into Languedoc viticulture. Josette rose from her seat and began a furious denunciation of the state's revised schedule of penalties that would be imposed on harvests of grapes whose alcoholic content exceeded state-approved limits (see chapter 7). She angrily decried the terms of the revised plan, declaring that it was simply another example of how the state discriminated against small producers and favored large growers. She urged growers to resist this measure: "we must find a way of fighting these policies. If we don't fight, we will not be able to live!" ("Il faut trouver un moyen de lutter contre ces politiques! Sinon, on ne peut pas vivre!")

For her efforts, she received a round of applause from half the people attending the meeting who cheered her on in a gathering which consisted mostly of men. The other half sat in an embarrassed silence, as it was rather unusual, according to one informant, for a woman to engage in such outbursts and blatant public displays. Indeed in contemporary Broussan, while the participation of women in such political meetings was exceptional enough, that fact that a woman was also openly inciting people to resist the exercise of state power was seen by some as beyond the bounds of the acceptable.

In the contemporary political struggles of smallholders then, women were indeed less visibly a part of the public acts and expressions of enmity against the state and the market than men. For the most part, all forms of protests from large-scale regionwide mass demonstrations to more localized protests and marches, tended to be organized and executed by men. In the realm of collective actions initiated through due political process, men by and large, were the main participants in the many formal organizations, associations, and unions through which family farmers pressed their claims and presented their demands. Moreover, in that other realm of political action that involved activities located outside due political process, very few women participated in that broad spectrum of confrontational acts launched by wine growers that included assaults and the sabotage of designated targets.

Although in the politics of Languedoc wine growers, men tended to act as the main agents in the political struggles initiated both within and outside due political process, this does not imply, however, that women were altogether absent from the political landscape. Women did indeed engage in a variety of acts of resistance. They participated in those everyday expressive forms of defiance and resistance lodged in the "hidden transcripts" of political practice. As I noted in chapter 2, everyday acts of defiance found women routinely participating with men in such practices as tax evasion, working in the underground economy, boycotting state programs, and partially complying with state directives. Women also frequently engaged in a variety of expressive acts that criticized and denounced large owners and the state in many different local gatherings as did Josette in the one village meeting. But by and large, in the present, the repertoire of women's political expression and action has become more limited, often being situated in a rather more "private" realm. Women tended to engage in political acts, but they tended to occur beyond the purview of the state and outsiders, and Languedoc rural women tended to avoid open and public confrontation with the agents of domination.

The hidden and rather private character of women's political activity in the contemporary context stands in contrast to the nature of women's participation in earlier periods. In turn-of-the-century rural Languedoc, women were not only consistently present in political encounters from union meetings to mass demonstrations and strikes, they themselves often initiated and engaged in a variety of public acts that displayed open defiance of the state and the authorities, while challenging the status quo (see chapter 2).

The discontinuities between the contemporary political activities and past political practices of rural women reflect significant transformations in the nature of women's work, gender relations, and the experiences of work that have accompanied the transition to capitalism. In this chapter, I focus the discussion around the changes in the gendered division of labor in the economy of vine cultivation that were brought on by the forces of capitalist rationalization of viticulture. I suggest that the shrinking of women's political universe can be linked to a process of the "domestication" of women, on the one hand, and a process of fragmentation of women's work experiences, on the other. Women in rural Languedoc have become increasingly associated with the domestic sphere as capitalist rationalization has meant the alienation of women from direct participation in the cultivation of grapes. Rural women have come to lose control over the principle means of livelihood as an economy of applying scarce means to obtain maximum ends has imposed an economic imperative to redeploy women's labor to the work of reproduction. This is reinforced by a moral imperative that prescribes the proper and primary identity for women of rural Languedoc to assume as housewives and mothers, whose primary responsibilities are to service the needs of husbands—the main income earners, and children, the future generation of workers. Simultaneously, however, with the loss of work in agriculture for women, many rural women have had to pursue their domestic responsibilities while both intensifying their labor in other livelihood activities and multiplying the means of making a living. In the context of rural Languedoc, rural women have not only found themselves inserted into many different sectors of the economy, performing both remunerated and unremunerated work as well as paid and unpaid work in the production of commodities and the provision of services.[1] But their multiple work activities are located in many different workplaces as their labor has become "freed" through a process of alienation from the land, and to a certain degree, as I will later explain, through a process of dispossession. The mobility of women combined with the processes of domestication, on the one hand and the fragmentation of their work experiences have imposed a limitation on the extent to which women can identify themselves with men as wine growers and smallholders and participate with men in their livelihood struggles. Moreover, in a context in which class politics and regionalism are privileged, the prevailing forms of political struggle fail to represent and express the experiences of domination suffered by women who were increasingly becoming associated with the domestic domain, on the one hand, and inserted into a series of different workplaces, on the other. As a consequence, women's modes of political expression became more and more attenuated as they have come to be increasingly removed from the process of vine cultivation. Moreover, their experiences of work, particularly those of domination and exploitation as women workers and wives is effaced by the dominant modes of political practice. The changes in work relations that have accompanied capitalist rationalization and the organizational dynamics of households in which women are engaged in the pursuit of multiple livelihoods will be highlighted through case material.

Past and Present

Many women in contemporary Broussan, by their own accounts, tended to avoid the political arena, seldom engaging in open acts of confrontation. While women's political dispositions and inclinations may not have been any less exigent or radical than those of their husbands, fathers, or sons, seldom were these sentiments translated into overt forms of confrontation. Many women insisted that they preferred to play a subsidiary and supportive role on the political stage. For the most part, their activities were confined to such contributions as manufacturing the symbols of protest. For example, women sewed and painted cloth banners and placards that were brandished in marches and protests. Before the mass demonstration of 1984, for example, Eliane Mas, the wife of one exceptionally active wine grower, was busily painting slogans on pickets and posters, placing them beside a huge banner emblazoned with the Occitan cross and various depictions of vines and grapes that they had used earlier in one demonstration in Brussels in the 1970s. Women also often contributed their labor to acquiring and assembling the materials needed for men to launch their guerrilla attacks, such as spray paint and canisters of gasoline. Women also commonly relayed information from household to household helping to coordinate protests and assaults. Though these activities and the contribution of women's labor toward the production of acts of protest were essential and indispensable, women tended to downplay the importance of such contributions and deny their political significance.

Eliane stated, for example, when assessing her work: "No, this is not really political work. I just do this as a favor for my husband, Marcel."

As I have stressed earlier, many authors have recently stressed the importance of redefining notions of the "political" to incorporate realms of activities and processes that lie beyond the bounds of narrow definitions political life. These critiques have been particularly significant for scholars who have been committed to analyzing the political practices of women in an effort to develop theoretical precision and comprehensiveness in their analysis of political processes (see for example, Kaplan 1982). These reconfigurations of the definition of the political realm have contributed toward expanding the realm of the political to include precisely those kinds of acts and activities practised by Eliane and locating them an evaluating them within the broader framework of their significance to more conventionally defined political acts.[2] However, irrespective of whether analysts or indeed, rural women, themselves counted such practices as political acts proper or merely actions that were an incidental contribution to some "real" political act, actions taken on by women in the context of rural Languedoc were seldom initiated as public and open confrontation. When informants were interviewed on the question of women and political participation, it was asserted unequivocally that, "Women don't get involved in politics." ("Les femmes ne s'occupent pas de politiques.") Both women and men subscribed to a representation in which women were disengaged and often dissociated from the world of politics. Notwithstanding, the rather totalizing quality of this view, the recent history of women's experiences of work and making a living in the early part of the twentieth century belies the absolutism of this representation. In the past, women, as well as men participated in a wide repertoire of forms of political action that spread across spectrum from the private acts initiated in a clandestine arena to the various form of open confrontation and direct resistance to power holders, landowners, and the state. While it has already been mentioned that women participated in the revolts and mass riots of the early 1900s (see chapter 2 and Frader 1991), open and direct contestation was commonly practised by women also at the more local level. Collette Castre, a former agricultural laborer described the actions she and other estate workers initiated in order to resist the wage cuts estate owners were attempting to impose as a result not only of a long process of rationalizing wine estates, but more immediately as a direct consequence of a market slump in the 1930s:

> We heard that the boss (le patron) was going to lower our wages for the same amount of work and this made all us workers very angry. Many of us started talking about this and we decided that we could not let the boss get away with this, so we organized a little march. After work one day, we gathered in one of the fields close to the boss' house but just out of his, his family and the steward's sight. There was quite a number of us, more men than women, but all the women day laborers (journalières) who worked on the land were there. After everybody arrived, we marched up to the house, singing the "International." We sang and sang from the evening until the small hours of the morning and we carried on singing for a good part of the next day. The boss couldn't stand the noise and finally came out of the house. We told him that we would not accept his cuts and that we were prepared to go on strike over this issue if he didn't back down. We talked together for quite a long time. Some of the workers got quite angry but in the end he gave in and we did not get our wages lowered—not that time anyway.

According to Collette, she and many other women of Broussan constantly resorted to strikes and were compelled to take up other forms of action which were occasionally very militant repeatedly in the past, as their bosses continually tried to get control their work routines, while paying them less than their due. The consistency with which women arose in the past to defend their livelihoods in vine cultivation through different forms of engagement reflected their immediate involvement in the process of vine production. Most notably before the arrival of the first tractor in the village in the 1950s, many women's knowledge of the practices and problems of vine cultivation was intimate garnered from their direct participation in the social relations of wine production. Moreover, the lived and direct experience of the relations of domination and exploitation contoured the lives of those women who toiled as workers on the estates.

Before and even while the process of capitalist rationalism was gaining momentum, women worked regularly alongside men in the fields both on large estates and on smallholdings of the region. They executed tasks that were in some instances different from those done by men. But in many other instances, both women and men performed the same tasks.

On the large estates of Lower Languedoc, the day labor force often included women (journalières), who with men made the daily journey to work from the villages. On the châteaux and domains, a division of labor prevailed and journalières worked at tasks that were defined by owners as lighter and more dextrous. In executing specifically women's tasks, they worked pinching buds, gathering and tying pruned stems into bundles for firewood, spreading fertilizer and sulfuring the vines, as well as cutting grapes during the harvest (Frader 1991, Fabre and LaCroix 1975). Before farms began to mechanise extensively, vineyard work for women also involved such tasks as applying treatments against chlorosis, a disease in which the green parts of the vine plant become blanched. Women often followed behind men pruning vines to paint over the surfaces of the pruned stocks with a solution of water, iron sulfate, and citric acid. In addition to performing such specific women's tasks, journalières also undertook many tasks that have come to be defined in the contemporary context as jobs done by men. For example, plowing, hoeing, and planting was undertaken by both women and men. Plowing was done with a tiller drawn by horses driven by both women and men. Before mechanization, women and men shared the tasks of applying anticrypto gamic, that is antifungal treatments (mainly against oïdum, a vine mildew) to the vines. This was done by manually sprinkling powdered sulfur directly onto the plant from atomizers worn on backs. Though some differentiation in the types of tasks performed by men and those done by women did exist in the past, many of the tasks in vine cultivation that have now come to be defined as men's work were once routinely done by women. The very sameness of the work done by women and men, however, did not constitute the basis for determining wage levels. Women were, in fact, customarily paid half men's wages.[3] It has been argued that grievances over this specific form of inequity provoked women to join in the riots and protests in the early 1900s and that the issue of the exploitation of women was a rallying point for women in that period of particularly heightened political sensibilities (see Frader 1991).

However, those episodes of the intesive political engagement of women were considered over. This has become evident not only by the conspicuous absence of women from the public political stage but also their quiescence in everyday life. Contrasting the past and the present, Collette, admitted great differences between women and their political commitments then and now. She remarked: "Women don't seem to make politics anymore. They stay in their little houses—inside their little worlds."

Domestication and Fragmentation

The contraction of women's political universe can be linked to the changes in social relations, work experiences, and divisions of labor that have accompanied the capitalist transition of Languedoc agriculture. The process of rationalization of Languedoc viticulture begun in the mid-nineteenth century has involved altering work routines as well as the physical layout of viticultural enterprises to achieve economies of scale. Over the century or so of capitalist transformation, the shift from labor intensive to more capital intensive forms of farming changed the nature of work done on the estates and the composition of workforces (see chapter 1). Technical and technological change resulted in an overall reduction of the need for day laborers on local estates.

The most significant item of capital equipment introduced that brought on the most drastic changes in these regards was, of course, the tractor. While, in general, day laborers were losing their employment as skilled vine dressers on local estates with the deskilling of work and the emergence of groups of common laborers (*terrasiers*) that accompanied the the adoption of capital intensive systems of production as well as mechanization of viticulture, women were often the first to lose their employment. *Journalières* were no longer were hired to perform the many tasks they once undertook.[4]

On estates as well as on smallholdings, the adoption of capital intensive techniques of production eliminated the need for the labor of women as higher levels of productivity could be reached with reduced inputs of labor. With the adoption of the tractor, for example, on smallholdings plowing were done by one man and one tractor. The treatment of vines against various diseases came to be done by men driving tractors that pull mechanical sprayers. After tractors were adopted en masse, more recent technological innovations had the identical effects. For example, on some of the most technologically advanced farms in contemporary Broussan, women seldom worked in the fields during pruning season to collect and bundle fallen vine shoots. Instead, a vine-shoot crushing machine has come to be adopted and another piece of equipment has had the effect of displacing women's labor on local estates and smallholdings alike, as wage labor has suffered an overall decline in the context of Languedoc viticulture.

As tractors and various types of capital equipment replaced women in the vineyards, rural women not only loss a source of employment on local estates but became alienated from both the process of production and the products of labor. Their involvement in the work and the economy of vine cultivation and their knowledge of the problems and consciousness of issues surrounding it have increasingly come to be mediated by men as men have come to dominate virtually all aspects of wine growing. Capitalist rationalization through mechanization then contributed to a process in which the division of labor by gender came to be more rigidly defined than in the era of horse power. Work in the home came to be associated with women, while work in the fields came to be associated with men and farmwork defined as a sphere of men's activity and social relations. In present day Broussan, men tended to be primarily responsible for the production of vines and the agricultural sphere of work was considered the proper domain for men. Women were considered to be primarily responsible for carrying out duties in the domestic sphere. An ideology of domesticity and definitions of women's proper place came to be reinforced by the process of capitalist rationalization.

The result of this was that in contemporary Broussan, women tended to position themselves consistently in the occupational universe first and foremost as a "housewife." This identification prevailed despite the fact that domestic work tends for many women to represent only one of the many forms of work that women pursued. Women became subjected to a process of domestication,[5] in which they came to be identified increasingly with the domestic domain, becoming "les femmes au foyer" (housewives) in the face of the loss of a measure of autonomy gained through having an independent income from their work, as well as their identity as ouvrières. The more rigidly defined division of labor combined with its prescriptions contributed to a great degree of dissonance in many women's attempts to define their subjectivity and locate themselves within a social and political universe as they struggled to reconcile their everyday experience of work with prevailing definitions of their identity. This is reflected in the differing attitudes to the kinds of changes that circumscribed women's lives in the context of capitalist rationalization that appeared among different classes of women.

Lament and Liberation

In Broussan, many of the poorer people in the village lamented the loss of estate work as one source of income and avenue for employment for women became unavailable. Among this segment of the population, as I later illustrate, the closing of one avenue of employment for women set into motion a process of multiplying livelihood seeking activities as well as intensifying work in activities in order to make a living. By contrast, other groups within the village that had more resources at their disposal saw agricultural technology as a force that "liberated" women from the drudgery of fieldwork.

Eliane, the 45-year-old wife of Marcel Mas who operated a fairly substantial farm, expressed a view held by many of the women of her class in the village that while they occasionally "helped" their husbands, as in the fields, they did not do so by preference. In fact, many women stated that they preferred to do housework and were pleased not to be involved in any sustained way in farmwork. Eliane's attitude toward fieldwork was rather disparaging and she diminished her contributions to the farm:

> I just help out my husband in the fields. I don't do it often and I don't do it much—a little bit here and a little bit there. I don't want to do more work in the fields. I don't like it. It's dirty and too hot in the summer and too cold in the winter. You have to do a lot of back-breaking hard work. It's dangerous for your health, when you breathe in all those chemical sprays. It's fine for men to do that kind of work but as for me—no thanks—I'd rather stay in the house and do my work in the house to keep it clean and tidy for my family.

The work history and indeed, the views of farmwork held by many of the older women in the village who worked as agricultural laborers contrasted sharply with many women such as Eliane, who were both younger, more prosperous, and whose work history incorporated no period of wage work. Indeed, many of the elderly women's work histories often included periods of sustained wage work on local estates as *ouvrières*. Work in the vines was undertaken and combined with domestic work, as well as participation in a series livelihood seeking activities outside vine cultivation. For example, 80-year-old Agnès Peyre outlined her own experience of work in the fields and stressed the importance it held for her in her life:

I worked for five years as an agricultural laborer on one of the nearby estates when I was in my early twenties. I met my husband Jean there who was also a laborer. Together, through this work we managed to save up enough money and put together a vineyard, bit by bit. I stopped working as a laborer when my first child was born. Many women were losing their jobs anyway, at that time and I felt that sooner or later I would be fired so I thought that I may as well quit. My husband continued to work on the estate. Over the years, our holding grew very slowly from a few acres to 5 hectares. For all our lives, I worked on our land alongside Jean, when I was not preoccupied with the care of the children. Today, I still manage to do all the necessary work on our little holding. We have handed over most of our land to our children. But we keep a few acres for us to work for as long as we are still able and this makes all the difference to our lives.

In contrast to Eliane, Agnès spoke of her laboring past with a measure of pride. She saw it as dignified work and for many women of her class and generation, it was the norm. Moreover, though her period of work as an agricultural laborers was brief, that experience of direct production served to unite both Agnès and her husband in their work, activities, and concerns. Both Jean and Agnès participated in several strikes that were initiated on the estate where they worked in the 1930s and Agnès identifies herself as an agricultural worker and a wine grower. For many women, like Agnès, who operated holdings too small to sustain a household, mechanization resulted in the serious loss of a means of making a living.

So while mechanization of wine growing was greeted by many women in the village as a development that "liberated" women from the drudgery of fieldwork, it also "enslaved" smallholding women and men to seek means to support a cycle of expenditures required to purchase, operate, and maintain the new technologies that were becoming the *sine qua non* of vine cultivation. Tractors, for example, are one of the most expensive items of machinery owned, and expenditures to buy tractors locked growers into cycles of debt and unending interest payments.[6] Many growers now hankered after a mechanical grape harvester, a highly coveted but for most individual owners prohibitively expensive piece of machinery. The escalating level of desire for new and advanced technologies combined with periodic crises in the market for wines, in fact, contributed toward ensnaring women and men in diversifying income seeking activities in order to generate revenues to finance their increasing wants. In these ways, smallholders came to be increasingly involved in the "simple commodity squeeze" (see chapter 1). This process also had other effects that were differentially experienced by women and men. For men, mechanization and the displacement of women from farmwork actually meant an intensification of work in the fields. In fact, with the advent of tractors, the length of the workday and the intensity of work has increased. Farmers often worked continuously throughout the day for 10 to 12 hours and took shorter breaks for meals than their predecessors who used horse power. For tractors unlike horses do not need to be rested or fed. Moreover, some of the manual tasks that women once performed were now taken on by men, in the time freed up by the quicker execution of other tasks done using machinery. Because mechanization has also virtually eliminated permanent wage work for women in agriculture and because of the dynamics of the simple commodity squeeze, women were driven to intensify other livelihood activities to put together a living as well as engaging in domestic work.[7] Women and men then not only worked more intensely on their farms and in the homes, but were also driven to multiply the means of obtaining incomes.

Women in the Economy of Pluriactivity

Women and men, therefore, put together a livelihood through their involvement in a diverse array of economic activities. Both before the transformation of the economy of Lower Languedoc into a commercial monoculture and in the present, women worked occasionally, part time and very often full time in a variety of nonagricultural wage jobs. They often found employment in the service sector of the economy as housekeepers and store clerks, or as wage earners in local factories. Many women also brought in an income by cultivating home gardens of fruits and vegetables destined both for home consumption and also for sale in local markets. Historically as well as in the contemporary context, women in smallholding households were often responsible for raising small animals, as well as tending to vegetable and fruit gardens. Chickens and rabbits were raised and eggs sold by women in local market centers. Market activity was an important means for augmenting household revenues and some women worked as *revendeuses* (literally "resellers") purchasing fruit, vegetables, and secondhand clothing, in bulk and reselling them in the market. Other women were engaged in forms of wage-earning activity that involved them in work as seamstresses, laundresses, dressmakers, and midwives. Cash was also brought into the household economy by women who grew, prepared, and sold food (Frader 1991). Many village women often combined many different activities in their efforts to put together a livelihood.

Agnès Peyre, for example, described her mother's efforts to maintain her family during the early 1900s.

> My father worked all his life as a day laborer for a large landowner. My mother sometimes worked there with him. On top of that, my mother did different things to earn some extra money. She used to do laundry for other people in the village. Of course, there were no washing machines at that time, so she carried big baskets full of laundry to the wash tubs in the village square. Sometimes she went to the river to wash the laundry. She took me with her and I would watch her scrub and slap them against the rocks to get them clean. That was just one of the things she did. Of course, she took care of us. And that's work, isn't it? She also used to cook meals for some people in the village. Actually she got quite good at it. She started out preparing meals for a few men in the village who were widowers and she got the reputation for being a very good cook. Occasionally when one of the bourgeois families had a party, she was asked to prepare the meal for them. She would shop and prepare the meal at home and then deliver it to the customers in early evening. Then she would come home and prepare an evening meal for the family. Later she would go and clean up after the party. I would go along with her sometimes to help. It was hard work for her, but it helped to keep us all clothed and fed.

Agnès herself began to pursue a number of different livelihood activities after she had been just about laid off from her work as a day laborer. She claimed that she was going to quit anyway because she was about to give birth and was thinking of other ways of making a living that would accommodate raising children. Following her mother's example, Agnès began work preparing meals for other people in the village and cleaning houses. She undertook this work while also working on her smallholding.

While Agnès's narrative refers to a period during which the capitalism was becoming well established in rural Languedoc, it nonetheless suggests an extensive history of pluriactivity in the region and the central position occupied by women in diverse economic activities that were and remain crucial in efforts to sustain a family and family-based farming. Agnès's account then not only offers us a glimpse of the kinds of activities undertaken by women in an economy of multiple livelihoods, but it also provides one example of how work was divided between women and men during a period in which the Languedoc peasantry was largely involved in a subsistence-oriented polyculture.

In the more contemporary context of Broussan, most households put together a living by combining farm with a multiplicity of other forms of earning an income both in farming and outside farming. Broadly speaking well over 60 percent of all households derived incomes from operating businesses, selling home-grown products as well as wage work both in and outside agriculture. However, only roughly 10 percent of all households put together a living combining farmwork with some form of wage work outside agriculture. In what follows I present a case that illustrates the organization of a household whose members derive revenues from a combination of wage work outside agriculture and farming itself. The case of the Campagnac household provides an example of the interrelationships that obtain between the gendered and generational divisions of labor in households that combine work in and outside agriculture. In the Campagnac household, the men of the domestic unit worked on the farm, while the women earned an income through employment in the wage sector of the economy and tended to domestic work. In contrast to the Peyres, discussed earlier, there was little unity or commonness in the work experiences between the women and the men of the household. This lack of commonality was reflected in the differential participation of household members in political activities. While Marc Campagnac claimed to have always heeded the call to take up action, Nathalie, his wife, simply stated: "The call is for Marc, not for me."

The Campagnacs

The Campagnac family owned a vineyard consisting of 15 hectares. Marc worked full-time in the fields, while Nathalie, his wife, worked full time as a postal clerk in Béziers. They had one daughter, Amandine, who was married and lived in the new housing development in the village and worked as a secretary in

Béziers. Marc and his wife lived together with his elderly parents, Louis and Claire. Louis, a former agricultural laborer, was now a retired wine grower who managed to amass a property of 10 hectares by the time of his retirement. This property was given to Marc, his only son, when he took retirement. Five additional hectares were bought by the Campagnacs per hectare with a bank loan and savings.

While Marc worked in the vineyards everyday, Louis still helped him from time to time in some of the labor-intensive and skilled operations required in viticulture. Marc claimed that his father was especially helpful during pruning season since he was familiar with all the special shears and techniques required in pruning. For the moment Louis was still able to help, but his health was failing and he found it increasingly difficult to get out to the vineyards. As Marc could no longer rely on Louis to work in the vineyards on a continual basis, he was forced to hire a laborer from time to time for some of the heavy tasks that required more than one person to complete. The laborer was usually one of the unemployed residents of the community or a someone seeking to earn an extra bit of money. The work was undeclared and Marc paid the laborer, depending on the task either on a piecework basis or with a wage below the set minimum. Also, Marc frequently enlisted the aid of Amandine's husband who worked in Béziers as a mechanic. In this case, no payment was made. Amandine, herself, was seldom asked to "help" as she, so Marc claimed, was not expected to take up wine growing as an occupation because she was a woman. Marc and Nathalie felt that it would be better for her to develop her secretarial skills and be able to make a living from work outside farming. Still Amandine stood to inherit the entire family holding and Marc was counting on his son-in-law to take up viticulture. Since Louis's farming days were almost over, Amandine's husband was being groomed to take over the farm. While Louis was still working on the farm, however, there was no need for extra family labor—neither Nathalie's nor Amandine's.

Living in an extended-kin unit clearly paved the way for Nathalie to take up full-time wage employment. Marc's mother saw to the daily round of domestic tasks. Claire's daily round began at about 6 or 7 A.M.. After preparing the early morning meal, she cleared up, swept, dusted, and washed clothing as part of their daily routine in the home. When Amandine was young, Claire also delivered her to the village school in the morning and picked her up for lunch. Claire's morning tours of duty also involved stopping off at the local shops to pick up small provisions required for the meals at midday and in the evening— fresh bread, some small quantities of meat, vegetables and cheese—whatever she could fit into her shopping basket. When she returned and after the morning round of tidying was done, she would begin the preparation of the midday meal—the main meal of the day.

Almost exactly at 12 o'clock on the dot, when village shops closed and parents, grandparents, and babysitters rushed to pick up children from school, the sound of a wide variety of motor vehicles—cars, trucks, tractors, and mopeds announced the return of Marc and other men heading home from the fields for his midday meal. Though Nathalie had a two-hour break for lunch, she found herself dashing home for a midday meal and returning to Béziers for work too hectic and preferred to lunch in town. Many women who worked in nearby towns or villages, however, did return home to serve the midday meal, which often has been prepared in advance, either the evening before or early in the morning. Claire then prepared the midday meal for Marc, Louis, and herself. Around 1:30 and 2 P.M. or later in the hot summer months, Marc again headed out to the vineyards often joined by Louis. In the afternoon, Claire took up the various domestic projects such as ironing, more washing, washing floors, and tended to the home garden. Then later in the afternoon, Claire started to prepare for the evening meal, which often consisted of soup and bread and was eaten around 8 P.M. after Nathalie and Marc had arrived home from work.

This domestic arrangement suited the entire household since it appeared to Nathalie, when she first entered into the household, that the contribution of her labor to the home was redundant. With Claire in charge of the domestic domain, it was suggested to Nathalie that she could serve the family well by finding work, which she promptly set out to do quite soon after she and Marc were married. The fact that Nathalie pulled in a wage was seen by the family as critical since the additional income helped in the purchase land, agricultural inputs, machinery, and items needed for daily consumption as well as in the repayment of debts.

In the Campagnac household, then grandparents made a substantial contribution of labor toward maintaining the household as a domestic unit and the household as an enterprise. Because of pursuing diverse income-obtaining strategies, over a relatively short period of time the size of their holding had increased from 10 to 15 hectares. Moreover, because Louis and Claire had only one son, the entire holding was kept intact.[8] The combined labor of the father and son in the vineyard and of the mother in the home "freed" Nathalie to work for wages in town.

The combination of paid with unpaid work was also critical in the reproductive strategies of the household enterprise. Exchanges of unpaid labor in the household and on the agricultural enterprise facilitated the pursuit of wage work, while the pursuit of wage work buttressed the household economy both in production and consumption. The example of the Campagnac household again illustrates how growers who relied on family labor were keenly aware of the value of labor power and demonstrates the ways in which elements of instrumentality and calculation prevailed in the household (see chapter 4). Moreover, it illustrates the ways in which households often moved into and out of commodity relations as extra labor was sometimes unremunerated or and unpaid, while in other instances it was paid. While in this particular case, an instrumental rationality existed in the organization of household, exchanges between members were not reduced to a market calculus. Labor and resources were pooled and shared on the basis of commitment to a common family project.

With a multiplicity of income sources, the possibilities of the reproduction and expansion of the smallholding enterprise among households such as the Campagnac's appeared greater than among the households of independent cultivators discussed earlier in chapter 4 whose revenues were derived solely from the vineyards. Though women's contributions were often critical to the process of accumulation, mitigating against the possibility of expansion, however, was the fact that while women brought in income to the household, they were employed mostly in the lowest-paid jobs in the economy. Large amounts of capital were thus not generated through wage employment. Like households of independent cultivators, extra income among pluriactive households was also secured through share tenancy and also, constant expenditures had to be made for the purchase of agricultural supplies and machinery and for their maintenance, as well as for the needs of the members of the household, that is, in both productive and individual consumption.

In the village, among households that combined farmwork with other wage-earning activities, then there was considerable variation in household composition. Both nuclear units and extended household arrangements were found. The Campagnac family was one example of a configuration that combined several generations of kin. In such households, elderly men and women often made a significant contribution of labor toward maintaining both the domestic unit and the farm. Moreover, the retired members of the household also brought in an additional income in the form of pensions and a portion was turned into the common household fund for daily consumption.

Though the kinds of wage work that were pursued among pluriactive households generally included both agricultural and nonagricultural forms of work, women tended to obtain paid work largely in the nonagricultural sector. This was the case as illustrated by Nathalie. Women tended to secure positions in the service sector of the economy and like Nathalie often commuted into Béziers to work in a variety of jobs as secretaries, clerks, housekeepers, waitresses, maintenance workers, and shop assistants. In the village itself, cleaning was the major form of paid employment undertaken by women. Women worked cleaning the homes of large landowners and the elderly or the offices in local businesses. Women also worked as shop assistants in the local grocery, butcher, and hardware stores. Some women were employed as receptionists in the village medical and legal offices. These jobs were relatively scarce and therefore difficult to obtain. Wage employment in the village was preferred over work in Béziers as proximity to the home for married women facilitated carrying out domestic responsibilities especially for women who had young children and husbands who worked the vineyards. For example, one woman in the village, Jacqueline, quit her job working as a seamstress sewing military uniforms and outfits for postal workers in a factory in Bédarieux, a small town located north of Broussan. After her second son was born, she decided that commuting such a distance to work created too much stress for her family and she preferred to put together a living by cleaning houses, as well local shops such as the bakery (*la boulangerie*) where she also worked part time as a shop assistant. Between her husband working practically around the clock in the vineyards and her early departures and late arrivals from Bédarieux, Jacqueline felt that the coherence of family life was being undermined as the children were shuffled off from one baby sitter to another. Moreover, with the cost of purchasing child care and travel, she felt that there was a high monetary as well as emotional cost to maintaining such work activities. Jacqueline, like Agnès, then experienced a shift in work routines with the demands of motherhood and of family life. While to a great extent Agnès's shift was imposed or at least coincided with large scale economic change, Jacqueline's was more determined by the prescriptions of the gendered division of labor that constructed women as first and foremost wives and mothers, whose primary duties are to see to the social reproduction of the family and only secondarily to its material reproduction. Men, then were primarily responsible for its material reproduction, that is, bringing in the wages and income to sustain the family as few men altered their work commitments to accommodate such changes in the demographic cycle of the family.

The Home and the Field

In Broussan, then a boundary was often drawn between women's work and men's work. The domestic domain was considered the territory of women, while the fields were considered the territory of men. Nonetheless, as I suggested earlier, women did on occasion work in the fields, as did men undertake various forms work in the domestic domain. Within each of these fields of work, however, there tended to be a division of labor that was strictly maintained. Men generally undertook those tasks that were to be done on an intermittent basis. They included such jobs as home repairs, renovations, and gardening. Other domestic tasks done on a more continuous and daily basis such as food preparation, house cleaning, washing, ironing, and so on were mainly women's tasks. This division of domestic work was reflected in many people's ideas of work and the responsibilities of domestic life. For example, Marcel Mas's notion of when his workday began and ended coincided with his crossing the boundary that demarcated the home from the field: "As soon as I reach the doorstep after a day in the fields, that's it—I stop work. I take my shoes off and relax. My work is finished for the day."

Marcel's insistence that he actually finished work at the doorstep of the household, obscured his own contributions of labor in the domestic domain. Because the home is considered the sphere of women's work and the field the sphere of men's work, men and women tended to overlook, underestimate, and diminish the importance of their labor contributions when they crossed the boundaries and enter into each others' respective work domains (see also Narotsky 1989). In agricultural production, women continually spoke of the insignificance of their contribution to farm-work and in each instance insisted that they were performing a minor almost incidental operation—"just help-ing out"—as Eliane earlier put it, rather than actually working.

As much as the domestic sphere in Broussan did not in reality exists as an exclusive arena for women's work, the fields were seldom a territory that precluded the contribution of women's labor. While many women worked on family enterprises from time to time, a significant number of women in the village laid claim to that territory by identifying themselves as "viticultrices"—women wine growers. They were registered as owners of vineyards. Al-though vine cultivation and agricultural work was defined as "men's work" between one-eighth and one-fourth of wine growers in Broussan were women. However, while they identified themselves in village records and interviews as viticultrices, in fact, very few of these women actually committed their labor to the cultivation the vines. Some women earned the designation as wine growers, simply by virtue of holding the title to vineyard property (see below). They maintained the vineyards through hiring workers or have the land rented out. In these respects they are properly defined as members of a rentier class, not engaged in the direct cultivation of land. Still, despite the forces of capitalist transition and the prescription of the division of labor, not all women were so continuously removed from the process of vine production. A small minority of viticultrices were directly involved in the sus-tained production of wine, executing all the necessary tasks.

Women Wine Growers

Josette Bonnefoy, who stood up to denounce state policies, was one of the few women owner-operators in the village. She ran a fairly sizable holding along with her husband and at the age of 39 was the mother of two very young children. After their birth, she continued to work full-time with her husband, Hervé, on the family holding of 25 hectares divided between two rather distant locations. Josette explained how they divided up their time:

> While 17 hectares of our farm are located in Broussan, we have another 8 hectares near Narbonne, which is about 60 kilometers southwest of here. I am from Narbonne origi-nally and those were my parents' vineyards. We go to Narbonne every other weekend and try to do all the things we need to do in that short period. We split up our lives like this because, I am the second youngest of four sisters in our

family. There are no brothers and without any male children and I inherited one-quarter of the family wine holding, that is to say I got 8 hectares. Hervé inherited 10 hectares and over the years we managed to buy an additional nine hectares. I do everything that he does on the farm, from driving a tractor to tearing up vines.

Talking of the nature of work in wine growing, Josette maintained that there was no reason why women cannot do the same work as men. Nonetheless, she complained that after having children at such an advanced age in life (she had her first child at 35), she was no longer able to keep up the pace of work followed before her pregnancies. Still, she conscientiously went out to the vineyards every day while one of her children attended school and the other was cared for by Hervé's parents. The substantial but not insurmountable difficulties of combining mother work with farmwork were encapsulated in a story told to me about Josette soon after she had her second baby. Alain, a distant neighbor recounted how he had been home one Saturday and observed how Josette drove her tractor back and forth, every three hours or so past his house to her mother-in-law's house and back to the fields again. In the late afternoon, he finally stopped her and asked if some piece of machinery had broken down and could he help in any way. She replied that she did not have machinery problems and the only way he could help was by growing breasts. Josette was rushing back and forth from the fields to breastfeed her baby. Unlike Agnès and Jacqueline, Josette's work routine remained virtually unaltered after the birth of her children.

Josette, through her own and her husband's efforts ran a fairly successful operation. This contrasts in a number of ways with the case of Paulette Macou another *"viticultrice."* Paulette was the divorced mother of four adult children of whom only one, Pierre, lived in the village. He worked as a day laborer at Château X. Paulette worked full time as a housekeeper and aid to several disabled people in the community and ran a holding of about 2.5 hectares. In the late afternoons and on the weekends, she could be seen heading toward the vineyards on her moped. Though her son helped her out occasionally, she performed all the necessary operations mainly on her own using very rudimentary tools. She was unable to afford a tractor.

Divorce, widowhood, and lack of male heirs forced many women to defy the strictures of a gendered division of labor and work as wine growers. In the first case, for example, the responsibility for farming the family holding was taken up by Josette, one of four daughters in a wine-growing family with no male heirs. She continued to work in the fields even after marriage to a wine grower. It was more common for women in these circumstances to abandon farmwork on marriage or remarriage, however, in Josette's case, it was regarded as more cost effective for the family for her to continue to work as part of the unpaid domestic labor force rather than to hire a laborer, especially as her level of skill in viticulture was high, acquired through years of running her parents' farm in the absence of male children.

Patriarchy, Patrimony, and Gender

From Josette's case, it becomes apparent that in Broussan, when succession issues arose, women were neither altogether exempted from the binding forces of the ideology of farm and family continuity, nor did they escape the dynamics of patriarchal domination in the home discussed in chapter 4. Though women did not usually work the land as wine growers, there were many cases of households with only female heirs. Daughters, in many of these cases, were subjected to the same types of pressure as male heirs. They were compelled by parents, usually fathers, to continue to run the holding or to marry a man who either himself had land or who would run the inherited farm. Deathbed pleas made by fathers and the promises made by children at the bedside often sealed the fate of women while securing the future of the farm. This deathbed drama was played out in case of Marie Pons, another of the few women wine growers in the community. This segment of her life story explains how she became one among the minority of women wine growers in Broussan:

> I am an only child and so I inherited a holding of 6 hectares. I also inherited a business running a hotel in a town not too far from here. When I was 35, I married Jérome who works as a supervisor of various public works projects. We have one daughter who is 14 years old. I continue to run this farm though the income from our vineyards is negligible, especially after paying the costs of production and our principle income source is the hotel business and my husband's job. [They owned 13 hectares and rented and additional 2.] With the ongoing crisis and the bleak future in wine produc-

tion, there is little sense in staying on as a wine grower, specially since I have another business.

The only reason that I am staying on as a wine grower is that I promised my father as he lay dying that I would never sell a single hectare of the family property. He was so sick for such a long time and while he was ill he kept urging me not sell the land. He felt that he poured is life blood into that farm. So, I have not to this day sold off any piece of his farm. I have suffered because of this promise. I married late in life because I was always too busy working on the farm or helping my mother with the hotel business she ran. I am proud of the fact that I can work that land but really this is not suitable work for women. I have never really been comfortable as a *viticultrice*. Your hands were always dirty. You smell and your skin gets coarse and wrinkled very fast. I would rather have just helped my mother in the hotel, but when my father was alive we really had no way of running the farm without my help. So I was made to go to the fields with him. I married Jérome because he was the only man I met who could stand to have a real wine grower as a wife. Other men wouldn't look at me.

Marie's case shows how a woman's life may be circumscribed by the imperatives of farm continuity. Some women were forced through the excercise of patriarchal authority to disregard the prescriptions of a gender-based division of occupations and often this nonconformity came at a price. According to Marie, her life as a grower had the unfortunate consequence of delaying marriage and motherhood, that is, of her assuming a more socially appropriate role for women. She felt humiliated that her presentation of self to the public world was as a woman who seldom conformed to the norms of femininity. It is also by no means a coincidence that Josette's life history involved delay in marriage and "late" pregnancies. The cases of women wine growers such as Josette and Marie, then represented exceptions that proved the rule of women "belonging" in the domestic domain. The forces of domestication rendered women more susceptible to the dynamics of patriarchy in the household, in the family and in the larger society.

Through Marie's narrative and from earlier accounts, it is evident that within the household, patriarchal power was commonly exercised when the fate of the farm was at stake. Father and husbands tended to try to control the course of the lives of both male and female children. Acting on the imperative to control, allocate, and retain labor for the continuity of the farm, daughters, like sons, were often subjected to patriarchal authority and forms of domination by the more powerful members of the household. However, the experience of domination for daughters was different to that of son. Sons eventually came to be established as the head of the household and the power differences between fathers and sons were but a phase in the life cycle of a male farmer. The power differential came to an end once the son inherits property. The situation of women in this context was rather different. The period of women's position as subordinates to the male head of the household and farm was more sustained and often reinforced both through social practice and through political and economic means. For example, while a system of partible inheritance was underwritten by law, the social practice of transferring ownership rights to men seemed to prevail. Sisters often sold their share to brothers or other male kin. Wives transferred control if not outright ownership to husbands. Other women had their holdings rented by male kin. The majority of agricultural holdings, therefore, tended to be registered in the names of men. One of the reasons for this was that the state reinforces the *de facto* if not the *de jure* male ownership of agricultural enterprises. Access to state subsidies, loans, and the dissemination of technical information was facilitated by registering property in the names of males. Since men were considered the rightful operators of any farm, this meant that credit facilities, subsidy programs were directed at men. The terms of loans, interests, and mortgage rates were more favorable to men, who were considered the primary income earners and property owners, despite the fact that in an economy of pluriactivity, it becomes very difficult to determine who brings in the main income. Nevertheless, ideas and practices that associated men with principle income and women with subsidiary or secondary incomes prevailed in census categories and officialdom. The juropolitical apparatus of the state therefore also supported an identification of women with the domestic sphere and promoted the economic dependence of women on men. The state then participated in the cyclical process of establishing males as household heads, reinforcing male power and authority by providing an economic basis for patriarchal authority (see Lem 1991b).

This was underscored by a joke one informant made when explaining the practice of involving retransferring titles to women. In taking up formal retirement, men often transferred the title either to their sons or their wives, if the wives had not yet reached retirement age. This allowed men to collect pensions while still receiving revenues from their work on farms. Yvon Rabou, for example, recently reached retirement age and reregistered the ownership of the family vineyards under his wife, Emilienne, who was 10 years his junior. Emilienne joked: "For years, I was his slave, now I own the farm. I am the boss and he is my slave." *("Je suis la patronne et il est mon esclave.")*

The male head's control over labor and family members was mediated through a variety of ideological devices, especially those associated with the sanctity of the family. Marie Pons's father impressed on Marie that his life blood was part of the soil on the farm. But that control over labor in fact gained real force through the head's control over property. Men also tended to control the products of that labor, the income generated from the production of vines was paid to the head of the household, the owner of that property who ultimately controlled its distribution. It is as dependents of the owner that members establish entitlement to the products of labor. In this sense, wives and husband exchange their labor on the basis of what has been called the conjugal contract (Whitehead 1981). However, because women tended to surrender control and *de facto* as well as *de jure* ownership of their agricultural property to their husbands, husbands and wives entered into the conjugal contract on very different terms. Men entered as the owners of the means of production and their own labor power. Women entered as the owners of labor power, only. The authority of the male head is sanctioned by ownership of the means of production and control of the economic resources on which the livelihood of the domestic unit depends. The dependent status of the other members of the domestic unit underlines the authority of the male head who may withdraw, apportion, and appropriate goods, services, and labor.

In these respects it is possible to speak of a classlike relationship prevailing in the domestic domain. This opens up the notion of "self-exploitation," which Chayanov associates with family-based production to some scrutiny. Caught in the simple reproduction squeeze discussed earlier, men not only intensified their own labor by working longer hours, they also increased the amount of work dome by members of the household by deploying labor from the domestic sphere to work in the fields, in the production of commodities. This is a class like relationship akin to the lord's diversion of peasant labor from the peasant plot to the market-oriented demesne land. Self-exploitation then often amounted to the exploitation of women expressed through increased pressure on women to lower costs of consumption by increasing autoprovisioning, the intensification of work on gardens and subsistence plots, making clothing in the home, rearing animals for food, as well as taking up more and more work in wage sector of the economy. While the labor of members of the domestic unit was deployed to maintain the family farm, identified so profoundly with the male head, the subordination of the interest of all to the "common family project" in fact became the subordination of the women and children to the male head. It is in this sense that relations within the domestic unit may be called patriarchal and the forms of domination in women's lives was experienced as the domination by husbands and fathers.

The changes in the division of labor that saw the domestication of women, on the one hand and the fragmentation of women's work expereince, on the other, which found women's labor redeployed to work in a variety of workplaces had particular consequences for women and the ways in which they engaged with their political worlds. In an era when women were regularly employed in agricultural wage work and struggles revolved around the cultivation of vines and work in the vines, the exploitation and domination of vine workers was part of the immediate experience of women. The immediacy of that experience of work stimulated women to engage in forms of open and direct confrontation with merchants, estate owners, and the state. A collective consciousness was built up around that experience in a universalistic vision that encompassed the experience of all workers and laboring people. In Languedoc history, actions, sentiments, and activities that focused on the domination of laboring women and men as members of the working class were galvanized by conditions in which radical politics and the politics of struggles as a class held sway. While forms of domination on smallholdings and the dynamics of patriarchal relations may have also prevailed in households and other work contexts in an earlier period, the fact that both women and men shared a common experiences of work and domination in the process of production, enabled women to contend with the conditions of exploitation at least in one field of their work lives. This then diffused the potential eruption and perhaps acknowledgment of domination in other facets of the lives as women who work in the domestic domain. For in that earlier period, the highly organic way in which the household economy operated, found women and men working in agriculture, reinforced the commonness of the common family project.

However, in the more contemporary period, the increasing differentiation of work experiences and spheres of work that accompanied capitalist transformation, in many respects led also to differentiated fields of political experience for women and men. The shifting fields of work occurred while the dominant modes of political struggle remained constant. By and large, the dominant forms of struggle in Lower Languedoc were concerned with viticulture and wine production. Modes of political expression centered class claims and regional specificities and as such they failed to articulate with the diversity of different workers' experiences, especially those of women who were experiencing forms of domination in workplaces at home and rather removed from the farm. The alienation of women from the process and relations of the production of wine combined with the primacy of a kind of political struggle that did not reflect the specificity of women's experiences then not only effaced women's experiences but also had the effect of removing women from the public field of collective action. The struggles of wine growers as a class and as Occitan growers and the issues that people confronted in the struggle failed to speak to the contemporary experiences of women whose lives have become contoured by the ideology of domestication and a process of fragmentation of work relations. Moreover, despite the prevalence of a more mechanical form of solidarity in which members of households have become increasingly differentiated in terms of work and roles, the primacy and the hegemonic status of the idea of the common family project persists. The imperatives of dedicating all efforts to ensure family and farm continuity impedes any attempts that may be made by women to resist domination and control by patriarchs, especially when the adversary is one that is located "within" the family. Any initiative taken by women to resist or contest the power exercised by men in the household may be construed as a repudiation of the family and a betrayal of the common family project. This became evident in the threats that were often used by fathers to compel children to take up farming discussed earlier (see chapter 4). Moreover, women's sense of collectivity and potential for acting in concert to resist the specific conditions of women's subordination were undermined by the dispersal of their work activities in both time and place. Many women worked in different locations, performing different types of work, often in solitary places and on a sporadic basis. Episodes of exploitation in the different work sites tended to be perceived as highly individualized and confined almost to a private experience, especially in the light of the failure of predominant forms of collective struggle to resonate with more diverse experiences of women as workers. So, when women express their enmity and engage in struggles, it is in the everyday, and often rather more quiescent arena. Hence the political universe for women has become narrower and women express their disenchantment and disaffection with the existing order by retreating into the world of private expression or everyday forms of protest. The absence of women from those public and collective moments of contention and their confinement and self-confinement to a subsidiary or supportive role reflected the fact that their own experience of domination has been subsumed by the more encompassing forms of class and regional struggle. By contrast, in an earlier period it was more integrated into dominant political struggles and concerns. The ambivalence therefore of women in Broussan toward class and regional struggles reflected a repudiation of the dominant political discourses. This, in itself, may be construed as a political act or, at least, an act of everyday protest. However, as a political gesture it was of little consequence, for it neither addressed the ways in which women experienced domination nor did it contribute toward changing the conditions and relationships that perpetuate the exploitation of women. In fact, it simply reflected the extent to which the political practices of women have been subordinated to and absorbed by forms of political practice that speak only in small part to the experiences of domination suffered by women as workers and wives living in contemporary Broussan.

CHAPTER 6

Between Friends, Among Neighbors

Nous sommes individualistes, egoïstes. C'est notre mentalité.
[We are individualistic, selfish. It's our mentality.]

—Emile (farmer)

Parfois, j'ai besoin d'un coup de main. Parfois, je donne un coup de main à mes camarades. Ça c'est l'entr'aide et c'est notre tradition.
[Sometimes, I need a helping hand. Sometimes, I lend a helping hand to my friends. That is what is called mutual aid and it is our tradition.]

—Roger (farmer)

Tradition and Modernity

The dichotomy between tradition and modernity has been upheld through various tropes in the study of rural life. In early anthropological writings on peasantries, for example, Redfield, (1956), spoke of the "tradition-" bound peasant community and the "modernity" of the impersonal world outside it. Alavi (1973), wrote of the "primordiality" of kinship ties among rural producers. Writers from diverse schools of in studies of agrarian society have both implicitly and explicitly held the view that while relations based on nonmarket categories represent ties of tradition, the contractual relations of the market embody modernity, itself. In studies of the small-scale farmers in political economy, furthermore, relations based on status are often seen to predate the advent of capitalism. For example, Scott (1976), stressed how the ethic and impact of the capitalist market breached the inherent morality of traditional relations within the peasant community, inciting peasants to act to restore what was the old order. Moreover, it has been argued that "old order" has to give way, since it acts as a fetter on the development of capitalism. Bradby (1975), for example, following Luxembourg (1951, 402),

165

referred to the "precapitalist" social and economic context as the "natural economy" that must be destroyed for the development of capitalism to be possible.

The dichotomy between the relations of tradition and modernity, status and contract, as well precapitalism and capitalism has also been reproduced in recent discussions of petty commodity production. It has been asserted, for example, that commodity production implies that "units of production are formed and maintained through non-familial conditions which do not depend on kinship or communal sanction" (Ennew, Hirst, and Tribe 1977). Further it has been argued that among petty commodity producers, relations between units of production tend to take the form of buying, selling, and competition as households of commodity producers become increasingly individualized (Friedmann 1987). The underlying modernist assumptions here are that what forms of "communal sanction" prevail in peasant society, actually do so as survivals from a precapitalist, premodern era, and moreover, are destined to be eroded under advancing capitalism. In this chapter I shall argue that not only do interpersonal ties persist in the process of production in an advanced capitalist context, but that the practices that those ties presuppose emerge from and respond to the vicissitudes of contemporary capitalism. A second assumption that often underlies such dichotomies are that social relations that are embedded the "morality" of community and friendship were free of the dynamics of competition, calculation, and exploitation. Furthermore, I shall illustrate using examples from Broussan that the character of such relations as they are maintained between households are in fact dimorphic, encompassing elements of competition and cooperation, simultaneously. Therefore, while ideologies of community and kinship invoke practices based on the principles of mutuality and reciprocity, such "traditional" relations are neither free from capitalist calculation nor devoid of exploitation.

Invented Tradition

Though the smallholders of Broussan have long been integrated into a market economy, ties based on the "primordialisms" of kinship and amity in production not only have persisted, but were in many respects consciously maintained between households. Relations outside the household remained embedded in a series of interpersonal ties that served as a medium for the reciprocal exchange of human labor and material resources. Cooperative practices involving a series of nonmonetary exchanges were, in fact, critical for the reproduction of the family farm and were deliberately sustained in a effort to resist the forces of deepening commodification. Not only did the material reproduction of petty commodity production in Broussan depend on the strength of kin ties and communal sanction, but the symbolic reproduction of social and cultural universe of village life was premised on participation in social practices that integrated one household with another.

Though analysts and subjects alike often represent social relations unmedited by the market as ties of "tradition" and "custom," or residues from a precapitalist past, cooperative practices in contemporary Broussan were in fact responses to novel situations that had only an implied continuity to the past. In the past as in the present, a tradition of seeking collective solutions to individual problems fostered practices that involved the non-monetary exchange of goods, labor and service on the basis of reciprocity. This served as the traditional framework into which practices that responded to the exigencies of making a living under contemporary capitalism were inserted. The content then of reciprocal practices have been altered and restructured in fundamental ways to meet the specific challenges of maintaining the family farm under the conditions of a highly developed market in both labor and goods, as well as the forces of economic modernization. While exchanges between kin, neighbors, and friends in the process of production, formally harked back to an earlier era when the capitalist market intruded less on their lives, substantively, they responded precisely and very specifically to each permutation of that intrusion. Social practices premised on communal sanction conformed more to what Hobsbawm and Ranger (1983) called "invented traditions," responses and habits that arise to meet the vicissitudes of the new than cultural "survivals" ill adapted to the economic and social conditions of modernity.

In these respects, social relations between households in Broussan have come to be contoured by the market and the effect of the process of commodification. Producers ever consciousness of the value of labor, and the costs of other factors of production in a highly developed capitalist market deliberately maintain exchanges of both labor and equipment outside the sphere of commodity circulation. On the one hand, this is pursued as each household follows a strategy of "cost minimization" (Redclift 1985). On the other hand, however, their efforts were also guided by a will to resist complete subordination of their world to a world of market determination. Such deliberate and conscious efforts were employed also to define the boundaries of community and galvanize communal solidarity in the face of the forces of transformation under capitalism and the development of modernity that favored the disappearance of all holistic control over the economy (Touraine 1995, 24). However, while the holistic bonds of kinship, community, and amity prevailed, the exchanges of goods, labor, and services secured through the idioms of community were nonetheless configured in specific ways by the rational principles of the market. Although transactions between friends and relatives seldom involved buying and selling, exchanges, nonetheless were inevitably subjected to a market calculus without necessarily being expressed through the market as commodities.

Instrumental Rationality and Communal Sanction

As a collectivity of petty commodity producers, the community of Broussan embodied a paradox. On the one hand, it was made up of producers who were tied to the market, therefore subjected to a market morality. Wine growers were petty commodity producers who sold the items produced on each of their enterprises on the market. Therefore, in the market each enterprise was pitted against the other in a competition to sell the products of their labor.

On the other hand, the people in each of the household units of production were also members of a community, tied to each other as kin, neighbors, and friends. People from individual households not only had to secure the means for their own individual material reproduction as well as the reproduction of the enterprise, but they also lived together as members of a "community." As members of a community, their obligations extended to reproducing the community and the social relations within it, that is to the symbolic reproduction of collective life. The family farmers of Broussan, then, were simultaneously engaged in relations of competition in the market, as commodity producers, and in relations of cooperation, as members of a community, governed by the forces of communal sanction. The moral strictures of collective life in Broussan prescribed amity, reciprocity, and cooperation in work as in other spheres of social life. The dimorphic quality of social relations then embodied a dialectical tension that governed the attempt to make a living under the ethic of the market, on the one hand, while living under the morality of "community," on the other. The dual character of social life in Broussan manifested itself in a paradoxical self-image and often the same individuals who decried their own narcissistic impulses, in the same breath maintained that a spirit of collective solidarity guided their interactions.

Narcissus in Broussan

In self-referential statements, many of the people in Broussan, such as Emile, above, alluded to themselves as "egoists" and as people who always try to take advantage of other people. *"Ici, tout le monde se profit de l'un et l'autre."* Frédéric Vias, a wine grower, who also drove a school bus for a living, remarked with a note of rancor in his voice:

> Most people prefer to keep to themselves and work out their own problems. They wait until they have enough money to buy what they need or they do without it. They think that's better than getting all complicated with other people.

Many villagers lamented that these attributes were the main reason for what they see as a dearth of organized collective ventures in Broussan. Such ventures, many maintained, would solve some of the most pressing problems experienced by smallholders, such as access to large, technologically sophisticated capital equipment. One of those items was the much-coveted mechanical grape harvester,[1] whose costs were usually beyond the means of many smallholders. Frédéric continued:

> We will never be able to get our hands on a grape harvester without a cooperative. But we will never be able to form a cooperative because people are not interested in doing things together. Even when people try to share small pieces of equipment, an argument always breaks out and people are asking each other for money to pay for damaged machinery or they suspect that they are being taken advantage of.

Farmers interviewed often denounced this unfortunate "mentalité" of the people of Broussan, holding that if they were only more cooperative by nature, they could form an association to buy equipment and expensive machinery as their predecessors had before them. Many smallholders felt that such collective action would be the solution to individual difficulties and crises. More-over, again like their predecessors, there was an inclination to combine collective action with an appeal to the state for assistance. Growers felt, in this particular instance, that what was necessary was the establishment of a Coopérative d'Utilisation de Machines Agricoles (CUMA)—a state-sponsored cooperative that would be established for the purchase and shared use of agricultural equipment. A CUMA, then would solve the immediate problem of gaining access to one of the most expensive and innovative pieces of equipment in viticulture. Still, while many farmers wished for a CUMA, most doubted the viability of such an organization, especially since the story of the rise and fall of one that had existed in the village served as a persistent reminder of their overpowering narcissistic inclinations.

The Legacy of Individualism

For a period of twelve years, a CUMA operated in the village. It was formed in 1946 after a local drought had wiped out a substantial part of the vineyards in Broussan. The growers were anxious to replant their vineyards in the shortest possible time using the latest technology available and as tractors were being widely adopted in rural France during that time, the most effective way of securing access to expensive mechanized equipment was through a cooperative arrangement. The CUMA was established through a government subsidy and it was administered through the vinification cooperative (see chapter 7). Over the years it bought a substantial amount of machinery including, American caterpillar tractors and a huge plows that were initially used to replant vineyards wiped out by the drought. After an early period of intensive utilisation, however, informants reported that the various pieces of equipment that CUMA owned came to be used less and less as the years went by. Problems of accessibility presented themselves as well as problems of maintenance. It was easier for growers to hire a plowing contractor to do certain tasks than to rely on the CUMA to coordinate and schedule the sharing of the equipment between all members. Indeed, most members of the cooperative had very restricted access to the equipment and soon the equipment itself fell into disrepair. Funds for their replacement expired as participants withdrew both their membership and fees. All the machinery owned by the cooperative was finally sold in 1960 and the CUMA dissolved amid accusations of corruption and incompetence. The directors of the CUMA were roundly criticized for having mismanaged the cooperative. Also, many of the villagers suspected that those who ran the CUMA abused their position of power. It was thought that they used the fees members paid to buy equipment, but gave themselves privileged access to the equipment.

Sébastien Cabanel commented on how the memory of that failure acts as a cautionary tale:

> There were never any meetings and the members were never kept in touch with what was going on. Its failure has been a lesson to everybody in the village. Everyone had talked about sharing and what a good thing a CUMA would be and, of course, it was a good thing in principle. But in practice human nature took over and the greedy ones who could hoard and keep hoarding the equipment did exactly that, without a thought to others who might need it. Nowadays, there was no question of establishing another one in the village. There was no question of buying a grape harvester. It's really a shame. You can't trust your neighbor. Everyone was in it for themselves. Nobody will get together to help each other out.

The specter of that failure was inscribed into the popular memory of the farmers of Broussan. In many of the self-reflective statements made by the growers, the collapse of the CUMA was cited as evidence for absence of spirit of collectivity and the tenacity of a tradition of individualism that beleaguers family farmers. This memory of "failure" of the CUMA, then, confirmed growers' worst images of themselves as narcissistic and uncooperative.

Not only was this representation pervasive among the wine growers themselves, but such a construction of the French farmer has also made its way into scholarly writings. The French farmer is often portrayed as being supremely individualistic and fiercely independent (see, e.g., Wylie 1956, passim). Moreover, for subjects and analysts alike, this representation has been elevated to the status of explanation as planners and policy makers have seized on this "mentalité," as the main culprit responsible for the failure of various forms of organization that involve cooperation. Moreover, when cooperatives are adopted or manage to succeed, it is noted that they do so despite the atomistic tendencies among French farmers (Groeger 1975, 300; 1981, 166).[2] While these representations exist, many other studies have cautioned against the elevation of a "folk model" or stereotypes of the character of French farmers to the level of explanation. For example, Yoon (1975) cites unwieldy bureaucratic structures of the state-sponsored cooperatives as more the factor responsible for such failures than the purported generic individualism of French farmer (see also Groeger 1981). Moreover, the existence in Broussan of alternative images and social practices advise against accepting self-referential statements as encompassing truths. In Broussan, social relations were suffused with notions generosity and collective solidarity and these to some extent belied the stereotype.

The Language of Kin and Community

Despite an avowed individualism, therefore, a great number of households in the community were continuously involved in a whole array of exchanges of labor, goods, and services, not mediated by cash. Reciprocal exchanges prevailed among people who committed themselves to the obligations of kinship (*le parenté*), friendship (*l'amitié*), and neighborliness (*le voisinage*). Loose coalitions of households were formed to share and pool resources. Reciprocal arrangements tended to be made on an ad hoc basis with a several different households making up loose network. Exchange networks were in a constant state of flux and its composition varied continually according to the different needs of the constituent households. While households moved in and out of exchange arrangements, the networks themselves tended to be framed overall by a set of common characteristics. They were often made up of households tied together on the basis of kinship. Villagers often spoke of getting a helping hand from their relatives (*les parents*). In cases in which kinship ordered exchange networks, households were joined by sibling ties, filiation, and collaterality. Kinship links were often forged through a process of extension in which distant kin were drawn into kin-based coalitions. Kinship however, acted as only one of social bonds that united people into exchange networks. Participation in local solidary organizations drew people into coalitions. Such participation served as the common ground that unites people in terms of their interest, but it symbolized a commitment to sustain the way of life in a rural community that contrasts with a world in which capitalist calculation and contract threatened to be all encompassing. The social practices that corresponded to these commitments then were premised on an ethos of mutual aid without monetary recompense and this ethos filtered into a variety of social practices in the reproduction of petty commodity production. Exchanges were negotiated through the language of kinship and friendship and series of different terms were used to refer to the practices involved—*"l'entr'aide"* (mutual aid); *"rendre service"* (doing a favor); *"dépanner"* (to help out); *"un coup de main"* (helping hand). One such practice was reciprocal labor exchanges.

Exchanges of Labor

Among the exchanges that took place between households of petty commodity producers, labor exchanges occurred most frequently. They were undertaken usually when a shortage of labor was experienced. Labor shortages in the household enterprise were due to both economic and demographic factors. In certain phases in the demographic cycle of the household, labor short-falls resulted from situations in which members were either too young or too old to contribute their labor. Migration and marriage, combined with neolocal residence were among other factors that also resulted in labor shortages. Moreover, the nature of specific tasks themselves often required more than one individual to execute, that is, spreading fertilizer, uprooting vines, pruning vines, and picking grapes. Labor exchanges between members of distinct household enterprises were undertaken to solve both the problem of labor shortages and demands for extra labor for the completion of specific tasks.

Wine growers then often approached a neighbour or friend (*un camarade*) or other kin to help out as a favor (*rendre service*). This occurred both on a sustained basis and on an occasional basis. Kin ties were particularly prominent as one of the means for securing labor between households. For example, the Fages household ran both their farm and their hardware business by activating a very direct kin tie. The Fages family operated a holding of 25 hectares and while Bertrand worked in the vineyards, his wife ran the hardware store. Both operations were run with the help of their son Grégoire and his wife, Suzanne, who themselves operated a holding of 6.5 hectares. Grégoire, Suzanne, and their children lived in a separate household that was really a self-contained apartment that adjoined the hardware store. While, technically, the Fages households operated separate holdings, as each held title to different units of land, their properties were run jointly, as of it were one enterprise. The income from wine growing was shared proportionately between the two households and was considered the joint family income. Much of the revenue from the hardware store was turned into land purchases and equipment upgrades. Another direct kin tie joined both these households to another very small unit of production. Bertrand and Grégoire contributed their labor toward the running of the small 0.5-hectare vineyard belonging to Bertrand's parents, Raymond and Catherine. Bertrand and Grégoire turned the small income that derived from this vineyard over to Raymond and Catherine. In exchange, Raymond and Catherine, offered their barn for the storage of the several tractors and other large pieces of agricultural equipment owned by these relatively wealthy members of the community. Also, Raymond and Catherine provided accommodation in their house during the harvest for the workers who have been hired by Bertrand to pick grapes on the family vineyards.

The immediate kin connection between the Fages households represented an important basis for the nonmonetary exchanges of goods, labor, and services. As the holding was worked as if it were one enterprise, family labor was mobilized without monetary recompense. Grégoire and Suzanne worked on the agricultural enterprise and in the hardware store without being paid. They helped themselves to whatever hardware items they needed in their parents' store. According to Grégoire, all the consumption needs of his family were met through the vineyard income that they pooled and shared, as little distinction was made between the part of the enterprise that belonged to him and his wife and the part that belonged to his parents. Bertrand's parents were also supplied with hardware goods at no cost from the store.

While it was apparent that very direct nature of the kin ties bound the different Fages households together, less immediate connections between kindred also serve in many cases to fuse different domestic units in both production and consumption. For example, Sébastien Cabanel, whom we discussed in the previous chapter, ran a holding of 8.5 hectares in part by hiring a wage worker, but also by deploying the help of his nephew (le neveu), Olivier. Sébastien's nephew was, in fact, the son-in-law, of his deceased wife's sister. Olivier was a retired ship's cook who worked in the French navy. Sébastien had neither children nor any siblings. After the death of his wife, his affinal relatives became his closest kin. They took him in almost as a full member of the household. Sébastien dined with them on a daily basis, but otherwise lived on his own.

The unpaid labor of Sébastien's "nephew" helped to keep the enterprise in operation by lowering the costs of production on the farm. Without this contribution of labor, a worker would have to be hired on a full-time basis and the problem of succession would have to be tackled. The nephew's family offered Sébastien the comforts of a family—meals, companionship, and care. The arrangement between Sébastien and his affinal relatives was based on a tacit understanding of reciprocity between the parties concerned that those taking care of the property owner in old age will receive some amount of land on the owner's retirement or death. Sébastien was noncommittal on the question of the future of his holding, saying only that he would not sell his vineyards. But, there were many hints that his nephew and his family stood to inherit his property. For example, Sébastien actively supervised his nephew, who was relatively new to the wine-growing milieu, in all viticultural tasks. Moreover, Sébastien, himself was the heir to the vineyards of his own uncle. Benoît, the brother of Sébastien's father, had no children and that left Sébastien as the sole beneficiary. There were grounds to suspect, therefore, that a similar pattern of the disposition of property would ensue, especially as Olivier was making a significant contribution of labor to maintain Sébastien's vineyards.

The case of Sébastien Cabanel illustrates how the ascription of kin terms through the extension of kin ties to individuals not immediately constructed as part of one's kindred serves as a way of incorporating them into a social universe in which particular moral strictures obtain. These strictures of kinship prescribe, as shown in the example of the Fages, that exchanges of labor, goods and services even between households be noncommodified. The mobilization of labor through such ties also poses limits on the extent of the process of commodification. Both the purchase of labor in production and services for consumption is avoided or, in some cases limited, that is, the laborer that was hired by Sébastien worked only part-time. While the kinship connections between households appeared less direct, the strictures appear to apply with equal weight.

In both Sébastien Cabanel's holding and that of Bertrand Fages, wage labor coexisted with the unpaid labor of kin members. Sébastien Cabanel ran a relatively small holding with both hired help and family help and in this respect, commodified relations existed alongside noncommodified relations. Similarly on the large holding operated by the Fages household, a worker was employed on a full-time basis. Bertrand and Grégoire together ran a holding that consisted of at least 31.5 hectares. (Actually, the total amount of land worked was 35.5 hectares as they also rented an additional 4 hectares.) The rule of thumb in viticulture was that one person and one tractor could run a holding of 8 hectares. The Fages admitted that while they worked their farm together often carrying on well into the night and on weekends, they could only manage their enterprise by hiring full-time help. However, they, like many other farmers were reluctant to expose the fact they resorted to hired help they tended to employ workers in the underground economy. Much of the agricultural wage work was undeclared and those hired in the informal economy were paid below the minimum wage. While one of the means through which the Fages farm reproduced itself involved the deployment of wage labor, shortfalls in labor were still experienced from time to time on this particular enterprise for several reasons. Because of the relatively large size of the holding operated by the Fages family, they frequently ran short of labor despite having full-time hired help. They also faced some difficulty completing work on the vineyards located at a distant from other vineyards. They lost time in traveling to these vineyards and found it hard to complete certain tasks on these vineyards within the requisite period without extra help, especially under unfavorable seasonal conditions. Such occasional labor shortages encountered by the Fages were remedied through two means. Frequently, casual labor was hired in the underground economy of the village. But often, the need for periodic help brought them to enlist the aid of Sébastien Cabanel who furnished them with a laborer from time to time. The exchanges struck between the Fages's and Sébastien Cabanel provide an illustration of how ties of amity and affiliation bind households together into type cooperative labor exchange that involves the exchange of commodified labor, but without the exchange of cash.

Sébastien on occasion "donated" his worker to the Fages household, for a day or half day or so at a time, claiming that his own holding did not always need his worker for the full number of hours contracted per week. The worker was employed by Cabanel on a part-time basis for 20 hours per week. Sébastien continued to pay the salary of his worker for the full 20 hours irrespective of whether the worker put in time on the Fages's holding or on his own. The request for this kind of favour from Sébastien. Cabanel was not made regularly, but only under rather urgent circumstances, when falling behind schedule posed a threat to the operation.

Sébastien insisted that he did not demand any form of recompense from the Fages, and his worker was donated as a favor. Though from time to time, he was furnished with various hardware items by the Fages family at no cost. Moreover, he was given access to the technologically sophisticated equipment owned by the Fages family. Sébastien's explanation for his generosity was that Bertrand Fages was his friend and they worked together on various local committees. He referred to the exchange that took place between him and the Fages as *"l'entre-aide"* between friends *("copains")*. In general, he felt that somehow he would be repaid and that it was not important to determine how and when in each instance. Sébastien's attitude toward the worker was that he got his salary for performing certain number of hours of work a week, irrespective of where that work is performed.

At one level, this exchange exemplifies the position of powerlessness occupied by the worker, who had no control over where he was to work and whom he was to work for. To some extent he represented a pawn in the game of neighborliness played by his employer. The worker, however, objected little to this arrangement. He received his usual wages and also was asked to work from time to time on the Fages enterprise outside the hours contracted by Sébastien. The worker was also able to borrow equipment (see below) from both Sébastien Cabanel and Bertrand Fages to operate his family's 1-hectare vineyard. Moreover, Sébastien also acted as a patron to the worker's family. Sébastien tutored the son of the worker in automechanics. Having no children of his own, he took on the young lad as a kind of protégé, prepared a learning manual for the boy, and had a keen interest in his training in automechanics at school.

Generosity and Generalized Reciprocity

From the above examples, it is evident that in Broussan, generosity and forms of generalized reciprocity then were not strictly confined to kinship networks. Some growers also lent a hand to other households without asking or expecting favor in return. For example, the Sillon household received a helping hand from their friends, the Mas's, from time to time. Marcel Mas helped to cultivate the Sillon vineyards without asking for anything in return. Michel Sillon, the male head of the household, became incapacitated by a degenerative nervous disorder and was paralyzed from the waist down. He still managed, nonetheless, to run a holding of about 8 hectares while his wife, Sylvie worked in a cafeteria at the hospital in Béziers. Michel operated his holding mainly by hiring an undeclared laborer. By combining the incomes generated from the vineyards and from his wife's employment they were able to maintain the farm and pay the laborer, but only below the minimum wage. He also relied on the help from a number of friends who regularly dropped by to offer their assistance. Michel claimed that his friends, Marcel Mas, Maurice Rey, and Joseph Seignol always helped him out without asking for a favor in return.

The example of the Sillon household illustrates that reciprocal exchanges of labor may in fact have a very long time component to them, which only makes sense in the context of the small-scale community, in which face-to-face interaction prevailed. The growers who helped out Michel viewed his helplessness in the same light as the helplessness created by old age or accidents. A degenerative disease can come to anybody, as sure as old age and such occurrences were fortuitous and beyond peoples' control, part of the general scheme of things. The same view is held on accidents in work and most growers have experienced some misfortunes in the vineyards that rendered them helpless and dependent on their neighbors for varying lengths of time. In the community, as many of the elderly or incapacitated were given such help (and those who grew old or were hurt could expect such help), labor was given freely to the Sillon's.

Notwithstanding the delay in returns, it was easy to construe these offers of help as motivated by selflessness or perhaps by pity. Without diminishing the significance of a spirit of altruism or charity that inspires such beneficent acts, however, it must also be noted that the social attributes of recipients and donors of such acts were critical in influencing whether such goodwill is expressed. Before Michel became incapacitated, he took on many of the responsibilities for running the cooperative, helped to set up the agricultural supply cooperative, and participated in many of the village organizations. Michel was an energetic actor in the social theater of the village. He also was involved in a series of "guerilla-like" campaigns in the defense of Languedoc wine growers in the years before he was stricken. Through such activity, he demonstrated commitment to viticulture and to community life, establishing by means of such public performance, his entitlement to neighborly goodwill. So his friends and associates from these village organizations, who were direct witnesses to Michel's efforts have rallied to help keep his enterprise in operation.

In the examples discussed, I have concentrated on labor exchanges in which there was seldom an expectation of a return or the expectation of an immediate return. By and large, labor exchanges were often repaid in kind by a direct return of labor. Direct exchanges of labor were particularly convenient between growers with adjoining vineyards or contiguous plots of land. In these cases, depending on the size of the plots of land that were owned, growers alternated between working one person's plot of land one day and the other person's the next day. This was the arrangement that obtained between Jacques, Roger, Raymond, and Jean mentioned in the Introduction. Commonly, however, the repayment in kind of such favors was deferred to a period when extra labor was needed, for example, during the harvest.

Reciprocity in the Grape Harvest

On all wine-growing enterprises, reciprocal labor exchange was most intensively practiced during the grape harvest, "la vendange." During late September and in early October, all available labor was mobilized to pick grapes over the short duration of the harvest. Most enterprises, except the very smallest holdings, that is, usually those under 5 hectares, utilized a paid as well as an unpaid labor force during this period of time. The smallest farms normally deployed only the labor of household members or other kin. Wives, sons, daughters, in-laws, as well as retired relatives were all recruited to help in the harvest. The work done by immediate family members tended to be unremunerated or token sums were often paid. The labor of distant kin who were recruited, that is, cousins, aunts, and uncles was often remunerated, but at rates below the market rates. Coalitions of households based both on kinship and amity who during the greater part of the agricultural years ran their enterprises as separate unit were often formed during the harvest. The workforces of the different households were combined and the work was accomplished by alternating between different enterprises to pick grapes.

On the larger holdings, a hired labor force often worked alongside a family labor force. Moreover, within the category of hired, a force of declared workers often worked alongside a force of undeclared workers. Formally declared and registered workers were labor laws and other forms of social security, and could not, for example, be expected to work more than 8 hours a day at regular wage rates. Any time put in after the regular workday was considered overtime and by law had to be paid time and a quarter for the ninth hour and time and a half, for any time over the tenth hour. These regulations, of course, did not apply to informal workers, who often worked longer hours without overtime pay. Immediate family members themselves often put in longer hours and worked more intensively than hired help. But this emerged out of a commitment to the family and the farm. More distantly related kin who were remunerated during the harvest were also often asked to work longer hours but often without overtime pay. On any single enterprise then during different points in the agricultural cycle, but particularly during the harvest, two forms of exploitation existed side by side. The production of surplus value intrinsic to a wage relationship, identified by Marx, coexisted with what Chayanov (1996) has called self-exploitation of the farmer and his family.

During the harvest, the demand for extra labor was especially high, however, as I mentioned previously, during certain other periods in the annual cycle of production, shortfalls were experienced by many farmers due to a number of factors. The mobilization of family labor or the labor of neighbors and friends was not available on every occasion that extra help was needed. To resolve the demand for extra labor, wine growers who could afford to do so, periodically hired laborers in the annual cycle of production. Most of the workers hired on an occasional basis were participants in the informal economy. Growers who followed a strategy of cost minimization used informal workers— *le travail en noir* (underground work)—without making a formal declaration to the authorities (see also chapter 2). The way in which the informal economy operated then often involved a form of cooperation between employers and employees in the conspiracy of silence that shrouded *le travail en noir*.

Cooperation in Conspiracy: Informal Work

In Broussan women and men not only worked during the grape harvest as members of an underground labor force, but also undertook a wide range of jobs that were not declared to state authorities. Earnings from this work were not recorded in tax registers, nor were payments made to the state for unemployment insurance and retirement pensions. All households seemed to participate in this economy and when discussing the work practices in the informal economy, growers roundly pronounced that "Everybody cheats." ("Tout le monde triche.") Members of wine-growing households participated simultaneously as both employers and employees in the informal economy. For example, while most wine growers hired some undeclared seasonal workers in the grape harvest and often, in other periods during the agricultural cycle, many of their wives worked temporarily as clandestine workers as fruit pickers in the melon fields, as well as the peach and cherry orchards in the village. Most of the women who worked as housekeepers in village homes were employed on an informal basis. Several women in the village worked as seamstresses for a local manufacturing company located in Béziers as undeclared homeworkers. Moreover, many agricultural laborers who worked full time were undeclared to the authorities. A considerable number of the independent tradesmen—the builders, carpenters, plumbers and painters worked entirely beyond the purview of the state. The informal economy also encompassed such activities as the marketing of products made in the home or produced on home gardens as well as the sale of a variety of services in farming. For example, agricultural contractors offered services "off the books" such as plowing land for those who lacked labor and machinery. Moreover, retired wine growers were often hired to help during pruning season. As pruning was both a labor-intensive and highly skilled operation, retired wine growers, with their long years of experience, were considered the ideal workforce in pruning. They were usually paid on a piecework basis, at roughly 50 centimes per plant. On the one hand, they earned extra income while continuing to receive pension benefits. The employer, on the other hand, was able to meet the demand for extra labor without paying the mandatory social insurance contributions.

In the village, women, the unemployed and retired people made up the bulk of the workers in the informal labor market.

A number of unemployed people continued to receive unemployment benefits while, occasionally, working on the side.[3] Both employers and employees alike claimed that informal work benefited both parties as they follow a strategy of cost minimization." For employers, *le travail en noir* kept the costs of production low. For workers, it ensured higher wages since the state was deprived of its claims over a share to each transaction. However, wage earners in the underground economy were highly susceptible to exploitation as the conditions of work were often precarious as was job security. The vulnerability of workers in the informal economy was encapsulated by the case of one of the housekeepers in Broussan who had switched employers several times within the space of a few months. She had been fired or quit several positions, hoping to secure work for someone for whom she "would not have to work her fingers to the bone for a pittance." She had hoped to get a position as a housekeeper in the formal economy, in each attempt she was unsuccessful as few employers were willing to hire her as a registered employee since they were required to pay the state charges. Workers accepted the employment in the informal economy, knowing their position of vulnerability within it on the grounds that they could maximize their incomes by circumventing the payment of income tax and the employee's contribution to state funds. Those who were employed on this basis asserted that because there was such a large degree of unemployment, there was little choice but to take available opportunities for employment. The hidden economy flourished in Broussan with the full knowledge and participation of local state officials as well and employers and employees, all of whom claimed to benefit from maintaining an economy outside beyond the scrutiny of the larger state (see chapter 2). In this respect, a considerable degree of tacit cooperation prevailed to maintain a conspiracy of silence around the hidden economy. While the informal economy served as one means of integrating households and individuals in the village, another less fraught means involved other types of informal arrangements that centered on the exchange of goods and services.

Equipment Loans: Intraclass Exchanges

The lending and borrowing of agricultural equipment was regularly practiced. It occurred as a mechanism that integrated households both within and between classes. Therefore, intraclass exchanges as well as interclass exchanges of material were commonplace. By and large small pieces of machinery and equipment was exchanged freely, however, a major obstacle to the fluency of the exchanges of larger items often presented itself. Some growers who owned large machinery were reluctant to lend out very expensive and large pieces of equipment, such as tractors and mechanical sprayers, fearing the misuse or damage of such costly equipment. However, while the anticipation of damage was seen as problematic, such fears themselves did not in every case inhibit machinery loans between households. In fact, such fears were often allayed by a lending practice in which the owner of a piece of equipment not only lends it to another household, but often accompanies the item in order to operate it. On the surface, this resembles the work performed by contractors in the village, however, no payments were made. Those who have loaned out equipment on these terms held that this was the best way of giving other people access to machinery, while assuring that the item was used properly by someone who was familiar with its operation. This prevented costly breakdowns and damage. Borrowers often made repayments contributing labor to work on the lenders' enterprise. But often, if the task done on the borrower's holding was simply and not time consuming, no repayment was demanded.

Such arrangements particularly suited owners of relatively small enterprises who could not afford expenditures on large pieces of machinery. The owners of small enterprises who borrowed equipment usually repaid the loan by offering their labor. In such exchanges, no cash changes hands. Without these arrangements, the owners of these very small properties would be forced to make an expenditure in renting machinery or to pay a contractor to perform the operation. For example, the Ibanez household ran a holding of 6 hectares and it did so entirely by using borrowed equipment. Jacques Ibanez claimed that as they had just taken up agriculture on a full-time basis their holding was too small, at the moment, to warrant large expenditures on capital equipment. They did not have the means to make large expenditures on both land and machinery and only owned a small truck, a motor-cultivator, and a manual sprayer. All other items used, both mechanically and manually operated, from rotatillers, to tips to tractors, themselves, were borrowed from friends. Jacques explained how he came to be installed as a full-time grower and how such loans were particularly critical for the running of the family vineyards:

I used to be employed full time as an agricultural laborer on one of the larger holdings in the community. While I was employed as a worker, I inherited a small vineyard consisting of 1.5 hectares from my father, in 1971. Later on, in 1976, we made a purchase of an additional 1.5 hectares with a loan from the Crédit Agricole and with the combined savings generated from my own and my wife's earnings. Marcelle, my wife, worked for a long time as a housekeeper in the village. Now our son, Robin, 22, who works as a bus driver also helps us out.

I was recently laid off. My employer explained that he could no longer afford to keep me on because of the high cost of labor, especially since the state charges are so high. Rather than face an uncertain future trying to look for other jobs laboring in the vines, I decided to turn to farming on a full-time basis. This is somewhat less uncertain than waiting for another vine worker job to come along and besides when my unemployment benefits are finished we couldn't manage on Marcelle's money.

The Ibanez household began this new undertaking by obtaining a bank loan to purchase the additional 3 hectares of vines that now make up their holding.

While Jacques worked as a vine worker, all the large machinery used on his small holding was borrowed from his employer. Now that he had been laid off, he no longer had access to his employer's equipment. Instead the family relied on equipment provided by friends and neighbors. At the moment, the Ibanez household did not own a tractor. Though indispensable for viticulture, it also represented the largest, most expensive piece of machinery used. Jacques was able to get by through borrowing tractors from several friends. He intended to buy a used tractor as soon as he could afford to do so. In exchange for this favor, Jacques offered to help out on his friends' holdings. As his holding was relatively small, it did not at the moment absorb all his working hours. So during the busy periods of the year, Jacques repaid these favors by helping in the harvest, pruning, uprooting vines, and spreading fertilizer.

The friends from whom Jacques borrows equipment included several households, who ran fairly large farms that required extra labor from time to time—the Mas household, the Rey household, and the Seignol household. The Rey's operated a holding of about 28 hectares of which 10 were rented. The Mas's were discussed earlier. The Seignol vineyards were about 10 hectares in size and 4 of these were rented. Each of these household enterprises for different reasons and in different periods experienced labor shortages and called on Jacques among members of other households that made up a loose network of exchange partners, which as I discussed in chapter 2, often coalesced in groups of political activists.

Negotiating Networks

In the particular network in which Jacques participated, the members of each of the households all claimed to be friends and had several features in common. The experience of work for each of the men in the households followed a similar pattern. It included a phase of work as a day laborer, followed by independent proprietorship and work as full-time wine growers. The experience of the women of the households included periods wage work combined with domestic work, as well as work in the fields. Moreover, each of the enterprises, started out as a fairly minute vineyard and through a variety of means, each household managed to put together a workable full-time unit of production. This was accomplished through such varied means as inheritances from the husband and the wife's side of the family; land purchased through bank loans, share tenancy, as well as savings from wives' earnings.

Moreover, aside from the common work histories and the trajectories of development of each of the enterprises, members of each household had consistently participated, though at different times, in a number of village organizations—the cooperative administrative council, the municipal council, the commissions of the municipal council, rugby association, as well as the boules club. The most striking attribute of each of these households, however, was that they were all members of Mouvement pour la Défense de l'Exploitation Familiale (Movement for the Defense of the Family Farm) (MODEF)—the farmers union that was devoted to the defense of the specific interests of family farmers in France. Furthermore, all the men of the households were members of the Communist Party, the political party that supported MODEF (see chapter 2). Shared interests and commitments as demonstrated by the participation of these households in local associations were important in binding households together in reciprocal exchange networks. The basis on which many such groups were united in the nonmonetary exchange of human labor and material resources involved participation in common in the "modern" institutions of political parties, unions, and also variety of state-sponsored organizations. In this respect such "modernist" avenues of association then facilitated the mobilization of interpersonal or "traditional" relations for the "antimodernist" struggle that groups of Occitan guerrillas in which Roger and his friends were involved (see Introduction).

The Coownership of Equipment

Following a strategy of cost minimization in production also brought members into other forms of cooperation between households. The coownership of machinery and other smaller pieces of equipment was frequently practiced especially among the very small household units production. It allowed producers to minimize expenditures on both the purchase and rental of equipment. On the enterprise of the Gizard family, for example, almost all pieces of equipment were coowned. While they owned one truck, they shared a tractor with one other household. The Gizards also coowned a fertilizer spreader and a pulverizer with two other households. They jointly owned an augur with seven other households. Pascal Gizard had been the mayor of Broussan since 1974 and professed to be completely committed to the principle of cooperation. He stressed: "Cooperation is the only way, we wine growers can hope to survive." As the long time mayor of Broussan, the way he ran his own enterprise was meant to serve as a model for cooperative practices in the village and to spearhead cooperative ventures in Broussan. Moreover, it was a concrete manifestation of his devotion to the principle of cooperation and also of his politics as a member of the Communist party, which privileged the collective over the individual.

The cooperative network in which Pascal participated like the network in which the Ibanez household was involved, included households which belonged to MODEF among other village associations. The Gizard household jointly owned a tractor with the Terray household. The Terray household ran a holding of 9 hectares and Pascal, the male head of the household, had been a long-time member of MODEF, the Communist party, and sat on the municipal council for one term. Marc Terray was also involved in helping out at the agricultural supply cooperative, on a voluntary basis.

The coownership of machinery and other equipment was also practiced widely among very small growers who also worked as agricultural laborers. On a number of such enterprises, all the equipment used was either coowned or borrowed. For example, in the Dupré household which operated a holding of 2 hectares, every piece of equipment was either coowned or borrowed. Their tractor, rototiller, spraying machines, and tips were all jointly owned with several friends, who all belonged the Confédération Général des Travailleurs (CGT), the national workers' union. The Duprés also borrowed some equipment from Château X, where the son worked as a day laborer.

The coownership of machinery could only be undertaken within the class of petty commodity producers. All instances of equipment coproprietorship were found to exist amongst the households of small holders, only, that was to say among units of production that were structurally similar, the one to the other. The coownership of equipment and machinery was seldom practiced in interclass exchanges between landowners and laborers. Equipment that was used most infrequently in vineyard work, such as fertilizer spreaders, manual herbicide sprayers, rotatillers, tips, augurs, and a variety of small tools such as pruning shears were the kinds of items that was most frequently owned in common. Tractors tend to be coowned less frequently since they were more or less in constant use. However, among the smallest petty commodity enterprises, joint ownership of this item did indeed occur, since no one enterprise needed the tractor consistently on a daily basis.

Coalitions of households that owned equipment in common were formed usually on an ad hoc basis, according to the needs of individual households. Enquiries tended to be made among relatives and associates on village committees in order to search for parties interested in such an arrangement. Monetary resources were pooled among the households for the purchase of items and if sufficient capital was lacking, one of the households arranged credit through the local bank and made payments on behalf of the others members of the network. The networks, however, were in a continuous state of flux and, in fact, dissolved frequently. Problems that lead to their dissolution revolved primarily among machinery maintenance and access. When coalitions became too large and equipment became damaged or when it became too difficult to coordinate access, households hived off and either made financial arrangements to buy their own equipment or other coalitions were formed.

Equipment Loans: Interclass Exchanges

While the joint ownership of equipment represents an example of intraclass exchanges, nonmonetary reciprocal exchanges often also took place between landowners and day laborers who operated their own small vineyards. These exchanges mainly included loans of large equipment and agricultural implements. Such loans were made on weekends and at the end of the day, when the equipment belonging to the landowners was not in use. The example of the Duprés, a pluriactive household, illustrates several of the ways in which interclass exchanges took place. Florence Dupré a store clerk described how she and her husband, Richard, an agricultural laborer, managed to run their holding and buy a house with the help of Richard's employer:

> We run very small holding of just over 1 hectare in size. Richard is employed full-time by Max Théron who owns a holding of about 19 hectares. Until two years ago, we lived rent-free in a house owned by Richard's employer. This house was offered to us to entice Richard away from working for another landowner in the village.[4] In 1955, after we were married, he accepted the offer and began to work on the Théron enterprise. We now own a home in the new low-cost housing development on the outskirts of the village. It is only with the savings made possible by having a rent-free apartment that we were able to place a down payment on a building site and, eventually, to construct our new house.
>
> We manage to run our very small holding with little agricultural equipment. We only have a couple of hand-operated sprayers. All our other equipment from the tractor to the tip used in the harvest is borrowed from Richard's employer, Max Théron.

Without such equipment loans, the Duprés would have had great difficulty in keeping the small vineyard in operation. Their holding was so tiny that it did not warrant expenditures on a tractor or other pieces of large equipment. However, with the patronage of his employer combined with their pluriactive pursuits, they hoped to able to expand the family holding, bit by bit.

Patrons and Clients

While the such ties of patronage served as a very important means for the reproduction of petty commodity enterprises, the patron-client relations were, in fact rather diffuse and weak in this context, little resembling the more systematic forms of patronage found in other Mediterranean societies (see Silverman 1965; Weingrod 1968; Littlewood 1980). While patron-client relations in Broussan emphasized social hierarchy and power differentials between in the landowner and laborer relationship, the patron seldom necessarily maintained a position of formal power by acting as a mediator between the local population and the state. In contemporary Broussan landowner-employers did not play a significant role as mediators between laborers and the state, neither politically nor economically as did in an earlier era. The community was highly integrated into the state apparatus and the state itself did not appear to represent an unfathomable or necessarily alien structure to the members of local populations.[5] Most villagers, unlike their predecessors, therefore, neither relied on large landowners to deal with the state nor to market their products that since the 1960s has been done through the cooperative (see chapter 7). Moreover, these exchanges were seldom undertaken in order to mobilize a following in local-level politics (cf Bailey 1969), since small landowners themselves did not appear to dominate municipal politics and seemed to wield as little or as much power in the village as other members of the population.

Still, there was a clear hierarchy based on wealth differences between landowner and laborer and employers did profit from extraction of surplus value from the laborer. However, the perception of exploitation in these relations was to some extent limited by several factors. To begin with, the differences between such social classes were attenuated since they shared interests as wine growers or aspiring independent wine growers. Also, by and large, such wealth differentials in most cases were not great. Moreover, agricultural wage work often represented a phase in the work history of many landowners and many of the small landowners in Broussan had children who still labored on the estates and class distinctions were in many cases seen as temporary. Finally, many of the landowners who operated their enterprises using day laborers, also made a direct contribution of their labor to the cultivation of vines and, often, working alongside the laborer, doing exactly the same tasks. To some degree, these reinforced the sense of association between the employer and the employee, concealing the economic relationship that bound them together. The close degree of identity between the village landowners and laborers also mitigated against placing landowners at the apex of a power hierarchy in the village.

In some cases, even in which the employer made no contribution of labor to the land, practice of lending equipment to laborers is, nonetheless, followed. This was done for a variety of reasons. Generally, the lending of agricultural equipment by landowners, as an act of patronage contributes to the definition of owners as decent and good members of the community. The prevalence of loans of agricultural equipment to laborers was well as other acts of patronage represented a payment of what G. Smith (1989) has referred to as "social rent"—a performance to demonstrate the rightfulness of one's inclusion as a member of the community, that is to be defined as a "moral" person. The landowners of Broussan were subject to the strictures and sanctions of community life. As members of the community, their obligations involved extending various acts of goodwill toward their employees. On the one hand, these social performances were important to uphold where personalistic and face-to-face interactions prevailed in both work and living contexts. On the other hand, on enterprises even where the wage relation predominates, landowners had to use various nonmonetary or extra-economic means to secure labor and to guarantee the continuity of the enterprise. It also ensured the compliance, loyalty, and efficiency of day laborers. Edmond S., the owner of Château X, continually lent his machinery to the day laborers that work his vineyards. Though, Edmond was less bound by the moral strictures of community life, living both geographically and socially outside the village and somewhat beyond the reach of communal sanction, he still consistently offered his equipment to village day laborers. It was evident to the workers, why this was done. One of the day laborers who worked at Château X commented:

> First of all, when you rely on the boss for his machinery to run your farm, it ties the worker to the employer. It prevents all important social movements such as strikes from taking place. The worker obviously can't borrow this equipment to work on his own vineyard if he was in the middle of a strike. So, while you're busy striking and losing pay, you're vines were also dying.

Thus through such acts, the employer at the château, was able to secure a dependent and reliable workforce, offsetting threats to production on the estate. It was also commonly acknowledged that among some of the smaller landowners, loans of equipment were undertaken to secure the compliance of workers. A day laborer who works for one of the smaller landowners commented along lines similar to the statements made by the estate worker:

If the day laborer relies on his boss' equipment to keep his own vineyard going, then you can't go on strike. When you go on strike, or something like that, of course, your boss isn't going to lend you his equipment. So you not only lose your wages but you lose money because your vines start to die. No worker was going to risk that.

Patron-client ties whether seen as extra-economic means for the coercion workers, or a economic tie that benefited both laborers and landowner, were absent on the impersonal capitalist estates that were owned either by an absentee owners or by a company or a bank, and run by a steward. Loans of agricultural implements to the day laborers who work on these estates was not practiced in what was an impersonal employer-employee relationship, divested of the strictures of community obligation.

The Politics of Performance

Each of the examples discussed illustrates as how social relations bind together apparently different households in a series of exchanges. Both direct and less direct kin ties, as well as associational ties link households together into coalitions involved in intersecting exchange networks. The examples also illustrate how households were often neither coterminous with the family nor with the enterprise. While the household is a unit of production and consumption in family farming, the boundaries of that unit are loose and permeable to chains of interpersonal relationships that between different domestic groups and enterprises. These examples, then caution against conceptualizing households as marked by a boundary that separate the domain of market ties from the domain of non-market ties.[6]

Households in Broussan then were bound together in reciprocal relations on the basis of *"l'amitié"* or *"le voisinage."* As shown in several of the examples, one of the important means through which a friend or a neighbor is defined involves participation in political parties and community organizations. While the coalitions of households were very loose and being formed on an ad hoc basis, these networks were often not randomly tied together by relations of amity. In the example of the mutual help network of Ibanez household, the three constituent families were all members of the Communist party and of an organization that aimed to defend the interests of the small-family farmers in

France, MODEF. Michel Sillon, the handicapped wine grower, was helped by Marcel Mas, both of whom were also members of the Communist party of France and MODEF. Both men had been long involved in a number of village councils concerned with administering the municipality to administering the cooperative. Marcel was actively involved in coaching the village rugby team (*le sport du pays d'Oc*), the national sport of the land of Oc, and in organizing the village band. Political parties, family farmers', unions sport associations, however, different in orientation and thrust, nonetheless have in common a concern to keeping community life vital and the local economy of family viticulture viable. The participation of community members in these organizations represented a public demonstration of these commitments.

Calculation and Equivalence

From the cases discussed, it appears that not only was the mobilization of the unpaid labor of household members important, but the mobilization of unpaid labor and reciprocal relations between households played a critical role in the reproduction of the petty commodity enterprise. Although the market has intruded in the domestic arena, the pervasiveness of market calculation and monetary ties outside the domestic sphere was limited. Relations between such petty commodity units of production in contemporary Broussan remained embedded in interpersonal ties. The status of individuals set limits on the extent to which market calculation is practiced in economic exchanges. Still the commodification effect influenced the ways in which reciprocal exchanges were executed. Exchanges of material resources and human labor between households involving nonmonetary exchanges were nonetheless subject to calculations based on a monetary model. For example, reciprocal exchanges took place on the basis of what might be called an idea of equivalence rather than on the basis of relative market price.[7] For example, the recipient of a donation of a day's worth of labor to spread fertilizer in the vineyards did not necessarily repay a neighbor through exchanges in kind—labor. But repayment might involve the substitution of involving the loan of a piece of equipment for labor. What was vital in the exchange of use values was that one item or service was seen as equivalent to another item or service irrespective of their varying market prices. Hence the exchange of unpaid labor, for example, took place on the basis of what was considered equivalent to that labor in terms of use value. Interpersonal relations of kinship and amity intervene to assure that whenever a good or service was exchanged, it was done so *below* the market price. Such exchanges reflected the specific status relationship between the parties concerned, while the market guides their calculations in so far as equivalence must always remain *below* that price, since the growers consistently followed a strategy of cost minimization. In these exchanges, the calculations of the amount of goods and services that flowed between households then involved an implicit reference to their price on the market.

Methods of reckoning equivalence involved a variety of calculations. For example, the parties to an exchange of labor often kept an account of hours worked and the number of times one individual may have worked for the other. If the exchange involved the performance of different tasks on different enterprises, some agreement was reached as to equivalence. Growers kept an account of the duration of a loan of a piece of equipment and the amount of time and effort saved by borrowing machinery to carry out a certain task that would otherwise have to be done with hand tools or by hiring someone. Clearly it was difficult to determine exact measure of equivalence, because of the variety of forms of exchange. Labor and machinery was often allocated to different tasks, carried out at different points in the seasonal cycle of work. The type of reckoning that requires measure for measure was not an altogether important aspect of the relations of exchange between households. Among friends, neighbors, and kin, some measure of what was considered to be equivalent was arrived at and if there was a disparity, the difference could be made up in another agreed fashion or in exceptional instances in cash. The substitution of cash for labor or a service in order to make up a disparity was regarded as undesirable for, as Marcel Mas pointed out, it breaches the morality of these ties:

> You need friends to survive these days and your friends need you. Of course many of us could afford to hire people to do all sorts of jobs in the fields but only those who have no friends and who don't help out other people have to resort to this. Also it isn't the most economical way of doing things. When you have to hire somebody you have to pay the going rate. It's the law of the market. But with friends even when you have to use money to make up the difference

sometimes, you pay less than the going rate. Also, you know that you could build up credit with your friends and they could build up credit with you, when there was a difference in how much you've done for them and they've done for you. You could repay them later by helping them out. If you have to hire somebody and you don't have the cash. You're out of luck.

Thus the market entered into numerous calculations in many of the exchanges and each participant gave and received. Such exchanges served to integrate households into the community in a context in which the market introduced forces of disintegration.

In the examples, I have emphasized that reciprocal practices prevail in both intraclass and interclass exchanges. In a context in which a community is significantly differentiated in terms of class, cooperative practices between households of different classes often disguise unequal relations. As I mentioned above, the language of community and kinship, interpersonal relations often intervened to envelope the idea of equivalence in a cloud of vagueness. This served often to disguise the unequal benefits that accrue to large and small producers in cooperative exchanges. For large farmers, cooperative practices acted as a means of securing labor from smaller growers. Cost minimization strategies often translated into forms of petty accumulation and exploitation, especially since definitions of equivalence were ill-defined. Nonetheless, the limits on exploitation are to some extent set by the market. Because all household participated in the market for labor, goods, and services, there was a high degree of familiarity with the market costs of production. The parameters of the market, ironically, guided participants in their reckoning of equivalence, potentially setting limits on the exploitative tendencies inherent in intraclass exchanges.

The Tradition of Invention

The social practices discussed play a critical role to in keeping petty commodity production viable under the vicissitudes of making a living in late capitalism. In the examples discussed, the practices of cooperation reflected contemporary responses to the conditions of making a living under contemporary capitalism. To characterize social relations unmediated by the market as ties of "tradition" or "precapitalism" inevitably evokes an image of practices from "the past." By interrogating the relations of production between households in Broussan, I have suggested that such elementary dichotomies between the past and the present, tradition and modernity cannot be upheld. Moreover, to cast such relations as "survivals" was to imply that they were out of step with the political and economic times. However, I have argued that it was precisely because these practices in Broussan met the demands of the times that makes them economically and culturally potent. Such ties of "tradition" then have been consciously maintained and deliberately reinvented as part of a political as well as economic strategy to resist the domination of the market. The form of that reciprocity implied some continuity with the past. However, the content of such exchanges have been consciously and collectively refashioned to meet the exigencies of the present. The petty commodity producers in Broussan, participated in a tradition of invention, in which they respond to the exigencies of novel situations through a creative reconstitution of the past.

CHAPTER 7

Harvesting Disenchantment:
Cooperatives, Control, and Alienation

The general spirit of the bureaucracy is the secret, the mystery preserved within itself by the hierarchy and against the outside world by being a closed corporation.

—Karl Marx, 1943

In the early 1900s, the convergence of the rise of socialist ideals and syndicalism combined with growing class antagonism in the Languedoc countryside spawned a tradition in which collective and direct social action came to be seen as a means of defending the powerless against the forces of the capitalist market.[1] Unions held sway among wine growers and agricultural laborers. While growers joined such unions as the Confédération Générale des Vignerons (General Confederation of Wine-growers) and many agricultural laborers joined the workers' union Confédération Générale des Travailleurs (General Confederation of Workers) to defend and negotiate remedies for problems such as wage levels and security of employment. Notions of forming unions to seek solutions to the problems faced by smallholders who were also agricultural laborers surfaced in a period that fostered an inclination to form collective associations in order to deal with the economic crises and new demands posed by the transition to monoculture. While a spirit of banding together prompted small-holders to organize autonomous mutual aid groups and collectives at the local level, they were also provoked to negotiate help from the state to form cooperatives to deal not only with problems of wine production, but also marketing and storing increasing quantities of wine. In previous chapters, I discussed a tradition of collectivism that prevailed among smallholders confronted with problems in vine cultivation; in this chapter, I examine how difficulties presented in the marketing and manufacture of wine were addressed through one form of collective organization—the

197

vinification cooperative. I argue that the cooperative that this institution, which was once heralded as a great collective solution to the many problems that growers faced in embarking on the production of wine as a commodity, ultimately became a mechanism that facilitated and extended state control over the lives of small growers, on the one hand, while fostering class differentiation, on the other. The cooperative in Broussan and (in Languedoc, general) which was rooted in the autonomist forms of collective organization represented a striking example of how those institutions and initiatives that become incorporated by the state are submitted to a process of growing bureaucratization. The expanding bureaucratic apparatus of the cooperative encouraged the alienation of people from the fruits of their labor by incarcerating power and knowledge within a hierarchical structure that extended from the local level to the state. As a consequence of the powerful role played by such an institution in local life, producers became alienated from the product and imprisoned by an institution that ultimately served the interests of the state. So while the emergence of the cooperative in Broussan succeeded in loosening the ties of dependency between land owners and laborers that incorporated laborers and smallholders into a hierarchical system of patronage that prevailed on the estates, the cooperative itself also became a means for the hierarchical integration of small growers into a state determined to realize its modernizing agenda. The power once held by landowners and the rural elite became transferred to an apparatus that facilitated the encroachment of the state onto the local level.

Small Growers and the Market

Small growers who, in many cases, were newly established wine growers in the early 1900s, generally faced three sets of problems once grapes were harvested (*la vendange*). First, small growers generally lacked the necessary equipment to vinify the larger harvests produced in monocultural viticulture. Second, the facilities to store increasing amounts of wine were on the whole inadequate. Most smallholders in the Lower Languedoc village possessed rudimentary equipment, such as, small presses, one or two tanks, and casks. With this basic equipment, growers could adequately vinify and store a small amount of wine but for domestic consumption only. However, with the increase in the number of hectares on each holding devoted to viticulture that accompanied the transition to commercial monoculture, the larger harvests produced required equipment that would not only vinify larger quantities, but also, in the least amount of time. Finally, as newly installed commodity producers, small growers lacked familiarity with commercial circuits, and therefore, experienced great difficulty in marketing wine produced.

Before the advent of cooperatives, small growers, tended to rely on several means to gain access to the necessary vinification equipment and storage. Through a system of patronage, day laborers working on the estates of the large landowners relied on maintaining good relations with their employers in the attempt to secure and maintain access to the equipment and facilities of the estate owner. Their own harvests were brought to the cellars of their employers and mixed with the harvests of the estate vineyards. While this arrangement ostensibly accommodated day laborers, landowners often abused their advantageous position vis-à-vis the dependent worker, in several ways. Landowners divided the receipts based on the amount of grapes brought to the estate by the day laborer to be vinified. But landowners usually subtracted a charge for the use of estate equipment and facilities from the receipts due to the day laborer. They often charged what was considered by the workers as very high fees for the use of their services and equipment. Moreover, as frequently no account was taken of the different varieties of grapes harvested or of the sugar content of the grapes, landowners could easily lower the amount due to day laborers. In fact, when the smallholder brought grapes grown on the family vineyard to the estate, control over the harvest was completely surrendered to the large landowner, who acted as the intermediary between producer and broker. As a result, the worker was often neither able to discuss the selling price of the wine with the broker nor choose the time of sale. The landowner, then, thoroughly dictated the terms of sale to the day laborer, when the harvest could be brought in and set the price that would be given to the day laborer irrespective of the market price (Molinier 1983, 10). These prices were usually set lower than the market price and landowners were thus able to speculate on the small harvests of the day laborers.

Sébastien Cabanel, whose father worked as a day laborer from the early 1900s until World War II, remarked that:

> the worker always lost in putting his wine in with that of
> his employer. At that time, workers had very little power

and were really exploited. When they suffered such abuses, they had no way of taking action. They were in no position to discuss this with their employers for fear of creating bad relations with someone who could provide them with the services they needed for the next year's harvest.

Under the system of patronage on Languedoc estates, power was still embodied in and personified by landowners and it was expressed through the control over the marketing of their clients' products.

Developing absenteeism on the estates however exacerbated the difficulties encountered by smallholders and day laborers in gaining access to equipment and storage facilities. As the transformation of large farms into commercial capitalist estates progressed over the late 1800s and early 1900s, large landowners began to establish residences in commercial and financial centers of the region. As a result the system of patronage on the estates became eroded since it depended on the maintenance of personal ties. Large landowners who once formed the rural elite of Languedoc villages, abandoned their role in the community political structure in favor of pursuing investments and profits in regional commercial centres, leaving the management of their estates to stewards. Community sanctions and obligations left little impact on the stewards, who were simply hired by estate owners to run the enterprise. The depersonalization of relations between large landowners and agricultural workers on the estates thus deprived small growers of the services and equipment to which they once had access.

One solution that emerged endogenously to the problem of the lack of access to equipment and storage facilities emerged in the void created by decline of the patronage system in Broussan. Village smallholders banded together to share and pool resources among households. What vinification equipment was available came to be shared among households. Those who had no equipment helped to manufacture the wine for those who had in exchange for the use of equipment. Small producers pooled monetary resources and labor to construct tanks in tiny cellars that had been used once as animal sheds. Agnès Peyre, a former vine worker described the system of exchanges that took place before the advent of the cooperative:

> In the old days, those who didn't have a wine press went over to help a friend who did. We helped do the job of putting up the wine press and pressing grapes. This was a job

that took several hours to complete and was usually done at night, after supper. It required at least five people to do. One person went into the tank and using a large fork, threw the "marc" (the peels, pips, and stems of the grape) toward the lower trap door. Another person takes the marc and fills a *comporte* with it (a wooden tank of about 75 liters with two handles). Two people then carried the tank and emptied the marc onto the press. The last person climbed onto the heap. The hardest job of all was in the tank where the person was subjected to the heat from the fermenting grapes and breathing in the gases. The job that required the most skill was pressing because if it was not done properly the pile came to be too compressed and the marc was not pressed. In exchange for this help in pressing grapes, the owner lent his pressor to those who helped him.

These autonomous and endogenous forms of mutual aid and organization also facilitated the way for the development of larger forms of cooperation, since organizing institutions of cooperation and collectivity were a familiar response to crises and need. Prior to the development of cooperatives, then small growers and vine workers experienced a number of handicaps not only in vinifying their small harvest but also in storing and marketing wine. The lack of storage facilities meant that stocks of wine could not be amassed and kept in order to be sold over a period of time but whatever was produced in a given year had to be sold immediately. In other words, small wine growers were neither able to spread out the sales of the product nor distribute their income evenly over the year. Wine had to be sold quickly for fear of spoilage. The problem of spoilage was further exacerbated by poor vinification facilities and the unsanitary conditions under which wine was prepared and stored. While this was due in part to limitations of equipment, it was also due to the lack of familiarity with oenological techniques.

Merchants and Brokers

Recognizing the vulnerable position of the small grower in the market, wine merchants and brokers took advantage the need for small growers to sell their product quickly. They offered the lowest prices possible, also arguing that they were purchasing an inferior product. Small growers were obliged to accept the offers made by merchants, since at the end of the harvest their financial reserves were severely diminished by expenditures made for extra labor during the harvest, needed for a variety of inputs and for treatments for the vines. For these reasons, wine traders were considered by petty producers, as the arch-exploiter of those who made their living by growing vines. Traders were seen as even more exploitative than large owners, as they were interested only in making the largest of profits entirely at the expense of the petty producer (Pech 1975, 473–74). The traders rarely dealt directly with the producers, themselves. They were represented in the villages by a broker, who was usually a fellow villager in need of an additional income.

Brokers, were usually marginal members of the community or those who did not get on well with other people in the village. Brokers were expected to know all petty producers and to gather information about who made the best wines in the village. They were also expected to be familiar with the financial situation of as many petty producers as possible. As the agent of a trader, he was expected to get the best deals for his employer. As an intermediary, he rarely disclosed the name of the merchant to whom the producers sold their wine, thus ensuring the complete dependence of the small grower on the broker. This also acted to ensure that small growers would remain unfamiliar with marketing networks. The tactics used by brokers to compel producers to sell at low prices involved a series of underhanded actions. They often scared them with the possibility of a stagnant wine market, while predicting an overabundant harvest. Brokers also persuaded growers to sell at low prices by encouraging them to believe that there was dearth of buyers precisely at the moment when producers had exhausted their financial resources (Pech 1975, 478). In this way they profited by the fears generated by competition in the market. The formation of cooperatives by groups of growers, then began to emerge as an attempt to combat the effects of market crises and to solve the more mundane problems of yearly production faced by the small growers.

Waves of Socialism

Cooperatives throughout the wine-growing region of southern France are considered the offspring of a general movement for cooperation and unionism that emerged in the early 1900s (Yoon 1975, Pastor-Barrué 1981). In Languedoc efforts to establish cooperatives were initiated under two waves of socialism. The first wave occurred in the aftermath of 1907. Then, collective ideals and social action fueled a concern to address the individual problems faced by the small grower in the market and the antagonisms that had developed between classes in Languedoc villages, sharpened by the differential impact of the crisis in the early twentieth century on large landowners and smallholding enterprises. However, very few cooperatives actually appeared in the region before the 1920s. This was due to several factors. Cooperatives could only be established through state subsidies and loans. However, the deteriorating the economic conditions under which many small growers produced their vines in the slump of the early 1900s prohibited them from taking advantage of state subsidies and loans to mount cooperatives. Growers who had been ruined by or weakened by eight years of market slumps, were reluctant to contract loans and mortgage their already uncertain future to the banks. Despite the law of 29 December 1906, guaranteeing long-term credit for the establishment of cooperatives, only 19 were formed before 1914 in the entire region of Languedoc-Roussillon. However, they came to be more widespread between 1931 and 1939, under socialism's second wave in France, as growers desperately sought means of protection from a further slump after a period of economic recovery in the 1920s. The vinification cooperative in Broussan was founded amidst these conditions of economic crisis.

While growers actively sought to establish cooperatives, the state saw cooperatives as a means for realizing its own agenda. It sought to increase its control and intensify the means for regulating the market for wine. Cooperatives would serve as the mechanism that would accomplish this end. Through the cooperatives, therefore, the state would be able to implement some of the measures outlined in the Statut Viticole of 1935.[2] The Popular Front government thus increased state aid to help in the formation of cooperatives, advancing 25 percent of the amount of money necessary for constructing a cooperative. Loans over 20 years at 3 percent interest were provided as teams of rural engineers were sent out to the region to help plan and construct the cooperative building. The state's effort to regulate the market through its subsidy program, then, greatly accelerated the process of cooperative formation and in the 1930s there was a rush in Languedoc villages to establish these organizations (Pech 1975, 481–82). The cooperative of Broussan was formed in 1938 under the system of incentives through subsidies offered by the state. While on the one hand, it was seen as an institution that emerged from a tradition of collectivism, on the other hand, it was experienced as an instrument that facilitated state control over their lives. Because of its rather mixed origins the small farmers of Broussan expressed profound ambivalence to it and regarded it with a mixture of pride and disenchantment.

The Cooperative in Broussan

The initiative for the creation of a cooperative in Broussan was taken up amid much antagonism to the whole principle of cooperation. The opposition came from large growers and small independent producers alike. Small growers in many villages abhorred the thought of mixing their grapes with the grapes of others: "Mix the wine from my vines with the wine from vines of my neighbor—what sacrilege!" (Molinier 1983, 23). This view was informed by the belief that neighbors' vines were doubtlessly inferior to one's own. Opposition also came from large growers, brokers, and merchants who feared that their monopolistic position would be undermined and their bargaining power reduced as prices would become fixed.

During the mid-1930s, appeals to the villagers to form cooperatives were made on many grounds apart from the purely practical advantages cooperatives offered in resolving the problems faced by growers after the harvest. The possibility of realizing socialist ideals presented itself at the time with the newly elected government of the Popular Front, under the presidency of Léon Blum. Sébastien Cabanel commented on the attitudes prevailing in the village during this second wave of socialism, which ushered in a left government:

> The victory of the left in the elections really gave rise to a new state of mind to people in the village. For the first time in France there was a government made up of a majority of the left and all state organizations favored the development of cooperatives. Finally there was the possibility that the problems faced by workers and small growers in making wine were going to be dealt with. This political climate made people take the initiative to group together to find a collective solution to their individual problems.

The first experiments in cooperation that were tied to efforts at forming unions in the countryside in the early 1900s under the influence of the first wave of socialism in the region and succeeded in bestowing to the small grower the ideals of solidarity in the face of adversity and throwing their lot in with the effort to form cooperatives. The idea became prevalent that "Instead of each person for himself and God for everyone, the principle became all for one and one for all."[3] The cooperative came to represent an institution that would ideally stand for the autonomy of petty producers, loosening the grip of the relations of dependence between landowner and laborer and exploitation by brokers and middlemen. The manifest objective of the cooperative was not to accumulate profit, but to share receipts uniformly among it adherents, who represented the weakest in the community. The smallest growers in the village would thus be placed in a position of greater strength. All these appeals to the idea of the collective were presented in terms of a coherent ideology, but they were also translated in fact into practical advantages such as the reduction of the physical hardship and worry at the end of the harvest and the improvement of the quality of the wines produced. The notion of cooperation and mutual aid translated into lower costs of production for each grower. The collective ownership of equipment meant that purchases could be made of the most efficient vinification materials and storage facilities, ensuring against the risk of spoilage (Molinier 1983, 17–18).

A number of small and medium producers grouped themselves by agreeing to place a portion of their harvest into the cooperative in order to provide enough hectoliters to qualify for the state subsidies required for its creation. In 1938, there were 134 members who provided about 1,194 tons of grapes, vinifying 7,780 hectoliters of wine. This represented roughly 6 percent of the total for the village in that year. Some 50 years later, there were roughly 540 members of the cooperative and it vinified approximately 116,500 hectoliters of wine or 66 percent of the total harvest in the area. Only about 40-odd wine growers did not belong to the cooperative. This group was mainly made up of the very small growers and large owners.

At its inception and for several decades later, the cooperative restricted itself to gathering the harvest of its members for vinification only, while the sale of the wines rested with each individual member. In 1962, however, the cooperative took on the task of selling wine in common. The sale of wine in common remained an option until 1964, when it became obligatory for all members.

Cooperation in Principle

The ideals of cooperation came to be underwritten by several principles that appeared in the legislation on cooperation, for example, in the law of 10 September 1947. The first principle of cooperation set out an "open door" policy in which membership to the cooperative was unrestricted. Second, the general democratic principle of "one person, one voice" appeared also in the legislation and the statutes of the cooperative. All cooperators, irrespective of the amount of capital brought to the cooperative, exercise an equal right in matters concerning the cooperative. The third principle guaranteed a just price to each member, with any profit generated above this price shared among members. The whole notion of profits was replaced by the notion of service to its members. Finally, cooperatives were to follow a principle of economic progress at the lowest cost to members (Molinier 1983, 19–20; Pastor-Barrué 1981, 226). These principles were formulated on the basis that wine growers consisted of a homogenous group, with common and unitary interests. Yet it was precisely because the cooperative operated on the principle of the homogeneity of classes in a class-divided context that led some villagers to criticize the institution for its bureaucratic constitution that served not only the interest of the state, but also as body that tacitly supported the interests of large growers against the small. Moreover, the bureaucratization of this institution was reinforced by its embeddedness in a capitalist market. Despite, the professed commitment to service above the notion of profit, the continuity of the cooperative in a competitive market relied to a large extent on its ability to operate along capitalist lines. It was imperative to generate profits for reinvestment in the means of production, in equipment and land. While, ideologically all such profits "belonged" to the members at large, control over those profits rested in the hands of the administrative council, whose members were considered as servants to the state bureaucracy, despite, the fact that it consist of men elected by the cooperators.

The Bureaucratic Apparatus

The administrative organization of the cooperative consisted of a General Assembly of all cooperators, which met once a year to select the administrative council. The president of the cooperative was elected by the council, who consulted with the director who was paid by the state, out of the general funds of the cooperative. The cooperative secretary was also paid by the state to assist the director and the council. These positions were appointed by the administrative council. The paid director was considered the manager of the cooperative, while administrative council was seen as the general body responsible for the management of the cooperative. The administrative council met regularly, usually once a month, and made decisions governing all aspects of the cooperative, including investments, loans, equipment purchases, and the implementation of policies. As the general assembly convened only once a year, many of the cooperators were seldom aware of the major decisions that the council and the director have undertaken and of the nature of the state policies that have channeled through the cooperative. While the director was charged with keeping members in touch with these decisions, there tended to be no formal means by which members were informed on a regular basis of cooperative affairs. Also, few growers seemed to seek out this information, except at the annual meeting. For these reasons, the meeting of the general assembly often erupted into arguments and accusations that the administrative council seldom consulted the membership-at-large over, decisions which governed their livelihood. The administrative council was seen to monopolise knowledge and control the dissemination of information through its commissions.

Mandatory sale in common alleviated the competition between producers, who prior to this, were responsible individually for the sale of their product, once it had been vinified by the cooperative. Before sale in common, growers would rush and gather at the cooperative after the wine was vinified or even before the harvest was brought in to wait for offers made by the brokers. Offers to purchase certain quantities of wine at a certain price were made by brokers at the cooperative, itself, not directly to each cooperator. Interested producers would register at the cooperative to sell their product for the advertised price. Taking advantage of the fears harbored by each producer that the product on his or her own enterprises would not be sold and that other growers would be quicker to accept the offers, brokers offered the lowest possible prices. The merchant would then appear at the cooperative to claim amount of wine bought and to pay the producer. Mandatory sale in common, in which the cooperative represented all members of the cooperative, allowed the growers to enjoy better terms of trade. It reduced the fears generated by a process in which each had to confront the market, individually, with the hope that the sale of its products would not be preempted by contracts made between traders and other households. The development of a marketing commission and sale in common, reduced competition between producers in the sale of wine. However, that competition came to be channeled in other directions provoked through the state policies that were implemented through the cooperative.

The Commercialization of the Cooperative Wine

The cooperative produced three types of wine—red, white, and rosé, which are classified into VDQS, Vin de Pays, or VCC.[4] Vin Délimité de Qualité Supérieur (VDQS) wines are those that yield approximately 50 hectoliters per hectare and have an alcoholic content of 11 percent to 13 percent. These were sold either in bulk (unbottled) to large wine merchant distributors, in a long commercial circuit, or in a shorter circuit, in which the cooperative sold directly to centers of consumption, such as restaurants and retail outlets. In the longer commercial circuit many intermediaries formed links in the chain between producer and consumer, each claiming its share of the product.

The Vin de Pays class of wine first appeared as a designation in 1974. These are of an intermediate quality between inferior VCC (Vin de Consommation Courante) and superior *VDQS*. There were fewer constraints on the production of these wines. For example, the maximum yield for this category is relatively high, set at 100 hectoliters per hectare. Merchants usually buy this in bulk from the cooperative and bottle the product and often it will be sold to consumers in bottles with a local label and personalized label in order to enhance its value to the consumer. Most of the wine in the cooperative is sold in bulk as VCC without any label to the distributors and a very small amount is marketed directly under the local label. Broussan did not produce AOC wine.

Before the 1960, there were two types of wine merchants in the longer commercial circuit. First, there were the shippers who bought the wine from the cooperative, and cut the wine usually with imported wines and then transported it. The second type of merchants were the distributors. Distributors were responsible for the bottling and the distribution of the final product to retailers.

After the 1960s this circuit came to be modified as large businesses began to assume both the shipping and distribution function and the large chain retail stores also began to take on the function of distribution as well as retail. A series of intermediaries virtually disappeared after the development of common sale and sale by contracts. Also, the cooperative itself has taken on a brokerage function. These two developments have allowed a more direct link between the cooperative and the consumer by eliminating brokers and shippers. At the same time, new types of trading enterprise have emerged to maintain direct links with the cooperative. They exert considerable influence in the production of wines since their knowledge of the market and consumer patterns aids in directing production according to demand for certain types of products. These businesses bottle wine and supply the large retail outlets such as supermarket chains. The shortening of the commercial circuit benefited both the new trading enterprises and the cooperative who share between them the profits that would have otherwise been taken by the shippers and distributors. There has thus been a simplification of the circuit, primarily due to the process of concentration in the commercial sphere, as the number of traders has declined with the growth in scale of commercial units. A tendency toward integration has also occurred, as these large trading enterprises have become multifunctional. These businesses were also often involved in the trade in other products (Puijk and Vaagland 1983, 65–66; Boulet 1976).[5] The impact of these developments was to link producer to consumer more directly and to reduce the dependence and subordination of producers to a specific chain of commercial intermediaries. Prior to this, for example, the bankruptcy of a merchant who dealt with a particular cooperative meant disaster to the cooperative, itself. Not only would the establishment of a new chain of intermediaries be required, but there was no recourse to obtaining reimbursement for payments already made to the merchant. As Pastor-Barrué remarks, under these circumstances: "The growers always suffer the consequences where bankruptcies are regulated in court of commerce (who are made up of a number of representatives of trade) not a civil court" (Pastor-Barrué 1981, 250).

In an even shorter circuit, wine was also sold by the cooperative directly to the centers of consumption. It was sold directly to the consumer at the cooperative itself, by taking orders through correspondence and at fairs. The amount of wine sold in this manner was relatively small. This mode of sale was undertaken by employees of the cooperative and by volunteers. The volunteers were recruited from among the cooperators but few were eager to take on this responsibility as it often takes producers to quite distant commercial centers in order to advertise the wine produced in the locality. This method of marketing wine ensured the maximum return to the producer as it effectively bypassed the intermediaries in the commercial network.

The Noncooperators

There were approximately 40 growers in Broussan who did not belong to the cooperative. They consisted of a rather heterogenous group. On the one hand, there were the large private wineries in the community whose enterprises do very well without belonging to the cooperative. Indeed, the reputation of Château X to a large extent rests on staying outside the cooperative circle. The château wine was marketed as a product having a higher and more distinctive quality than the wine produced in the village cooperative. On the other hand, there were small producers who do not produce enough wine to pay the membership fee in the cooperative, which was approximately 4,000 francs (about $900) or the equivalent in hectoliters of wine. There were very few of these growers, the noncooperators were mainly the large landowners of the locality.

Edmond S., the owner of the château, contrasted the conditions of his estate with those on his neighbors' farms in the village and revealed a highly individualistic attitude toward viticulture:

> The future of wine-growing in France is very bad except in some areas such as the Cognac Region, Armagnac region, and here, at Château X. While I agree that the state should help the smaller wine growers to try to survive the crisis, I am not affected by it, nor am I really worried about it. All I care about is that X survives and so far it has been doing exceptionally well. I am only interested in finding my own solution to the problem. Part of the problem lies in the fact my neighbors do not know how to make wine. You can't make wine in a huge cooperative, using such vast quantities and expect it to taste any good. Quality is the only thing that sells and you can't convince my neighbors of that. They have an archaic view of the market and poor old-fashioned equipment. Moreover, most people who take up wine grow-

ing today are people who can't get work doing anything else. They are urban rejects. These people don't know how to produce wine, let alone use the latest equipment. They may become obsolete as wine growers, but X will survive. It produces the best wine in the area and has a good international reputation. People from all over Europe come to buy my wine and I exercise strict controls on how vines are grown and how wine is made.

S.'s operation, for example, produced several types of wine under each classification and the best wine produced on his domain has earned the designation "Appellation d'Origine Contrôlée," and was marketed as a château wine.

In contrast to S.'s operation, the smaller private wineries used capital to a large extent for the maintenance of machinery and equipment rather than make investments in the most recent innovations. The equipment and storage facilities of these growers were often inferior to those in the cooperative and their efforts to improve the quality of the wine produced by planting new varieties of vines was costly, as they were not entitled to the subsidies that were restricted to cooperative members. Many of these growers who were once politically opposed to the concept and principles of cooperation, have been driven by economic necessity to join the cooperative. Eduard Mathe, for example, the owner of a 30-hectare farm, joined the cooperative after many years of showing little interest as he had marketed his wine privately for decades. Several members of the village regarded this as an act of pure economic self-interest as he bided his time until it was demonstrated that the cooperative could survive and prosper, before he, himself, became a member.

Private wineries sold their wine mostly in bulk to merchants. While the largest wineries bottle and label their own wine, those financially unable to undertake the bottling of their own product, sell wine in bulk along with the label to merchants. Small private wineries, which experience more difficulties in selling their wine often sell entirely in bulk to merchants through the few local brokers who remain in business.

Direct sale was also undertaken to some extent by some of the large private wineries who bottle and label their own wine. Selling wine in this way has transformed the owners of large estates into merchants and retailers in international and national fairs and markets. Another method of marketing wine produced on private wineries was through the conferring of wine to representatives who were hired on a commission basis to sell the product.

Not only were good commercial links important to cultivate for private wineries, but it is also important to establish a faithful clientele through good public relations. The operation of private wineries requires substantial financial reserves which only the largest holdings in the community have. According to Pastor-Barrué (1981, 256), one of the major advantages in the way in which wine is marketed by the large private wineries is that the growers and owners of large estates can follow the trajectory of the wine from the point of production directly to the point of consumption. This enables not only the supervision and control of the product at every point along the circuit but a larger degree of familiarity with the entire marketing network. The major disadvantages were the difficulties that were attendant on the individual entry into the market and also undertaking both the production and commercialization functions. The cooperative, while overcoming some of the problems in vinification and the marketing of wine, acted as a barrier between producer and consumer.

As the cooperative was charged with the sale of most village wine, dealing directly with brokers and traders, the growers, themselves were seldom aware of the ultimate destination of their product or of the complexity of the circuits of exchange into which their product enters. The family farmers who belonged to the cooperative entered the market in direct competition with some of the village private wineries. To some extent the market for the wines of the region was divided between the market for industrial alcohol and the beverage market. There were few private wineries in the village that resembled Château X either in scale or in the quality of the wine manufactured, and most of the château wine was sold on the beverage market. In contrast, the wine manufactured both in the smaller private village wineries and in the cooperative was sold in part on the market for industrial alcohol and, in part, on the beverage market. A portion of the wine sold on the beverage market appeared as wine from the cooperative of Broussan, but for the most part it was used to cut wine made in other regions of France.

The commissions and the administration of the cooperative were not only responsible for overseeing the different operations undertaken by the cooperative, but they also were the primary agents at the local level charged with the implementation of the state's policy of improving the quality of the wines produced and rationalizing the production process in the region. This policy influenced not only how vines themselves were grown in the fields, but entire cycle of viticulture, from the planting of the vines to the vinification process, itself.[6]

The Long Arm of the State

The overarching objective of the policies that governed the production of Languedoc wine was to manufacture a higher-grade product that would compete effectively on the national and the international markets, while eliminating crises of overproduction. This involved initiatives to encourage the production of higher grade wines and to prevent the glutting the market with vast quantities of low-grade wines. These have been the policy motives behind a series of state interventions in the wine-growing economy of the region. The first systematic intervention in the wine market was the implementation of the wine law of 1935, mentioned earlier, in which the distillation of surplus on the market was made mandatory and blockages were put into effect (Pech 1975, 481). This intervention occurred in period in which cooperatives were being established on a grand scale in the region. The most significant measures taken since the war however occurred in three phases.[7]

From 1953 to 1959, measures to eliminate low-grade wine and to reduce the volume of production were introduced. Surplus wine was blocked from sale and eventually sent to the distillery, while taxes were introduced on any alcoholic product produced from the marc after fermentation. Certain varieties came to be designated by the state as "recommended," "authorized," "tolerated," and "prohibited" for each region. A system of subsidies was introduced to encourage the tearing up of prohibited and tolerated vine varieties. Moreover, planting new vines without tearing up an equal number of old vines became prohibited. This last measure was repealed after the frost of 1956, which destroyed a considerable number of vineyards, and from that year onward growers were able to buy the right to plant new vines without tearing up old vines.

The second phase, 1960 to 1964, was marked by the state's attempt to organize the wine market by stockpiling and spreading out the volume of wine sold over the entire year. The wine produced above a certain yield limit (e.g., all the wine produced above 100 hectoliters per hectare or a certain percentage of the harvest) was considered as *hors quantum* and separated from *quantum* wine. The quantum wines were put on the market every 2 months in equal portions, from the first of January, onward. Hors quantum wines had to be used in industry for making juice, vinegar, and so on. In order to regulate supply, it then became possible to stockpile both types of wine in the cooperative through subsidies and thus to wait for an acceptable market price.

The third period, from 1964 to 1970, was notable for primarily as the period in which preparations were made to enter common market, founded on the principles of free competition and the interdiction of subsidies. The objectives of the interventions during this period were to reduce the supports, while improving the quality of the wine produced in France. The system of quantum, hors quantum wines was replaced by a system of blocked wines and free wines, which was less restrictive in nature. By 1969, a system of blocked wines was no longer in effect.

In 1970, the wine market in the EEC was organized and according to the Treaty of Rome, the circulation of wine between members states was to take place freely, without customs duties, export supports, and quotas. In order to eliminate differences between regions in the EEC, certain exceptions to these regulations were allowed. For example, because of climatic differences, the common market was divided into five wine-growing regions. Chaptalization is permitted in certain areas. In one zone, which includes Germany and the northern regions of France, it is legal to add sugar to wine. In the region of the Midi, however, because of the ample sun, adding sugar to wine is illegal.

Wines also came to be classified into different categories by alcoholic content. Wine prices were to be determined on the free market, however, orientation and intervention prices were fixed in Brussels for each category of wine. In order to avoid market surpluses, short- and long-term contracts came to be established. When the market price fell below the intervention price, producers could sign contracts—against a subsidy—which assured that their wine will not be sold in the following three months. If market prices exceeded the intervention price, such contracts were not allowed, but those already signed were valid for a period of three months. Long-term contracts were taken when the surplus for the month of December exceeded the demand over four months. These contracts were valid for a period of nine months. The last measure used to balance supply and demand as was the measure of the mandatory distillation of large quantities of wine.

Despite these interventions, wine prices did not increase substantially and there was a constant surplus on the markets (see Boulet 1976a, 30) and growers in the 1970s increasingly expressed their dissatisfaction with Common Market and the French government. Demonstrations and protests in the region, in Paris and in Brussels during the seventies came to be a frequent occurrence as the interventions and participation in the EEC did little to ameliorate the wine-growing economy, but rather exacerbated the conditions of wine production in Languedoc (see chapter 2).

"Double Binds"

The French government then attacked the problems of overproduction and low market prices by offering a series of incentives through subsidy programs and aid administered by the cooperative. For example, subsidies were offered to growers for tearing up old vine stock and replanting with approved higher quality varieties. The first step in the arduous road to quality[8] was to replant with vines that produced lower yields but with higher alcoholic content. However, small growers were inevitably caught in a double bind for if subsidies were accepted, it was done so at some cost.

The policy of tearing up vineyards then met considerable opposition especially from small growers. Some small growers were reluctant to tear up old vineyards and replant with new stocks, as vines required about three to five years, before they bore fruit. The intervening years implied the loss of income and the subsidies granted only cover the costs of the year of replantation. Jonathan Verdier, whose family, ran a 14-hectare vineyard commented:

> I don't believe that policy of improving wine is going to help anybody. Nobody has proved that quality pays. Besides it is impossible to make good wine with the amount of grapes that cooperative handles. Also you have to be a bit of an entrepreneur to tear up your vineyards. You have take a big risk. It is risky enough trying to make a go of it growing vines that produce high yields and inferior wines, let alone tearing up these vines, waiting for a few years before collecting an income from growing vines that produce better wines. Who knows if they will sell.

The smallest growers were the most reluctant to innovate on a massive scale, on these grounds alone, though some small growers applied for a subsidy from the cooperative to replant their holdings, bit by bit, with new and improved stocks since vines had to be replaced every 20 or 30 years. Opinion was indeed divided among growers as Jules Pages, a refrigeration engineer and part-time grower remarked:

> Sure quality always pays in the long run. Each wine-grower knows it and want to produce better wine. But they all count on their neighbor to tear up their vineyards. Everyone satisfies himself by producing the largest harvest possible. Nobody wants to get caught in a hole.

Medium growers, large landowners, and growers with relatively lucrative income sources were more able take advantage of such subsidy programs, having rather more resources to rely on than small growers. They could rely on income generated from that portion of their holding that has not been torn up in the interval before the vines bear fruit, as well as income generated from other forms of employment.

Alienation

The cooperative had in these respects fundamentally altered the process of production in family viticulture. The state has come to intervene in the process of production in viticulture and the direct producer has come to be increasingly less familiar with the destination of the product, once it entered into the cooperative and into the circuits of the market. Growers have increasingly become alienated from the products of their labor and their work has become transformed from an artisan-like undertaking to a kind of work that resembles factory work, in which workers produce one component of a product that is sold on the market. Many of growers in the community, while acknowledging the indispensability of the cooperative, lamented its role in the disappearance of a métier. Frédéric Vias, commented:

> Look at the growers these days. They call themselves wine growers but they have no idea how to make a bottle of wine. All they do is grow the grapes and dump the harvest at the cooperative and there—that's it. For the rest of the year they sit back and collect their paychecks. They're no longer wine growers. They've become state functionaries.

Cooperators were, in fact, paid by the cooperative in monthly installments according to the amount and quality of the grapes harvested on a particular enterprise. The amount corresponded to a calculated average sold in the previous year of production. Much debate took place in the general meetings and among the administrators on the issue of payments made on the basis of a differential payment scheme corresponding to the quality of the wine produced. Harvests of high-yielding grapes varieties brought in generally lower receipts for they produced inferior wines. For example, in the meeting of the general assembly held in February 1983, most members objected to the cooperative implementing a decision to reduce payments to producers whose grapes had a high sugar content, producing wine with an alcoholic content of 14 degrees. Many growers resent the unfairness of the higher payments made to growers who owned vineyards in the fertile plains who can, by virtue of location, produce better-quality wines. While growers who owned vineyards in the hills can produce more wine, it was of a lower grade and hence, they were penalized by lower payments. They insisted that this contradicted the principle of egalitarianism espoused in the statutes of the cooperative, for as André Bussières, one very disenchanted member of the cooperative maintained, *"It is always the small grower who can't afford to tear up vines, who gets penalized. The bigger guys always end up doing alright. So where is the idea of equality in cooperation?"*

Collectivism and Its Limitations

The cooperative of Broussan provided a solution to several problems faced by the small growers of the community and, indeed, throughout the wine-growing region of Languedoc. It solved the problem of storage, vinification, and of improving the quality of wine produced. The larger financial and technical resources of a pan-community institution have allowed the development of new and improved techniques in the storage of wines and in the fabrication of wine itself. These improvement have thus contributed to the viability of small producers, who otherwise would have been seriously threatened producing under erratic market conditions. It has promoted social mobility to some extent, as it has facilitated the transformation of many agricultural laborers into wine growers by minimizing the costs of production and vinification.

One of the largest advantages offered by the cooperative to the growers was that it acts as a means of defense in the sale of wine. By producing wine of a homogeneous quality and by diversifying the methods of marketing wine, the cooperative occupied a stronger position in the negotiation of prices with merchants. Merchants were no longer able to insist on paying low prices to individual producers because of varying quality of wine produced by individual growers, though still in place at the cooperative, there was a differential pay scale according to the class of the harvest each producers brings in. Merchants could also no longer take advantage of the competitive position that confronted each individual small grower in the marketplace, seeking to ensure the sale of their individual product over their neighbors'.

Nevertheless, while competition between wine-growing enterprises on the market has been tempered by the institution of the cooperative, it was displaced to slightly different sphere in the market. Many growers, who had the financial resources were following the directives of the cooperative and replanting with new and approved stocks, hoping to get an edge on their neighbors by producing a more saleable product. Some were attempting to ensure the viability of their agricultural enterprises by diversifying their products and entering into the market with these products on an individual basis. The production of different crops took producers outside the circuits of cooperation, both in production and in marketing. Many households, for example, have converted a small part of their property into artichoke growing and asparagus cultivation. Other enterprises have converted some hectares of land into fruit orchards, growing melons, peaches, olives, and almonds. Crop diversification was not undertaken on any great scale in the village, for the reasons stated in chapter 2, but to each of the households who were engaged in market gardening and the rearing of small animals, it represented a subsidiary income source and part of the survival strategy for their individual enterprise. Most of these products were sold locally by the producers themselves to local stores, in local markets, in their own homes, and on roadside. When a particular product was in season, the producers often competed with one another by undercutting prices and getting to market outlets before other producers. Also, a few households have undertaken to farm by contract. The mayor, Pascal Gizard, cultivated a small cherry orchard and some of the cherries were sold to a canning factory in Narbonne. One of the households in the village has also contracted to raise rabbits for a food company. In these ways, competition between households on the wine market has been channeled by crop diversification into the market for other agricultural products.

Some of the limitations of the cooperative were seen by growers to consist in the rising expenses and operational costs of the cooperative that results in higher membership costs and lower returns to the producer. Moreover, the programs and the policies that the cooperative subscribes to for the improvement of wine, especially the system of subsidies and penalties put into effect, were seen by the producers as an infringement on their freedom to cultivate their lands as they wish. Thus, one of the most important limitation of the cooperatives was that they were "imprisoned" by the statutes they themselves have created (Pastor-Barrué 1981:240). By uniting large and small producers and part-time growers in a single institution according to the principle of unrestricted membership, disagreements and opposition emerge according to the divergent interests of the different groups. For example, many of the large owners who belong to the cooperative, own vineyards located in the most fertile zones of the commune lands. While these growers were able to follow the policy of improving wine recommended by the cooperative more easily than smaller family producers, few were actually committed to such improvements, wishing only to get the maximum returns from their land. Those small-family producers, by contrast, who desired to improve the quality of the wines produced on their holdings located in the more marginal, low-yielding zones although to follow such a policy represented a higher risk to them. Hence, many of the small growers struggled to get better returns on the lowest yields of the lowest-grade wine, unable to take advantage of subsidies. Some of the smallest producers felt that these policies favored the larger producers who could afford to make the costly changes advocated by the cooperative. The programs thus reinforced the class differences among the producers and exposed the contradictory quality of the egalitarian and democratic principles of cooperative's statutes. Moreover, the entry of former private wineries into the cooperative, which the cooperative cannot legally prohibit, was seen as a purely utilitarian act on the part of large owners, in so far as the cooperative gives relatively prosperous holdings more of a competitive edge over small growers.

The admission of those part-time growers with large financial resources gained from business, law, and medicine, diffused the strength of any defense of wine growers interest on the basis of professional solidarity since, for these individuals, the purchase of land under vine cultivation was seen more as a source of investment than a commitment to wine growing itself. A final limitation of wine-growing cooperatives lay in the fact that the idea of private property dominated the idea of cooperation. All the cooperators were by definition owners of land who espoused an ideology of private property. Various development in the cooperative have, ironically reinforced this notion. For example, the development of sale in common, which appeared to oppose individual interests actually underlined and promoted the lack of interest in the cooperative, its undertakings, and the manufacture and sale of the final product. As was mentioned earlier, this development resulted in the alienation of the growers from the final product, transforming them into the recipients monthly paychecks after turning over the responsibility for production, manufacture, and marketing to the cooperative. It encouraged a process in which the product in the end, came to represent a paycheck and the growers expressed an interest only in so far as it affected their own personal accounts.

Conclusion

The overwhelming feature of vinification cooperatives are that they are a bureaucratic state-run institution. The movement to form cooperatives was given impetus by the state and accepted by local growers as a means of dealing with the economic crises. While cooperatives succeeded in assuring the economic survival of the small growers in Languedoc, they represented a means for the absorption of producers into the programs of the state. Cooperatives placed all aspects of the production process under the direct scrutiny and control of a state, which sought to enforce a program of modernization through encouraging the pursuit of quality. Each step in the cultivation and vinification of wines was subjected to state guidelines and conformity was encouraged through a system of penalties and subsidies. Considered by the growers as an instrument of the state, cooperatives were not seen as a means of *political* defense for the small grower. Having a mixed membership, it tended to reinforce differences between large growers and smallholders and through the implementation of its different programs it served to foster a process of increasing differentiation. The original ideals that inspired the formation of cooperatives under the first and second waves of socialism—principles of collective and direct action as well as solidarity—were now seen as very far removed from the reality of an institution which had furthered the state's agenda in the locality in encouraging the development of large-scale, so-called efficient, units of production. Moreover, the cooperative had simply replaced the patronage system as an intermediary between producers and the market. As modern institution, however, both power and knowledge came to be located in its bureaucratic apparatus rather than embodied in the person of the landowner. The result of the relationship between the powerful and the powerless, was nonetheless similar. The producers became alienated from the product and less knowledgable about its ultimate destination once it entered into the cooperative and later into the circuits of exchange.

Still, seen as the sine qua non of viticultural production, few growers criticized its crucial role in assuring the reproduction of farm enterprises. Yet, many growers tended to resist the package of interventions imposed by the state through the cooperative or accepted the subsidies with a wariness summarized by a view held the elderly Célestine Guy, a former agricultural laborer who experienced both the systems of patronage working on the estate and witnessed the increasing role played by the state in wine growing over a period of the 60 or so years of her working life. On the subject of state aid she declared: "What the state gives you with one hand, it takes away with the other." Cooperatives in the wine-growing region of Languedoc then came to be the instrument par excellence of state intervention, although ostensibly and ideologically, they were seen to have emerged from struggles of peasant workers in the early twentieth century that stressed collectivism and direct action in order to maintain and control production and their share of the market. While historically growers themselves often turned to the state in times of economic duress, seldom then did they count on the state to resolve their difficulties. The experience of the cooperative represented a case in point of how state intervention served as a means for appropriation of control and power. Because such institutions seldom served the interests of growers and small growers especially, wine growers continue to be locked into a struggle with the state to reassert some measure of control over the local economy.

CHAPTER 8

Subjects, Subjectivity, and Praxis in Late Capitalism

The Enigma of the Rural Subject

Small relatively poor farmers have long been an enigma for scholars and politicians alike in western society. From Marx (1913) and his contemporaries to more recent academics and even certain ministers of agriculture in France, for example, small farmers have been regarded as retrograde and hidebound. The image of the rural cultivator as politically inert and almost lifeless unless prodded by external forces persists despite much historical and contemporary evidence that proves the contrary. In fact, representations of the small farmers as politically active abound in the literature on agrarian societies and their radicalness has been amply recorded in the annals of history. However, according to Stern (1987), while such testimonies exist, records of rural political engagement, by and large tend to be confined to extraordinary moments or times of crisis which in fact lie outside the realm of the normal and quotidian life. When crises recede and the drama of those exceptional moments dissipates, rural people retreat from the political scene and it is assumed, they revert to their inert, undynamic mundane lives. While Stern's assertion may be criticized for underestimating the significance of a literature that attempts to portray petty producers as initiators and not merely reactors to processes of transformation (see,

223

e.g., Scott 1986, G. Smith 1989), his view is confirmed by Roseberry (1993) who suggests that studies that pose the question of rural activism in the field of agrarian studies tend to be exceptions rather than the rule. The scarcity of such interventions has led Stern to comment further that our understanding of the ways in which the rural subject has engaged with the political world, not only in tumultuous but especially in quiescent times, is in fact only beginning. If the perception that little is known about the nature of rural political activity prevails among two students of the peasantry, who specialize in an ethnographic region of the world, Latin America, for which there is a relatively voluminous anthropological and historical literature on agrarian unrest, their comments serve as a particularly strong indictment of agrarian studies in Western Europe. In that literature, the question of how rural people engage with their political worlds as initiators of change in ordinary, everyday life is seldom addressed.[1] To that end, when agrarian populations rise up and protest, these actions are regarded as extraordinary in the first place and reactive, in the second place.

Many academics who study the European rural subject and, indeed, many agents who have directed the course of change in Europe, then often worked with the unacknowledged assumption that a condition cultural stasis and political ineffectiveness typifies rural populations. The trend has been to be more concerned with family farmers as the problem rather than the problems faced by small-scale farmers. So, such developments as the French Revolution avoided the peasantry by being largely an urban affair, directed from Paris. Much later, after the World War II, what scraps from the table of state policy came their way were chiefly the result of a fear that an unprotected agrarian population would abandon the countryside and swell the ranks of the potential left-leaning urban proletariat.

While the problems of the rural subject and more urgently the fate of family farmers in general was far from center stage in many historical and political contexts in postwar French intellectual debates, it did arouse some interest among anthropologists and rural developmentalists. The work of Redfield (1956) and Arensberg and Kimball (1965), in North America produced a powerful cohort of students who conducted fieldwork on agrarian societies first in "developing" countries and later in the "developed" countries of Western Europe. Among rural developmentalists, the small, low-technology farm was seen as a curse, inhibiting the development of modernity. For all who studied agrarian societies in the immediate postwar period, the powerful ideology of the cold war, precluded any attempt to analyze the rural setting in terms of dynamic structures of class relationships. Petty producers were people with communities (possibly good) and traditional culture (definitely bad), not people experiencing progressive geographical marginalization and class differentiation.

By contrast, in the Russia and Germany of the early twentieth century, industrialization was sufficiently weak and the rural population sufficiently large, that those interested in social change were perforce concerned with agrarian populations in a more dynamic way. For this reason and because agrarian studies was ideologically constrained at its beginning in post–World War II North America, the debates that took place so long ago among European political thinkers, had such a powerful influence on rural studies in the more recent period first, in terms of the "Third World" and also in terms of small farmers in advanced capitalist societies such France. The very early students of agrarian society such as Lenin, Kautsky, and Chayanov addressed frontally the general question of how capitalism operates in agriculture and whether the peasantry could sustain itself once it had been drawn into the world of commodity and market production.[2] Questions about the sustainability of family farms launched many contemporary researchers into investigating the enigma of the rural subject that managed to continually withstand forces of disintegration. Drawing on the insights offered by the early scholars of agrarian society and economy, "capital-centric" (Roseberry 1993) forms of scholarship emerged that emphasized the structural logics that were at work in the economy of family-based agrarian enterprises. While one of the points of departure for this book originated in thinking about the "agrarian question" in the context of one region of France, I have attempted to stress that while certain logics do prevail in family-based production systems and in the economy of household-based producers, the ways in which they ramify through any single unit of production involves the conscious intervention of people as social actors whose actions are located in repertoires of cultural practice.

I have pursued this issue by illuminating the nature of the struggles that take place in the quotidian world of work, by interrogating the ways in which relations of work are embedded in networks of family and community and understandings, as well as conflicts over the meaning of emotive terms and intimate ties. My intention here was to illuminate how such relations were subjected to constant negotiation, manipulation, and re-alignments in the context of the different fields of power that contour agrarian life, not only within the domain of domestic and community life, but also within the confines of region and nation. Within those fields, the play of hegemonic forces pro-voked contests over the meanings and the obligations evoked by notions of family, friendship, citizen, peasant, Occitan, and work-ing class. I have been concerned then with the specific ways in which cultural practices configured work relations and in turn how relations of power authority, conflict, collaboration, and conflict were connected to the imperatives of making a living. As a study that focused on the varied dimensions of work, my project explored the implications of the observation made by Buroway (1985, 39) that:

> Any work context involves an economic dimension (produc-
> tion of things), a political dimension (production of social
> relations), and an ideological dimension (production of an
> experience of those relations) . . . The so-called economic realm
> is inseparable from its political and ideological effects, and
> from specifically political and ideological "structures" of the
> workplace.

My concern in this exegesis then was to study the question of how ordinary people acted within and against the structures of social life in their efforts to transform their political and eco-nomic environment. Simply put, I was concerned with the ques-tion of praxis in the everyday world of work and politics of one group of Languedoc farmers.

Politics, Structure, and Class

While I have tried to unravel the enigma posed by the persis-tence of family farmers in one small corner of France, the rather elusive quality of the rural subject is further underscored by the problem they present in efforts to define their class position. Petty commodity producers defy attempts to locate them within contemporary class structure, according to a strict structural definition of the "class." The unity of ownership and labor in the enterprise, as well as the participation of the household mem-bers in a variety of both agricultural and nonagricultural wage-earning activities mitigates against consigning them either to a class of owners or a class of laborers. Moreover, on the pluriactive family farm in Broussan, household members as often bought as sold their labor power in many different sectors of the economy. They were engaged in trade and commerce and participated in a whole range of land tenure arrangements that combined ownership, renting, and share-tenancy relations. Still, as farmers their experiences of the forces of market domination and subordination under capitalism inclined them toward identifying themselves as members of the proletariat and this was reinforced where smallholders and wage workers were one and the same. Both then represented social groups whose surpluses are appropriated by landlords, merchants, and the state. Given such characteristics, the case of smallholding farmers in the context of rural Languedoc emphasizes again the limits of strictly structural definitions of class. While they serve as a guide to determining the processes of class formation, a narrow focus on the relations of production is insufficient for understanding the class position of smallholders as well as the nature of the politics in which they become engaged.

To understand the process of class formation, requires some attempt to move beyond strictly structural approach, indeed to attend to one of the basic objectives in class analysis, itself—to determine the significance of differing kinds of political actions followed by particular groups in society and to identify the bases on which solidary ties are constructed in the overall process of the formation of collective identity. I turn again to Buroway who reminds us that:

> There is no "objective" notice of class prior to its appearance on the stage of history. Acting on the historical stage has to be conceived of as a moment in the constitution of class. Thus class becomes the combined effect of a set of economic, political and ideological structures found in all arenas of social activity. (1985, 39)

In this book, therefore, I explored the question of the class identity of the petty-commodity wine growers from the perspective of the specific struggles that were initiated and how their work experiences were conceptualized.

In my view this should not be seen in a deterministic way as the convergence of something called "economic interests" and something else called "political interests." The daily concerns of making a living *both* throw people into binding relationships with other people *and also* must extend beyond the daily "economic" interest of making money in the market, toward the longer-term "political" concern with preserving the conditions for life to go on. So relations needed to produce a livelihood uniting people into coalitions and a community of interests. I have sought to show, as well how this "commonality" is expressed both in class and in cultural terms: a sense of class crosscut by a community of those who share a common culture as Occitan people. Smallholders were thus a class and were bound together as a class by their structural position vis-à-vis the market as well as by the ties that are created in producing a livelihood. Yet the conflict was perhaps not as preeminently directed against capital as we might expect from the conventional working class, but was rather directed against *both* capital *and* the state (in the form of policies, tariffs, taxes, etc.). This combination meant that the shared identity was not just that of direct producers vis-à-vis capital, but also the entire region vis-à-vis the state. The practices of daily production in agriculture have important political consequences in fostering distinctive forms of ideology and collective identity both with and against members of the working class and, also with and against people of Occitania. In heeding Ortner's (1995) warning [and, indeed, one voiced by many other writers, influenced by poststructuralist and postmodernist thought] against monolithic representations, I have presented a case where the question of diversity among a peripheral people has particular political consequences. For while an identity in terms of class resonates with some facets of the experience of work in Broussan within a capitalist economy, regional sentiments articulate with other facets of the experience of a struggle for autonomy and control over a distinctive way of life that threatens to become governed by an ethic of modernization. Petty producers then positioned themselves in the cultural universe of France as Occitan people and practitioners of regional politics.

Occitanism, Nationalism, and the Politics of Minority Nationalism

In recent years, regional politics, nationalism, and minority nationalism in Western Europe has channeled attention toward the political and cultural dynamics of European "peripheries." The turn toward the political practices of people in the regions was due to a "discovery" that the salience of nationalism and regional minority nationalism belied what was held as axiomatic about modernized nations, states, and economies. Nineteenth-century social theories were used as the basis for an influential school of post–World War II theorists who believed that state formation and the development of modern capitalist society, would erode attachments to regional culture and local traditions.[3] Nevertheless, in the last quarter of the twentieth century, it is generally understood that in fact nationalism is a phenomenon that is peculiar to modernity, despite its relationship to what has been defined as "premodern" sentiments (Hutchinson and Smith 1994). So, in the context of Europe, with the emergence of Catalan nationalism and Basque separatism in Spain, the Northern Leagues in Italy as well as Breton and Occitan regionalism in France, however, it is now, widely acknowledged that ideals of national unity, the consolidation of a national identity, and the development of cultural homogeneity have not been achieved under the impulses of nation building and modernization and the integrity of many nation-states have become threatened by the pressures for regional self-determination and movements that promote separatism, as well as shifting loyalties from the nation to the region.

The question of why nationalist sentiments have resurfaced in recent years has provoked scholars to reexamine the nature of modern society and the process of modernization itself. Gellner, for example, has argued that the need for modern societies to create cultural homogeneity ironically promotes nationalism. The pressures created by industrializing societies for members of a "low culture" to shed the weight of custom by becoming absorbed into the "high culture" of modern societies is often accompanied by the genesis of alienation, resentment, and discontent among modernity's victims. However, the disadvantages of those who do not share the culture or language of the political rulers can be converted to an advantage for national or minority national culture becomes a means for the conceptualization and expression of grievances arising from melting-pot pressures (Gellner 1983). Nairn similar to Gellner focuses on the processes of modernization, particularly the development of capitalism and argues that nationalism is necessarily a populist form of politics that emerges from the processes of uneven development. It surfaces in those peripheries and margins of capitalism where modern capitalist development has not yet reached. This failure of diffusion combined with the concentration of the forces of control and leadership at the center is experienced as domination by the centre of the periphery. Nationalism emerges in those peripheries to defend regions against outside domination and, according to Nairn, it is a populist response involving the "conscious formation of a militant inter-class community rendered strongly (if mythically) aware of its own separate identity *vis-à-vis* the outside forces of domination" (1977, 337–41). This vision of nationalism which is seen as emerging from the forces of uneven development is similar to that of Hechter (1975 and 1985). Whereas Nairn discusses the emergence of nationalism internationally, Hechter focuses nationalisms that emerge within the boundaries of the nation-state and uses the concept of internal colonialism to explain the rise of nationalisms within the context of a nation-state. Hechter argues that "ethno regionalist" movements arise as politically potent force to challenge state authority and to reassert claims over material resources located in the peripheries.

In these pages, I have explored one case of minority nationalism which has emerged within the boundaries of the nation-state of France. Occitanism has became a politically potent form of regional consciousness in one rural periphery and it has emerged to challenge state control over regional resources contesting the state control over the regional economy and culture in a context in which development has consistently favored industry and the north. In this respect it has arisen in the context of uneven development in France. Efforts to correct that unevenness by devolving power and control to the regions have further galvanized regionalist claims and identities. On the one hand, Occitan culture, its metaphors, and idioms have become a means for expressing historical grievances and articulating the parameters of injustice. On the other hand, they have become a means for establishing claims for securing access to power and resource relinquished for the development of the regions. In France the renewed salience of Occitan consciousness coincided with plans for devolution and the revitalization of the southern regions that were already experiencing a cultural and economic renaissance was given impetus by the events of World War II.[4] Irrespective of the apparent instrumentality of sustaining a form of identity against the dominant nationalist identity, Occitanism has become a politically potent form of regional consciousness. Among smallholders, political efforts to defend rural livelihoods have become elided with struggles to defend the rediscovered Occitan culture and identity. However, in all its variants, Occitan nationalism is not invariably populist, transcending class division or uniting people across classes (cf Nairn 1977 and Anderson 1983).

Some writers, as I have stressed in the introduction, have emphasized that some forms of nationalism have a basis in class, expressing forms of class consciousness and sentiments (see also Hroch 1985.) I have focused on a case in which Occitanism is practised by a group of people who lay claim to being members of a subaltern class within the economic and cultural boundaries of the region, as well as outside it. This case, then reinforces the importance of making the attempt to identify the class basis of any instance of nationalist political practice, from those that have recently undermined contemporary nation-states to those that merely express sentiments of alterity.

While, as I have argued, Occitan regionalism represents a politically potent ideology, it is apparent to both analysts and subjects alike that the politics of Occitan regionalism as it is practised among petty producers would neither be likely to threaten the dissolution of France, nor in fact, result in the revolutionary transformation of French society. The recognition of this improbability has prompted some scholars to dismiss Occitan regionalism as politically and historically insignificant. This is seen to be especially the case when it is compared to other cases of European regionalism[5] which by and large are regarded by scholars and politicians alike as more politically potent or threatening to the established order (see Le Roy Ladurie 1977, Kielstra 1985, Loughlin 1985, Keating 1988). Occitan regionalism or minority nationalism is often overlooked and disregarded for several reasons. It is thought to lack the political coherence and the institutional structures that characterize Catalan and Basque nationalism. Occitanism is also seen as culturally deficient. Because Occitan culture is diffuse and the Occitan language is rarely spoken, it is seen to lack the cultural cohesiveness of, for example, Breton regionalism. Moreover, Occitan regionalist politics has failed to produce a coherent ethnic nationalist movement, in contrast to Basque nationalism. Added to this is the fact that Occitania cannot be located in space by distinct territorial or linguistic boundaries, since the region is geographically large and rather vaguely defined.[6] By contrast, other regions in France, such as Brittany and Corsica, are well defined both geographically and linguistically. Because of this cultural diffuseness and lack of unity, Occitan regionalism is therefore considered a force of little political and historical consequence, a weak imitation of "real" regionalism—it is deemed in essence a cultural commodity manufactured for tourist consumption. Loughlin (1985,

211 and personal communication, 1993) for example, has argued that Occitan regionalism is the domain of intellectuals and the elite largely preoccupied with the preservation of local culture and that often it is driven by a tourist economy. Touraine *et al* (1980) is also rather dismissive of Occitanism. After convening a conference of Occitan political groups, he concluded that the creation of a coherent Occitan movement would be impossible since the interests of the groups were essentially irreconcilable. Le Roy Ladurie also (1977) disputes the accuracy of representations of history in texts written by Occitan historians, privileging the accuracy of the product over the effects of the process of resurrecting that history.

In the light of these assessments or indices for determining the historical significance of political phenomenon such "deficiencies" do prevail in Occitan regionalism, especially when analysts examine this phenomenon through the filter of a positivistic approach to understanding political practice. Yet, in looking at regionalism and regionalist politics from the postpositivistic lens of the subjectivity of its practitioners, it is difficult to sustain an impression of its social, cultural, and indeed political insignificance. Occitan idioms permeated everyday forms of social intercourse. Moreover, in moments of heightened political activity, Occitan identity was wielded as a political weapon. Occitan sensibilities then configured the subjectivity of the small farmers in Lower Languedoc and a sense of being Occitan acted as a compelling force that incited people to take up collective action to resist forms of state domination, on the one hand, and to defend regional and local interests, on the other. Therefore, by attempting to decode the meanings attached to history, territory, and politics by those who embrace a distinctive Occitan consciousness is to approach an understanding of the social and political traditions of Languedoc small farmers. Those scholarly interventions that attempt to determine the significance of any political phenomenon simply in terms of institutional structures and the presence or absence of political movements properly constituted threaten to efface from history those moments of everyday struggle in which ordinarily people initiate change in their social and political worlds, as well as people's understandings of their experience of confrontation and periodic conflict in their day to day lives. Analysts who subscribe to formalistic formulations of politics then will continue to regard as extraordinary the kinds of "disorganized" politics practised at the margins. Here, I have attempted to shed light on how regional sentiments and regional expression and the symbols of regional culture become mobilized and politically charged. I have inquired into the processes through which subjects produce their identities in relationship to their work experiences and history. My discussion was devoted to exploring the internal dynamics of one example of Occitan regionalism and I argued that in order to apprehend the politically charged character of regionalism among the small farmers of Broussan, it was necessary to explore how regional subjectivity is inflected by daily struggles to make a living and by a tradition of collective mobilization or what Tilly (1986) has called "contentiousness."

I have also stressed that in order to apprehend the political discourses and practices of Occitan politics, it is important to understand the internal dynamics of how regional consciousness and identity has been produced by historical changes in the larger political economy. My attempt here to locate the culture of regionalism in terms of the material conditions of its production through history contrasts with approaches to regionalism that explain its salience in terms of the simple tenacity of regional culture. In many interventions, regional identities are privileged as a force that withstands the test of time and the processes of change and modernization (see Le Roy Ladurie 1975, Berger 1972) Moreover, regional culture and identity or culture in the regions is portrayed as a phenomenon sui generis through thick descriptions of cultural forms, practices, and texts (see, e.g., Urla 1988). While many such contributions go beyond the older notions of local culture and identity that see tradition as being static and posing some kind of premodern brake on change, discourses on culture and cultural difference are often discussed as detached from the material conditions and social practices that form the context in which they are constructed. Following Hobsbawm and Ranger's book on *The Invention of Tradition*, anthropologists have become increasingly interested in how "tradition" is constructed. Sider (1986), Roseberry (1991), and O'Brien and Roseberry (1989) all offer evidence of how traditions are not so much invented—implying a certain extrasocial strategy, perhaps on the part of politically ambitious local elites—but more interestingly, are produced and reproduced, disappearing and resurging in a dynamic relationship with political and economic forces through time. I have argued here that culture itself is produced and reproduced through specific relations with people in their everyday work lives and understandings through history. Through these avenues, then, I have presented a case in which what Sider (1984) has called "a culture of opposition" prevails among a group of small-scale farmers.

Culture, Class, and Opposition

The historical and contemporary experience of the smallholder of Broussan sustains and reinforces a "culture of opposition." According to Sider (1984), culture centers on social relations and it combines two kinds of ties. It combines and expresses the ties people develop *among themselves* in the context of productive labor, family, neighborhood, and market. Culture also combines and expresses ties *with others* of unequal appropriation of the social relations of production. In the contemporary setting, culture coheres around the ties people develop among themselves, through reciprocity in work relations, ties of friendship, and kinship and through the commonality of experience. In Broussan such ties were central in defining identity and contributed toward generating solidarity. That culture of the Occitan grower also expresses, ties *with others* of unequal appropriation, was reflected in the fact that smallholders were in a continual relationship of subordination in their efforts to maintain their share of the market and the product against competition from the capitalist sector and international trade mediated by the state. Hence, where smallholder already had a history of militancy and regional specificity on which to draw regionalism incorporated distinctive aspects of class interest and class identity incorporated certain facets of regional interests. The cultural expression of this solidarity may be in terms of "community," which expressed ties *among themselves*, in the everyday context. In the highly charged political context, it was expressed in the terms of Occitan regionalist discourses or forms of class struggle. To speak of a culture of opposition among the smallholder of Languedoc, then is to refer to the ties of unequal appropriation in the past and in the present that configure the work experiences of the petty producer so expressions of class and regionalism act as a rallying cry for political action.

In general and throughout this study, I have been concerned with exploring the ambiguities of identity and complexities of consciousness as well as the nature of praxis. It is now commonplace in treatises on the subject of identity to assert that collective identities are multiplex, shifting, emerging, and submerging (see, e.g., Hall et al 1996). *Cultivating Dissent* reaffirms this observation, in many respects but it very specifically addresses the question of the material conditions in which certain identities find expression and are strengthened or consolidated, while others become effaced, or occluded. This exegesis, in these respects, was a meditation on the problems of cultural unity and diversity in France and I studied these questions by stressing the conditions that contribute to the political, economic, and cultural resilience of a group of Languedoc family farmers. Indeed, the motifs of persistence, sustainability, continuity, and survival were prominent in *Cultivating Dissent*. However, this effort should not be read in any way as a treatise that forecasts the future of small-scale farming in France. I presented an essay that sought only to determine how people struggle to maintain control over the material and cultural conditions of their lives. While over the long term, such efforts may end in defeat, the point I wish to make here is that in the present, as well as in the past, the inevitability of decimation has been vigorously contested by the vine-cultivating smallholder in the village of Broussan who are heirs to an enduring tradition of acting in concert to resist forms of domination by the market, landowners, merchants, and the state.

In exploring the range of issues broached here, France represents a particularly apposite field, not only because of the continuing political and economic importance of agriculture but also because it has been and remains one of the most tightly centralized unitary states in European Union (Rousseau 1987). The efforts of people to resist the forces of hegemony living in a small community, located in a periphery of the country in which the dominant political trend has been to consolidate authority and centralize power, is particularly trenchant. I have presented a case, therefore, in which people do not represent the objects of the historical forces of transformation, engaging only in rearguard action against the immutable laws of capitalist development and integration by the state. But I emphasized throughout, how family farmers act as subjects who, with distinctive subjectivities fashion and refashion history through everyday practice.

Notes

Preface

1. *Midi* refers in a very general sense refers to the south of France where the sun soaks the landscape as if it were always midday. *Rouge*, of course, refers to the tradition of radical and left politics that is found in various regions of the south (see Judt 1979, Loubère 1974).

2. The linguistic and cultural differences that divide France into a number of distinctive regions or *pays* are acknowledged in Québec. In school curriculums, for example, Québecois educators have long emphasized differences between the north and the south of France in terms of history, language, and literature (C. Bélanger 1996, personal communication).

3. Kertzer in an address to the Society for the Anthropology of Europe discusses some of the complexities of this issue (SAE Newsletter, January 1995).

Introduction

1. It has long been noted that the term *peasant* lacks theoretical precision (Ennew, Hirst, and Tribe 1977; Kearney 1996) and its use in the context of western Europe may have especially pejorative resonances. It has been argued that categories such as family farmer, peasant, and smallholder are descriptive and conflate differences that exist between each of the groups as well as their relationship to the large economy. For example, Friedmann (1980) has argued that family farmers unlike peasants cannot withdraw from the market. They are locked into circuits of reproduction through the market, while peasants can reproduce themselves outside the circuits of market exchange. Technically, the people to whom I am referring are more precisely defined as petty commodity producers, since they have been locked into the circuits of market exchange for a period of at least a century, both producing commodities for the market and relying on the purchase of commodities

in the cycle of production, consumption, and reproduction (see Friedmann 1980).

2. Different members' agricultural policies have long been one of the greatest sources of discord in the European union. Suggestions by non-French members that France's agricultural policies are designed specifically to preserve an inefficient and antiquated rural economy, however, reflect more political afflatus than fact, as subsequent chapters of the book demonstrate.

3. According to Hoggart et al., roughly 78.9 percent of all farms in France are classified as "family farms" (1995, 40).

4. They are prevalent, for example, in the southeast—in a zone encompassing Lyon, Jura, Isère and Puy-de-Dôme. They are also found in the southwest—in the Dordogne, the Hautes-Pyrénées and the gulf of Gasconny—and in the southernmost reaches of the country—in its Mediterranean region. This contrasts with northern agriculture, in which capitalist production on a large scale tends to dominate, that is, in the Paris basin, Picardy, Upper Normandy, Centre, and Burgundy. Other areas of family-run farms include Alsace and Brittany (Duby 1976, 236)

5. Often the terms *nation* and *state* are conflated, complicating attempts to understand the meaning of "nation" and "state," as well as the relationships that exist between nation and state. For a discussion on the meaning of nation in relation to state see Connor (1978), who makes a distinction between the state as a territorial political unit that at times coincides with nation. Nation has been defined as both a subjective phenomenon and also positivistically. Subjectivity, it is often regarded as the expression in some sense of a moral community whose members are united by sentiments, attachments, and a consciousness of the ties that unite them. A positivistic approach to defining the nations is offered by Hroch (1985) who suggests that it is a concrete social group that combines several kinds of relationships including those of territory, economics, politics, language, and culture. In this study, I use the terms *nationalism, regionalism,* and *minority nationalism* interchangeably to convey the idea of loyalties, ties of collective solidarity, belonging, and identity. Where nationalist identity is focused on the nation-state of France, I will refer to this as French national identity. Where collective identity is focused on a territory within the boundaries of the nation-state, I will refer to this as regionalism or minority nationalism.

6. For some overviews of the ways in which the subject of nationalism has been treated see, for example, Foster (1991) and Williams (1989). Several anthologies now exist that extract classic works and recent studies on the question of nationalism and ethnicity. See, for example, Woolf (ed.) 1996 and Hutchinson and Smith (eds.) 1994.

7. In the case of France, for example, see the debate on politics and agricultural population in Berenson (1987).

8. For a recent discussion of the meaning of the market, see (Carrier ed., 1997).

9. Theorists of petty commodity production, in many respects take their inspiration from some of the insights originally offered by the Russian populists of the early twentieth century. Their arguments tend to lend support to the contemporary neopopulist strategies that promote the establishment of small-scale family-based enterprises that are seen as a way of encouraging sustainability and democratic structures of production in developing contexts (Lipton 1982, Kitching 1982, Adams 1993, J. Friedmann 1992).

Chapter 1

1. A department is an administrative subdivision of France that is administered by a prefect.

2. Languedoc is one of the three provinces, along with Provence and Roussillon, that form the Mediterranean region of southern France. Such provincial divisions are however no longer used for the purposes of administration, having been replaced by the smaller division of the department. Languedoc refers more to a region within France that consists of the departments of the Gard, the Aude, the Haute-Garonne; the southern parts of the Tarn, the Aveyron, and the Lozère; and part of the Ardeche. The coastal plain that surrounds the sea in Mediterranean Languedoc is referred to as Lower Languedoc (*Bas Languedoc*), while the hilly regions in the northern zones are referred to as Upper Languedoc (*Haute Languedoc*).

3. A canton is the administrative district below the departmental level that is made up of a number of communes. A commune is the smallest territorial division in French administration.

4. Phylloxera is a disease that attacks the roots of the vine plant. A full discussion of the impact of phylloxera and the measures taken for its eradication appears in Warner (1960).

5. For a full account of the transformation of Languedoc viticulture, see Warner (1969) and Pech (1975).

6. A good majority of Broussan households participated in the production of vines in some capacity. Out of roughly 700 households in the village, 400 contained at least one member who was employed in an agricultural profession, as either wine growers (full and part time) or agricultural laborers.

7. Between the years 1936 and 1954, the population of Broussan fell by 4.6 percent. Between 1954 and 1975, it fell by 6.8 percent. Between those same years, the number of people between the ages of 20 to 35 declined, while the percentage of the population between the ages of 35 to 60 rose, accompanied by an increase in the average age of the agriculturally active population (Bulletin Municipal de Broussan, 1983).

8. I prefer to use the term *pluriactivity* rather than other similar terms such as *multi-occupationality, part-time,* or *off-farm employment.*

It is a term that encapsulates the livelihood activities that may be paid or unpaid, part of the formal or informal economy, as well as a variety of kinds of work that exist outside employment (see Pahl 1984).

9. According to Bernstein (1979), the "simple reproduction squeeze" is a process in which the family farmer, faced with falling market prices for agricultural goods, must produce more to achieve the same return. An apparent solution is to borrow money and buy machinery, inputs, and so on, but which only increases the farmer's dependency (on the banks) and drives family members out to wage jobs in order to cover maintenance costs on machinery.

10. This was very often referred to as *"le métayage"* which translates as sharecropping, rather than share tenancy, which is *"le fermage."*

11. For a detailed account of the effect of capitalist rationalisation on Languedoc workers see Pech (1975).

12. This observation contrasts somewhat with Reiter (1976) and Rogers (1975 and 1985).

Chapter 2

1. Accounts of the Revolt of the Midi appear in Wright (1964), Napo (1971), Loubère (1974 and 1995), de Sède (1982), and Le Roy Ladurie (1982). See also J. H. Smith (1978) and Frader (1991).

2. The association that is made between the peasantry and mass or collective social movements may be traced to the fact that peasants had "clamored [*sic*] into history" (Kearney 1996, 39) as a the central historical actor in the major revolutions of the twentieth century. Wolf's (1969) classic study of peasant revolutions was key in fostering further studies of rural revolutions and rebellion.

3. The distinction I use here resembles a distinction made by Scott (1986, 28) between formal and informal forms of resistance.

4. Warner (1960, 32) describes the rising groups of middlemen that emerged during this period as well as the underhandedness of their dealing with growers.

5. It is beyond the scope of this ethnographic inquiry to include a comprehensive study of state policy and programs, however, many studies of legislation and programs governing farming and wine growers exist. For a detailed discussion of such legislation see Warner (1960).

6. See, for example, Keeler (1981) and Averyt (1977).

7. According to Averyt (1977), different laws present very different figures for farms that are deemed "unviable" or inefficient.

8. The series of taxes that were imposed on wine along with other items of trade that essentially remained unaltered from the Napoleonic era until World War I, when fiscal policies had to adjusted to the boom-and-bust cycle in the marketing of wines. Among these were the transport taxes, retail taxes, entrance taxes, and the municipal taxes. See Warner (1960, 65–67).

9. The CNJA came to dominate the FNSEA in the 1960s. Averyt points out that the CNJA is a good example of an interest group whose status and strength was bolstered by a government to serve its administrative and political needs. Lacking in a coherent agricultural program that could face the competitive pressures of the enlarged market of the EEC, the Ministry of agriculture turned to the young reformists of the FNSEA for their analysis of the needs of French agriculture. *Representativité* (the accreditation granted by the Ministry to the group, entitling it to participate in policy discussions) was conferred to the CNJA in the early 1960s. The government was thus assured of an ally among farm interest groups (1977, 27).

10. For a discussion of other organizations (see Keeler 1979, 13–14).

11. FNSEA and CNJA receive financial grants from the state for the pursuit of a variety of union activities; development subsidies; grants to train and enable union leaders to become competent in fiscal, legal, and social matters; and so on (Keeler 1981, 196–99).

12. Adulterated wines can be produced through a process called chaptalization. This involves the addition of sugars and hot water to the fermenting residue left in the vats after drawing off the first wines. When chaptalization is properly carried out, that is, adding sugar during fermentation to increase the alcoholic content of weak wines, the quantity of wine does not increase. When sugar is used with second wines, this process produces adulterated wines and quantities increase and fraudulent wine is produced (Warner 1960, 13).

13. From reports in national archives (Archives Nationales F/7/ 13883 on Agricultural Strikes 1927 to 1924).

14. The specific set of demands presented to the government are listed in Cazes (1976, 139–53).

15. Scott (1986, 7–8) cites several examples where such Brechtian, as he calls them, modes of resistance have had a significant effect on the course of history and the ambitions of states.

Chapter 3

1. A clear presentation of these arguments appear in Hall et al., 1996.

2. The name Languedoc, in fact, comes from the term *"langue d'oc"* [language of Oc] or the language that uses the term *oc* for *yes*. This of course stands in contrast to the language which is spoken in the north. This is called the *"langue d'oïl"* [language of oïl], the language in which *"oïl"* means "yes," now known as French. In contemporary French *"oïl"* has become *"oui."*

3. This interest in "popular culture" has been part of what has been referred to as the "French fashion" for folk culture emerging in the post-1968 era (see discussion in Rigby 1991). Many agents have participated

in the revival of Occitan culture and language as well as intellectuals (see, e.g., Touraine et al. 1980) each with their own agendas. Considerable folklore industries have emerged in which folk cultures have become encased and enclosed in national and local museums as a consequence of intellectual interests, while culture has become highly commodified as a result of commercial interests in the tourist trade.

4. The attention in this chapter is neither directed at Occitan regional politics, as a movement properly constituted with intellectuals at the vanguard, nor at movements for regional autonomy and linguistic movements, per se. I deal more directly with the issue of regionalism and regionalist politics in an earlier article (see Lem 1991a). I am more concerned with local manifestations and expressions of Occitan regional identity that may well have links to political movements proper but nevertheless have autonomous dynamics derived from local social and cultural relations and history.

5. Linguistic "consciousness-raising" through popular education has been a technique also used by Basque activists to promote a heightened sensitivity between cultural identity, history, and language (see Urla 1988).

6. Two studies point out how Socialist and Communist parties have particularly enjoyed support in this region. See Tony Judt's (1979) study of socialism in Provence and Leo Loubère's (1974) work on radical politics in Mediterranean France.

7. "Smicard" was often used interchangeably with "smigard." SMIG also referred to the minimum wage in France [Salaire Minimum Interprofessionel Guaranti]. In 1970 SMIG was changed to SMIC [Salaire Minimum Interprofessionel de Croissance].

8. It has been noted that a "new labor mentality" emerged in the early 1900s, when labor movements were gathering force in the region. J. H. Smith notes that a new term for vinedressers—*ouvriers agricoles* (agricultural workers) emerged for the first time after 1911 (1975, 381).

9. See Sider (1984).

10. These events prompted Alain Touraine to remark in *Le Figaro*, a national paper, that the concerns of sociological technocrats had turned disproportionately to the "conditions of consumption" while "conditions of production" had fallen off the agenda.

11. While some notion exists that there is a tie between language and "authentic" Occitan culture especially among regional activists, among small farmers Occitan identity is less bound up with the linguistic issue. Many think of themselves as Occitan without necessarily speaking the Occitan language. Urla (1988) also makes this point with reference to Basque identity.

12. This is not to say that regional bourgeoisie exempt themselves from regionalist politics and regional nationalist movements. The history Breton, Basque, and Catalan nationalism belies any such claim (see, e.g., Berger 1972). Regionalist politics may be appropriated by

right or left under certain conditions as, for example, Heiberg's 1989 study of Basque nationalism shows.

13. See, for example, Heiberg (1989) on Basque identity in Spain; Berger (1972) on Breton identity and politics; Rogers (1991) on rural Aveyron; Cohen (1982) on rural Northern Britain; Holmes (1989) on the Friulian peasant worker in Italy.

14. Holmes has suggested that this retreat into local culture accounts for the rise of a rural proletariat in the countryside without the formation of a working-class consciousness. (1989:29).

15. Judt (1979), Loubère (1974), and Agulhon (1982) focus their studies on the Mediterranean, which has had a strong tradition of voting socialist since 1849. Jones's (1985) study and also Rogers's (1991) work are located in a region of France, the Massif Central which has had a strong tradition of conservative voting. Weber's (1976) study is a treatment of France as a whole.

16. This is especially clear in Holmes's recent ethnography where he argues for a distinctive kind of "peasant-worker society"—neither peasant nor worker—yet remains caught in a discourse that insists on their radical separation.

17. See Roseberry (1989), Smith (1991), and Sider (1986).

Chapter 4

1. For a review of these debates see A. Scott, ed. (1986). See also Smith and Barker, eds. (1986); Collins and Gimenez, eds. (1991).

2. Scott (1986) points out that while theorists have identified the need to explore the ideological processes at work in studies of forms of household production, only "lip service" is paid to questions of culture and ideology.

3. I use a distinction made by Habermas (1984), in which material reproduction refers to the practices that produce things, and symbolic reproduction refers to the practices that cement group solidarity and reinforce cultural traditions.

4. Among the 85 households studied, at the time of the study, 44 households consisted of parents and their unmarried children; 14 households contained extended kin, either the wife's or the husband's elderly parents; 12 households consisted of husband and wife who were either childless or whose children had moved out of the parental home; 7 households of the sample were made up of a single, widowed, or divorced individuals who lived on their own.

5. The "stem family" has been the subject of debate in European demographic history. The debate centers on le Play's claims for the predominance of the stem family for several hundred, even thousands of years in Europe, especially in the south of France. Moreover, some

disagreement exists over its defining characteristics, as well as the nature of the rights associated with the form (see Laslett 1972).

6. No production unit merely reproduces itself without reinvestment in the means of production, which, in a strict sense implies expanded reproduction. However, Marx uses the notion of simple reproduction as an idealized form in order to explain expanded reproduction (see Marx 1976, 711–24). Simple reproduction refers to the consumption of the entire surplus value (i.e., it is entirely spent on the purchase of items of consumption). Expanded reproduction implies accumulation, where a proportion of the surplus value is used to purchase additional capital in order to increase the existing scale of production (Marx 1976, chapter 23).

7. The concept of hegemony as developed by Gramsci, clearly applies to the larger social world. However, in many respects the ways in which power, ideology, material relations, and consensus work together at the microscopic level of the household suggest that the processes of hegemony are at work at the microscopic level of the household.

8. Harris attributes these arguments to Meyer Fortes, 1969, *Kinship and Social Order*; London 1969; Maurice Bloch, 1971, "The Moral and Tactical Meaning of Kin Terms," *Man*, 6; and 1973 "The Long Term and the Short Term: The Economic and Political Significance of the Morality of Kinship," in J. Goody (ed.), *The Character of Kinship*, Cambridge.

9. Elsewhere, I have suggested that this engenders a "classlike" relationship between women and men in the household (see Lem 1991b).

10. See, for example, Friedmann (1980 and 1987) and Bernstein (1987).

11. Populist ideas have been embraced by politicians and state planners at various points in history in socialists countries such as China and Tanzania (see Kitching 1982). The World Bank has also adopted the discourse of the efficiency of the small scale (Cernea 1985).

12. The salience of a variety of types of petty commodity production have been noted in Asian contexts (see Smart 1989), Latin America (see Smith 1989), and Europe (Narotsky 1989).

Chapter 5

1. These are not all mutually exclusive forms of work and can be combined. For example, work that is unpaid and unremunerated encompasses much domestic work as well as agricultural production for subsistence and autoconsumption. However, unpaid work can include remunerated work. For example, work in agricultural production and in petty commodity production does not involve wages but producers receive compensation through the market. Wage work of course implies paid work, in which labor is sold as a commodity.

2. Kaplan's (1992) and (1981) studies stress that an understanding of the complexities of popular protest, anarchist, and socialist movements in urban Spain are premised on tracing the nature women's activities in creating solidary networks and coalitions.

3. Day laborers at that time earned a daily wage of about 1.75 francs during the winter and about 2.25 to 3 francs during the summer (Pech 1975, 42). Frader (1991, 84) puts the wages that women earned into perspective by noting that in 1862 women day laborers earned roughly 90 centimes a day. A loaf of bread at that time cost from 32 to 36 centimes.

4. A full description of the seasonal tasks in viticulture appears in Pastor-Barrué (1980).

5. For a discussion of the process of domestication, see Rogers (1980).

6. For some figures on rising costs, see Pastor-Barrué (1981, 152).

7. Seasonal and occasional work on smallholdings is still available to women. For example, women are often hired to pick cherries or peaches and of course during the grape harvest.

8. Rogers and Salamon (1983) maintain that in areas of partible inheritance, farmers tend to restrict family size in order to limit fragmentation of land.

Chapter 6

1. Mechanical grape harvesters were a highly coveted item among the family wine-growers, few of the smallholders actually owned such a machine. Grape harvesters were very expensive and out of the reach of most small growers. Though sought after, they were in fact ill-adapted to picking grapes in vineyards that were located on the sides of hills and planted haphazard fashion on small plots.

2. According to Groeger, in a report of the Fédération Départemental de CUMA (FDCUMA), individualism and "the irrationality of farmers' wives" posed obstacles to the formation of CUMA (1981, 166).

3. The table of statistics prepared in this chapter has conflated formal and informal work and is based on my own interviews and survey.

4. It might be useful to recall that in the period immediately after World War II, a shortage of skilled male laborers was still in evidence in the region, perhaps causing those who relied on hired workers to resort to these measures.

5. That is *not* to say, however, that the people from the village proceed dauntlessly in their dealings with the bureaucracy of the state. Rather, large landowners in Broussan no more have the magic elixir that melts away the layers of bureaucracy than do the smallholders and day laborers.

6. This example also underscores Harris's (1982) criticism that as a concept the household has become reified as census takers and government offices have elevated what may only be a statistically relevant category to the status of a socially relevant category.

7. This distinction follows a suggestion made by Groeger (1981, 171) in an article on cooperation and mutual aid in the massif central. However, I find her use of "equal value" for what I have called "relative market price" somewhat confusing as a contrast to "equivalence."

Chapter 7

1. For studies of the rise of socialism and radicalism in southern France see Judt (1979) and Loubère (1974).

2. This involved putting into effect a system of blockages on harvests that yielded more than 400 hectoliters and the compulsory distillation of the portion of the harvest that exceeded 185 hectoliters (Pech 1975, 482).

3. Robert Montagne (1964) "Coopération agricole" Judicial and economic study of cooperatives, Chambre of Agriculture Montpellier (quoted in Molinier 1983, 16). For a comparative study of cooperatives that focuses on the Bordeaux region, see Ulin (1996).

4. Wines were classified according to quality by alcohol content: Vin de Table (9°–>11° alcohol) is the lowest grade followed by Vin de Pays (>10°). VDQS (Vin Délimité de Qualité Supérieur–>11°), and AOC (Appellation d'Origine Contrôlée–>12°) are both higher grade wines. These are essentially state designations. The amount of vineyards that are permitted under each class is strictly regulated by the state in each wine-growing region.

5. For a chart that traces the circulation of wines in the market see Boulet 1976a.

6. For a description of the vinification process see Pastor-Barrué (1983).

7. This is based on Puijk and Vaagland (1981).

8. The quality of wine is reflected in the prices. The price corresponds to the alcoholic content of the wine produced. As a result, the prices are always expressed in terms of F/hl° (francs per degrees per hectoliter). For example, the price 10 F/hl°, 10,000 francs are payed for 100 hectoliters of wine of 10 degrees. The importance of degree of alcohol is the essential basis for their classification into wines of different categories. Other factors include the acidity, color, taste, and locality of production (Puijk and Vaagland 1983, 52).

Chapter 8

1. There are of course many notable historians and anthropologists of Western Europe who have studied questions of rural rebellion

and uprising such as Hobsbawm (1959); Tilly (1990), J. H. Smith (1975), Frader (1991), Collier (1987), Mintz (1982), Kaplan (1981), Magagna (1991).

2. For a detailed discussion of the contributions of Lenin, Kautsky, and Chayanov, see Banaji (1976a and 1976b).

3. See, for example, Lipset (1985) and Shils (1975). For France, see Weber (1976), Wright (1964), and Mendras (1970).

4. The revival of the regions was prompted by the German Occupation of France and the establishment of its center of power in Vichy. As the southern reaches of France were both geographically removed and physically cut off from the north, a Vichy "free" zone imposed virtual autonomy on the regions allowing southerners to begin to strengthen and shore up existing economic and cultural resources (Ardagh 1982, 123–27).

5. For a useful overview of approaches to regionalism, see Keating (1997).

6. Occitania includes the vast area south of the Loire, between the Atlantic coast and the Italian border, excluding the Basque country and the Catalan speaking areas. Linguistically, a large number of dialects of Occitan, such as Gascogne, Auvergnais, and Provençal were spoken in this area.

Bibliography

Adams, B. 1993. "Sustainable Development and the Greening of Development Theory." In *Beyond the Impasse: New Directions in Development Theory*, edited by F. Schurmann. London: Zed Books.

Agulhon, M. 1982. *The Republic in the Village: the People of the Var from the French Revolution to the Second Republic*. Trans. Janet Lloyd. New York: Cambridge University Press.

Alavi, H. 1973. "Peasant Classes and Primordial Loyalties." *Journal of Peasant Studies*. 1(1).

Amin, A., and N. Thrift (ed.). 1994. *Globalization, Institutions and Regional Development in Europe*. Oxford: Oxford University Press.

Anderson, B. 1983. *Imagined Communities: Reflection on the Origin and Spread of Nationalism*. London: Verso.

Anderson, P. 1974. *Lineages of the Absolutist State*. London: New Left Books.

Archives Nationales. F/7/13838. *Agricultural Strikes 1927–1924*.

Ardagh, J. 1982. *France in the 1980s*. London: Secker and Warburg.

Arensberg, C., and S. Kimball. 1965. *Culture and Community*. New York: Harcourt Brace and World.

Augé-Laribé, M. 1907. *Le problème agraire du socialisme; la viticulture industrielle du Midi de la France*. Paris: V. Giard and E. Brière Éditeurs.

Averyt, W. 1977. *Agropolitics in the European Community: Interest Groups and the Common Agricultural Policy*. New York: Praeger.

Bailey, F. 1969. *Stratagems and Spoils*. Oxford: Blackwell.

Bailey, F. (ed.). 1971. *Gifts as Poison: The Politics of Reputation*. Oxford: Blackwell.

Banaji, J. 1976a. "Summary of Selected Parts of Kautsky's *The Agrarian Question*." *Economy and Society* 5(1).

———. 1976b. "Chayanov, Kautsky and Lenin: Considerations Toward a Synthesis." *Economic and Political Weekly*, October.

Banfield, E. 1958. *The Moral Basis of Backward Society*. Free Press.

Bentley, J. 1987. *Languedoc*. Topsfield, Mass.: Salem House.

Berenson, E. 1987. "Politics and the French Peasantry: The Debate Continues." *Social History* 12(2) May.

Berger, A., and F. Maurel. 1980. *La Viticulture et l'économie du Languedoc du XVIIIe à nos jours*, Montpellier: Les Éditions du Faubourg.

Berger, A., and J. Rouzier, 1981. *Vivre et produire en Languedoc-Roussillon*. Toulouse: Privat.

Berger, S. 1972. *Peasants against Politics: Rural Organization in Brittany, 1911–1967*. Cambridge: Harvard University Press.

Bernstein, H. 1979. "Concepts for the Analysis of Contemporary Peasantries." *Journal of Peasant Studies* 6(4).

———. 1987. "Capitalism and Petty Commodity Production." London: The Open University, Development Policy and Practice, Working Paper No. 3. London.

Blim, M. 1990. *Made in Italy: Small Scale Industrialization and Its Consequences*. New York: Praeger.

Bloch, M. 1971. "The Moral and Tactical Meaning of Kin Terms." *Man* 6.

———. 1973. "The Long and the Short Term: The Economic and Political Significance of the Morality of Kinship." In *The Character of Kinship*, edited by J. Goody. Cambridge: Cambridge University Press.

Bottomore, T. (ed.). 1983. *A Dictionary of Marxist Thought*. Cambridge: Harvard University Press.

Boulet, D. 1976a. *La question viticole: essai d'analyse*. Montpellier: l'Insitut Nationale de la Recherche Agronomique.

Bradby, B. 1975. "The Destruction of Natural Economy." *Economy and Society* 4(2).

Brenner, R. 1985. "Agrarian Class Structure and Economic Development in Pre-Industrial Europe." In *The Brenner Debate*, edited by T. H. Aston and C. H. E. Philpin. New York: Cambridge University Press.

Brognetti, M. 1975. "French Farmers' Co-operatives in Crisis." In *Popular Participation in Social Change*, edited by J. Nash, J. Dandler, and N. Hopkins. The Hague: Mouton Publishers.

Bulletin Municipal de Broussan, 1983, mimeo.

Burawoy, M. 1985. *The Politics of Production*. London: New Left Books (Verso).

Campbell, J. 1964. *Honour, Family, and Patronage*. Oxford: Clarendon.

Carrier, J. (ed.). 1997. *The Meanings of the Market*. Oxford: Berg.

Carrière, R., and R. Dugrand. 1960. *La Région Mediterranéene*. Paris: Presses Universitaires de France.

Cazes, A., A. Castéra, J. Mestre et al. 1976. *La Révolte du Midi*. Paris: Les Presses d'Aujourd'hui.

Cernea, M. 1985. *Putting People First: Sociological Variables in Rural Development*. New York: Oxford University Press.

Chayanov, A. V. 1966. "On the Theory of Peasant Economy." In *Peasant Farm Organisation*, edited by D. Thorner, B. Kerblay, and R. E. F. Smith. Homewood, Illinois: American Economic Association.

Chevalier, J. 1982a. *Civilization and the Stolen Gift: Capital, Kin and Cult in Eastern Peru*. Toronto: University of Toronto Press.

——— 1982b. "There Is Nothing Simple about Simple Commodity Production." *Journal of Peasant Studies* 10(4).

Cohen, A. P. 1982. *Belonging: Identity and Social Organisation in British Rural Cultures*. Manchester: Manchester University Press.

———. 1987. *Whalsey: Symbol, Segment, and Boundary in a Shetland Island Community*. Manchester: Manchester University Press.

Collier, G. 1987. *Socialists of Rural Andalusia: Unacknowledged Revolutionaries of the Second Republic*. Stanford: Stanford University Press.

——— with E. Cowry. 1994. *Basta! Land and the Zapatista Rebellion in Chiapas*. Oakland, Cal.: Food First Institute for Food and Development Policy.

Collins, J., and M. Gimenez (eds.). 1991. *Work Without Wages*. Albany: State University of New York Press.

Connor, W. 1978. "A Nation Is a Nation, Is a State, Is an Ethnic Group, Is a . . ." *Ethnic and Racial Studies* 1(4).

Coulin, C., and F. Morin. 1979. "Occitan Ethnicity and Politics." *Critique of Anthropology* 4(13 and 14).

de Certeau, M. 1984. *The Practice of Everyday Life*. Berkeley: University of California Press.

Duby, G. 1976. *Histoire de la France Rurale*. Vol. 4. Paris: Seuil.

Durandeu, H. *Broussan et sa viticulture*. Unpublished manuscript.

Ennew, J., P. Hirst, and K. Tribe. 1977. "Peasantry as an Economic Category." *Journal of Peasant Studies* 4.

Fabre, D., and J. Lacroix. 1975. *Communautes du Sud*. Paris: Union Générale d'Editions.

Fortes, M. 1969. *Kinship and Social Order*. Chicago: Aldine.

Foster, R. 1991. "Making National Cultures in the Global Ecumene." *Annual Review of Anthropology* 20.

Frader, L. 1991. *Peasants and Protest: Agricultural Workers, Politics and Unions in the Aude, 1850–1914*. Berkeley: University of California Press.

Franklin, S. H. 1969. *The European Peasantry: The Final Phase*. London: Methuen & Co. Ltd.

Friedmann, H. 1987. "The Family Farm in Advanced Capitalism: Outline of a Theory of Simple Commodity Production." In *The Political Economy of Agriculture in Advanced Industrial Societies*, edited by F. H. Buttel and T. Murphy. New York: University Press of America.

———. 1980. "Household Production and the National Economy; Concepts for the Analysis of Agrarian Formations." *Journal of Peasant Studies* 7(2).

Friedmann, J. 1992. *Empowerment: The Politics of Alternative Development*. Oxford: Blackwell.

Geertz, C. 1994. "Primordial and Civic Ties." In *Nationalism*, edited by J. Hutchinson and A. D. Smith. Oxford: Oxford University Press.

Gellner, E. 1983. *Nations and Nationalism*. Oxford: Blackwell.

Gellner, E., and Waterbury, J. (eds.). 1977. *Patrons and Clients*. London: Duckworth and Co.

Goody, J. (ed.). 1973. *The Character of Kinship*. Cambridge: Cambridge University Press.

Groeger, L. 1981. "Of Men and Machines: Cooperation among French Family Farmers." *Ethnology* 20(3).

Habermas, J. 1984. *The Theory of Communicative Action*. Boston: Beacon Press.

Hall, S., D. Held, D. Hubert, and K. Thompson (eds.). 1996. *Modernity: An Introduction to Modern Societies*. Oxford: Basil Blackwell.

Harris, O. 1982. "Households and Their Boundaries." *History Workshop Journal* 13.

Hechter, M. 1975. *Internal Colonialism: The Celtic Fringe in British National Development*. London: Routledge and Kegan Paul.

———. 1985. "Internal Colonialism Revisited." In *New Nationalisms of the Developed West*, edited by E. Tiryakian and R,. Rogowski. Boston: Allen and Unwin.

Heiberg, M. 1989. *The Making of the Basque Nation*. Cambridge: Cambridge University Press.

Hobsbawm, E. 1973. "Peasants and Politics." *Journal of Peasant Studies* 1(1).

———. 1959. *Primitive Rebels: Studies in Archaic Forms of Social Movements in the Nineteenth and Twentieth Centuries*. Boston: Beacon Press.

———. 1990. *Nations and Nationalism Since 1780: Programme, Myth and Reality*. Cambridge: Cambridge University Press.

Hobsbawm, E., and T. Ranger (eds.). 1983. *The Invention of Tradition*. Cambridge: Cambridge University Press.

Hoggart, K., H. Buller, and R. Black. 1995. *Rural Europe: Identity and Change*. London: Arnold.

Holmes, D. R. 1989. *Cultural Disenchantments: Worker Peasantries in Northeast Italy*. Princeton: Princeton University Press.

Hroch, M. 1985. *Social Preconditions of National Revival in Europe*. London: Cambridge University Press.

———. 1993. Comments on Lem, W., 1993, "Rethinking Identities in Post Fordist Europe." Paper presented at the Opening Conference of the European Forum on National and Regional Identities at the European University Institute, Florence.

Hutchinson, J., and A. D. Smith (eds.). 1994. *Nationalism*. Oxford: Oxford University Press.

Hutchinson, J., and A. D. Smith (eds.). 1994. *Nationalism*. London: Oxford.

Jenson, J. 1988. "The Limits of 'and the' Discourse: French Women as Marginal Workers." In *The Feminisation of the Labour Force: Paradoxes and Promises*, edited by J. Jenson, E. Hagen, and R. Ceallaigh. New York: Oxford University Press.

Jones, P. M. 1985. *Politics and Rural Society. The Southern Massif Central*. Cambridge: Cambridge University Press.

Judt, T. 1979. *Socialism in Provence*. Cambridge: Cambridge University Press.

Kahn, J. 1982. "From Peasants to Petty Commodity Production in South East Asia." *Bulletin of Concerned Asian Scholars* 14.

Kaplan, T. 1981. "Class Consciousness and Community in Nineteenth Century Andalusia." *Political Power and Social Theory* 2.

———. 1982. "Female Consciousness and Collective Action: The Case of Barcelona." *Signs* 7(3).

———. 1992. *Red City, Blue Period: Social Movements in Picasso's Barcelona*. Berkeley: University of California Press.

Kearney, M. 1996. *Reconceptualising the Peasantry: Anthropology in Global Perspective*, Boulder: Westview.

Keating, M. 1997. "The Political Economy of Regionalism." In *The Political Economy of Regionalism*, edited by M. Keating and J. Loughlin. London: Frank Cass.

——— 1988. *State and Regional Nationalism: Territorial Politics and the European State*. Brighton: Harvester Wheatsheaf.

Keeler, J. T. S. 1981. "Corporatism and Official Union Hegemony: The Case of French Agricultural Syndicalism." In *Organizing Interests in Western Europe*, edited by S. Berger. London: Cambridge University Press.

———. 1979. "The Defence of Small Farmers in France." *Peasant Studies* 8(4).

Kertzer, D. 1995. "Presidential Address." *The Newsletter of the Society for the Anthropology of Europe*, January.

Kielstra, N. 1985. "The Rural Languedoc: Periphery to 'Relictual Space,' " In *Uneven Development in Southern Europe*, edited by R. Hudson and J. Lewis. London: Methuen.

Kitching, G. 1982. *Development and Underdevelopment in Historical Perspective*, London: Methuen.

Kriedte, P., H. Medick, and J. Schlumbohm. 1981. *Industrialization before Industrialization: Rural Industry in the Genesis of Capitalism*. London: Cambridge University Press.

Lagrave, R. 1987. *Celles de la terre*. Paris: Editions de l'Ecole des Hautes Etudes en Sciences Sociales.

Laslett, P. 1972. "Introduction: The History of the Family." In *Household and Family in Past Time*, edited by P. Laslett and R. Wall. London: Cambridge University Press.

Laurent, R. 1978. "Les Quatre Ages du Vignoble du Bas-Languedoc et Roussillon." *Economie et Société en Languedoc de 1789 à Nos Jours*. Published in agreement with the Centre National de la Recherche Scientifique. Paris: Editions du CNRS.

Le Roy Ladurie, E. 1982. *Histoire du Languedoc*. 4th ed. Paris: Presses Universitaires de France.

———. 1977. "Occitania in Historical Perspective." *Review* 1(1).

Lem, W. 1991a. "Classe et région: identité sociale chez les petits viticulteurs du Languedoc." *Ethnologie française* 21.

————. 1991b. "Gender, Ideology and Petty Commodity Production: Social Reproduction in Languedoc France." In *Marxist Approaches in Economic Anthropology*, edited by H. Gates and A. Littlefield. Monographs in Economic Anthropology, No. 9. New York: University Press of America.

————. 1988. "Household Production and Reproduction in Rural Languedoc: Social Relations of Petty Commodity Production in 'Broussan.'" *Journal of Peasant Studies* 15(4).

————. 1997. "Restructuring, Work and Identity: Perspectives on Class, Region and Gender in Southern Europe." In *The Political Economy of Regionalism*, edited by M. Keating and J. Louglin. London: Frank Cass.

Lenin, V. I. 1946. *Capitalism and Agriculture in the United States*. New York: International Publishers.

————. 1974. *The Development of Capitalism in Russia*. Moscow: Progress Publishers.

Lipset, S. M. 1985. "The Revolt against Modernity." In *Consensus and Conflict: Essay in Political Sociology*. New Brunswick: Transaction.

Lipton, M. 1982. "Urban Bias in Development Theory and Practice." In *Rural Development*, edited by J. Harris. London: Hutchinson University Library.

Littlewood, P. 1980. "Patronage, Ideology and Reproduction." *Critique of Anthropology* 4(5).

Loubère, L. 1974. *Radicalism in Mediterranean France: Its Rise and Decline*. Albany: State University of New York Press.

————. 1978. *The Red and the White*. Albany: State University of New York Press.

————L. 1995. *The Wine Revolution in France: The Twentieth Century*. Princeton: Princeton University Press.

Loughlin, J. 1985. "Regionalism and Ethnic Nationalism in France." In *Centre—Periphery Relations in Western Europe*, edited by Y. Mény and V. Wright. London: Allen and Unwin.

Lüdtke, A. 1995. "What Happened to the 'Fiery Red Glow'?: Workers' Experiences and German Fascism." In *The History of Everyday Life*, edited by A. Lüdtke. Princeton: Princeton University Press.

Luxembourg, R. 1968. *The Accumulation of Capital*. New York: Monthly Review.

McDonald, M. 1990. *We Are Not French*. London: Routledge.

Mackintosh, M. 1988. "Domestic Labour and the Household." In *On Work*, edited by R. E. Pahl. Oxford: Basil Blackwell.

————. 1981. "Gender and Economics." In *Of Marriage and the Market*, edited by K. Young, C. Walkowitz, and R. McCullogh. London: CSE Books.

Magagna, V. 1991. *Communities of Grain: Communities of Grain: Rural Rebellion in Comparative Perspective*. Ithaca: Cornell University Press.

Margadant, T. 1979. *French Peasants in Revolt*. Princeton: Princeton University Press.

Marx, K. 1913. *The Eighteenth Brumaire of Louis Bonaparte*. Charles H. Kerr. Chicago (originally published in 1852).

———. 1976. *Capital*. Vol. I. New York: Penguin.

Meillassoux, C. 1973. "The Social Organization of Peasants: The Economic Basis of Kinship." *Journal of Peasant Studies* 1.

Mendras, H. 1970. *The Vanishing Peasant: Innovation and Change in French Agriculture*. Cambridge: MIT Press.

Mies, M. 1986. *Patriarchy and Accumulation on a World Scale: Women and the International Division of Labour*. London: Zed Books.

Miliband, R. 1969. *The State in Capitalist Society*. London: Weidenfield and Nicholson.

Mintz, J. 1982. *The Anarchists of Casas Viejas*. Chicago: University of Chicago Press.

Molinier, M. 1983. "Etude Sociologique de la Cooperation Viticole, A Travers une Cave Cooperative de Vinification: Broussan." Université de Montpellier I, unpublished M.A. thesis.

Le Monde. 28 May 1985.

Montagne, R. 1964. *Coopération Agricole*. Montpellier, France: Chamber of Agriculture.

Mouzelis, N. 1976. "Capitalism and the Development of Agriculture." *Journal of Peasant Studies* 3(4).

Muth, H.P. 1970. *French Agriculture and the Political Integration of Western Europe*. Leiden: Stijthoff.

Naim, T. 1977. *The Break-Up of Britain: Crisis and Neo-Nationalism*. London: New Left Books.

Napo, F. 1971. *1907 La Révolte des Vignerons*. Paris: Privat.

Narotsky, S. 1989. " 'Not to Be a Burden': Ideologies of Domestic Group and Women's Work in Rural Catalonia." In *Work Without Wages: Domestic Labour and Self-Employment within Capitalism*, edited by J. L. Collins and M. Gimenez. Albany: State University of New York Press.

O'Brien, J., and W. Roseberry (eds.) 1991. *Golden Ages, Dark Ages: Imagining the Past in Anthropology and History*. Berkeley: University of California Press.

Ortner, S. 1995. "Resistance and the Problem of Ethnographic Refusal." *Comparative Studies in Society and History* 37(1).

Pahl, R. 1984. *Divisions of Labour*. Oxford: Basil Blackwell.

Pastor-Barrué, M. 1981. *Viticulteurs en crise à Laure-Minervois*. Paris: Éditions du C.N.R.S.

Pech, R. 1975. *Entreprise viticole et capitalism en Languedoc Roussillon du phylloxera aux crises de mévente*. Toulouse: Publication de l'Université de Toulouse—le Mirail.

Piore, M., and C. Sabel. 1987. *The Second Industrial Divide*. New York: Basic Books.

Poulantzas, N. 1975. *Class in Contemporary Capitalism*. London: New Left Books.

Puijk, R., and J. Vaagland. 1983. *Notre vin et notre patois*. Bergen Occasional Papers in Social Anthropology, No. 23, Department of Social Anthropology, University of Bergen.

Rapp, R., and E. Ross. 1979. "Examining Family History." *Feminist Studies* 5(1).

Recensement Général de l'Agriculture. 1979–1980. France: Prosper, Hérault, Communes.

Redclift, N. 1985. "The Contested Domain: Gender, Accumulation and the Labour Process." In *Beyond Employment: Household, Gender and Subsistence*, edited by N. Redclift and E. Mingione. Oxford: Basil Blackwell.

Redfield, R. 1956. *The Little Community and Peasant Society and Culture*. Chicago: University of Chicago Press.

Reiter, R. 1976. "Men and Women in the South of France: Public and Private Domains." In *Toward and Anthropology of Women*, edited by R. Reiter. New York: Monthly Review Press.

Renan, E. 1996. "What Is a Nation?" In *Nationalism in Europe 1815 to the Present*, edited by S. Woolf. London: Routledge.

Rigby, Brian. 1991. *Popular Culture in Modern France: A Study of Cultural Discourse*. London: Routledge.

Roach, A. 1997. "Occitania Past and Present: Southern Consciousness in Medieval and Modern French Politics." *History Workshop Journal* 43, Spring.

Rogers, B. 1980. *The Domestication of Women: Discrimination in Developing Societies*. London: Kogan Page.

Rogers, S. C. 1975. "Female Forms of Power and the Myth of Male Dominance: A Model of Male and Female Interaction in Peasant Societies." *American Ethnologist* 2(4).

———. 1985. "Gender in Southwestern France: the Myth of Male Dominance Revisited." *Anthropology*9(12), May–December.

———. 1991. *Shaping Modern Times in Rural France: The Transformation and Reproduction of an Aveyronnais Community*. Princeton: Princeton University Press.

Rogers, S. C., and S. Salamon. 1983. "Inheritance and Social Organization among Family Farmers." *American Ethnologist*, August.

Rokkan, S., and D. Urwin, 1983. *Economy, Territory and Identity*. London: Sage.

Roseberry, W. 1989. *Anthropologies and Histories: Essays in Culture, History and Political Economy*. New Brunswick, N.J.:Rutgers University Press.

———. 1993. "Beyond the Agrarian Question in Latin America." In *Confronting Historical Paradigms*, edited by F. Cooper et al. Madison: University of Wisconsin Press.

Rousseau, M. 1987. "France: The Bureaucratic State and Political Reforms." In *Regionalism and Regional Devolution in Comparative*

Perspective, edited by M. Rousseau and R. Zariski. New York: Praeger.

Sabel, C. 1982. *Work and Politics: The Division of Labour in Industry.* Cambridge: Cambridge University Press.

Sayer, D. 1991. *Capitalism and Modernity: An Excursus on Marx and Weber.* London: Routledge.

Schurmann, F. J. 1993. "Introduction: Development Theory in the 1990's." In *Beyond the Impasse: New Directions in Development Theory,* edited by F. J. Schurmann. London: Zed.

Scott, J. 1976. *The Moral Economy of the Peasant: Rebellion and Subsistence in South-East Asia.* New Haven: Yale University Press.

———. 1985. *Weapons of the Weak: Everyday Forms of Peasant Resistance.* New Haven: Yale University Press.

———. 1986. "Everyday Forms of Peasant Resistance," *Journal of Peasant Studies* 13(2).

———. 1990. *Domination and the Arts of Resistance.* New Haven: Yale University Press.

———. 1994. "Domination, Acting and Fantasy." In *The Paths to Domination, Resistance and Terror,* edited by C. Nordstrom and J. Martin. Berkeley: University of California Press.

Scott, A. 1986. "Introduction: Why Rethink Petty Commodity Production," In *Rethinking Petty Commodity Production,* edited by A. Scott. Special Issue of *Social Analysis, Journal of Social and Cultural Practice* 20.

de Sède, G. 1982. *700 Ans de Revoltes Occitanes.* Paris: Plon.

Sewell, W. 1980. *Work and Revolution in France: The Language of Labour from the Old Regime to 1848.* Cambridge: Cambridge University Press.

Shils, E. 1975. *Centre and Periphery: Essays in Macrosociology.* Chicago: University of Chicago Press.

Sider, G. 1996. "Anthropology and History: Opening Points for a New Synthesis." *Focaal* 26/27.

———. 1986. *Culture and Class in Anthropology and History: A Newfoundland Illustration,* Cambridge: Cambridge University Press.

———. 1984. "The Ties that Bind: Culture and Agriculture, Property and Propriety in the Newfoundland Village Fishery." *Social History* 5.

Silverman, S., 1965. "Patronage and Community-Nation Relationships in Central Italy." *Ethnology* 4(2).

———. 1975, *Three Bells of Civilization.* New York: Columbia University Press.

Smart, J. 1989. *The Political Economy of Street Hawking in Hong Kong.* Hong Kong: Hong Kong University Press.

Smith, C. 1984. "Forms of Production in Practice: Fresh Approaches to Simple Commodity Production." *Journal of Peasant Studies* 11(4).

Smith, G., and J. Barker, (eds.). 1986. *Rethinking Petty Commodity Production.* Special Issue of *LABOUR, Capital and Society* 19(1).

Smith, G. 1989. *Livelihood and Resistance: A Study of Peasants and the Politics of Land*, Berkeley: University of California Press.

———. 1991. "The Production of Culture in Local Rebellion." In *Golden Ages, Dark Ages: Imagining the Past in Anthropology and History*, edited by Jay O'Brien and William Roseberry. Berkeley: University of California Press.

Smith, J. H. 1984. "Family and Class: The Household Economy of Languedoc Winegrowers, 1830–1870." *Journal of Family History* 9(1).

———. 1978. "The French Winegrowers' Revolt of 1907." *Past and Present* 79.

———. 1975. "Work Routine and Social Structure in a French Village: Cruzy in the Nineteenth Century." *Journal of Interdisciplinary History* 3.

Stern, S. 1987. "New Approaches to the Study of Peasant Rebellion and Consciousness: Implications of the Andean Experience." In *Resistance, Rebellion and Consciousness in the Andean Peasant World, Eighteen and Twentieth Centuries*, edited by S. Stern. Madison: University of Wisconsin Press.

Tilly, C. 1986. *The Contentious French*. Cambridge: Harvard University Press.

Touraine, A. 1995. *A Critique of Modernity*. London: Basil Blackwell.

———. 1985. "Sociological Intervention and the Internal Dynamics of the Occitanist Movement." In *New Nationalisms of the Developed West*, edited by E. Tiryakian and R. Rogowski. Boston: Allen and Unwin.

Touraine, A., and F. Dubet. 1981. *Le Pays Contre l'Etat: Luttes Occitanes*. Paris: Edition du Seuil.

Ulin, R. 1996. *Vintages and Traditions: An Ethnohistory of Winegrowers' Cooperatives*: Washington, D.C.: Smithsonian Press.

Urla, J. 1988. "Ethnic Protest and Social Planning: A Look at Basque Language Revival." *Cultural Anthropology* 3(4): 311–394.

Vergopoulos, K. 1978. "Capitalism and Peasant Productivity." *Journal of Peasant Studies* 5(4).

Warner, C. K. 1960. *The Winegrowers of France and the Government Since 1875*. New York: Columbia University Press.

Weber, F. 1989. *Le Travail à-côté: étude d'ethnographie ouvrière*. Paris: Editions de l'Ecole des Hautes Etudes en Sciences Sociales.

Weber, E. 1982. "Comment la Politique vint aux paysans: A second look at peasant politicization." *The American Historical Review* 87.

Weber, E. 1976. *Peasants into Frenchmen: The Modernization of Rural France 1870–1914*. Stanford: Stanford University Press.

Weeks, J. 1987. "Questions of Identity." In *The Cultural Construction of Sexuality*, edited by P. Caplan. London: Tavistock.

Weingrod, A. 1968. "Patrons, Patronage and Political Parties." *Comparative Studies in Society and History* 10.

Whitehead, A. 1981. " 'I'm Hungry Mum': The Politics of Domestic Budgeting." In *Of Marriage and the Market: Women's Subordination in International Perpective,* edited by K. Young, C. Walkowitz, and R. McCullagh. London: CSE Books.

Williams, B. 1989. "A Class Act: Anthropology and the Race to Nation Across the Ethnic Terrain." *Annual Review of Anthropology* 18.

Williams, R. 1983. *Keywords.* New York: Oxford University Press.

Wilson, T. 1993. "An Anthropology of the European Community." In *Cultural Change and the New Europe,* edited by T. Wilson and E. Smith. Boulder: Westview.

Wolf, E. 1969. *Peasant Wars of the Twentieth Century.* New York: Harper and Row.

Woolf, S. (ed.). 1996. *Nationalism in Europe: 1815 to the Present.* London: Routledge.

Wright, G. 1964. *Rural Revolution in France.* Stanford: Stanford University Press.

Wylie, L. 1956. *Village in the Vaucluse.* Cambridge: Harvard University Press.

Yoon, Y. S. 1975. "Provençal Wine Co-operatives." In *Beyond the Community: Social Process in Europe,* edited by J. Boissevain and E. Friedl. The Hague: Department of Education and Science of the Netherlands.

Zeldin, T. 1983. *The French.* London: Fontana.

Index

absenteeism 34, 40, 200; absentee owner 30, 191; *"les proprietaires"* 34–35

agrarian societies x, 224; studies of 14, 165–66, 223–25. *See also* petty commodity production

agricultural policies 24, 49, 50, 51, 52, 53, 64, 94

agricultural laborers 10, 16, 25, 28, 30, 34, 37, 38–41, 43, 54, 57, 72, 73, 85, 119, 123, 125, 126, 127, 141, 146, 147, 151, 181, 184, 186, 188, 197, 217, 221

Alavi, Hamza Ali 165

alienation 19, 99, 216–17, 220, 229; of workers 221. *See also* women

antimodernization 53; strategy 52; struggle 186

Bailey, Frederick 132
Banfield, Edward 11
Bernstein H. 32, 106
Bourdieu, Pierre 96
Bradby, B. 165
Brenner, R. 88
Buroway, Michael 226, 227

Cabral, Amilcar 11

capitalism ix, xi, 7, 72, 73, 79, 86, 95, 106, 134, 149, 165, 166, 194, 225, 227, 229; Cold War 4; commercial 57; development of ix, 6, 165, 166, 229; logic of 18, 106; penetration of 16

capitalist 87, 89; agriculture 51; calculation 13, 15, 108, 166, 172; character 34; development 5, 49, 100, 110, 235; economy 17, 107, 228; farmers 4, 10, 19, 33; farms 6, 31–34, 72, 84, 134; growth 5; interests 52; market 89, 165, 167, 197, 206; modernization 91, 117; penetration 110; rationalization 40, 139, 140, 142, 145; society 98, 101, 225, 229; systems of production 95; transformation x, 7, 39, 40, 134, 139, 144, 156, 163, 168, 200; transition 34; viticulture 19. *See also* domination; market

Carnaval 93–95

Centre National des Jeunes Agricultures (CNJA) 52, 60. *See also* unions

Chayanov, Alexander 87, 161, 180, 225

Chevalier, Jacques 106

class 9, 13, 19, 34, 35, 42, 77, 78, 79, 82, 85, 87, 100, 111, 125, 146, 147, 156, 162, 163, 164, 182, 187, 226, 231; antagonism 57, 197, 203; claims 85; consciousness ix, 12, 78, 79, 83, 98, 99, 100, 231; culture 8; differentiation x, 10, 78, 198, 225; division 33, 85, 95, 100, 189, 194, 206, 219, 230; exploitation 69; formation 227; homogeneity of 206; identity 87, 95, 227, 228, 234; interest 234; notion of 78, 101; politics 12, 140; positions 129; relations 82, 86, 87; resistance ix;